A Life Distilled

A Life Distilled

GWENDOLYN BROOKS, HER POETRY AND FICTION

Edited by Maria K. Mootry
and Gary Smith

UNIVERSITY OF ILLINOIS PRESS
URBANA AND CHICAGO

Illini Books edition, 1989
© 1987 by the Board of Trustees of the University of Illinois
Manufactured in the United States of America
1 2 3 4 5 C P 5 4 3 2 1

This book is printed on acid-free paper.

Library of Congress Cataloging-in-Publication Data

A Life distilled : Gwendolyn Brooks, her poetry and fiction / edited
   by Maria K. Mootry and Gary Smith. — Illini Books ed.
      p. cm.
   Bibliography: p.
   ISBN 0-252-06065-2 (alk. paper)
      1. Brooks, Gwendolyn 1917–   —Criticism and interpretation.
   I. Mootry, Maria.   II. Smith, Gary, 1949–   .
   [PS3503.R7244Z74 1989]
   811'.54 — dc19   88-26151
                                                            CIP

Also available in cloth, ISBN 0-252-01367-0

This book is dedicated to Gwendolyn Brooks.

Conduct your blooming in the noise
and whip of the whirlwind.

Gwendolyn Brooks

CONTENTS

III. *"Daughter of the Dusk"*: Maud Martha

Madimba: Gwendolyn Brooks

Music is its own heartbeat

Double-conscious sister in the veil,
Double-conscious sister in the veil;
Double-conscious sister in the veil:
Double-conscious sister in the veil.

You beat out the pulse with your mallets,
the brown wishbone anemones
unflowered and unworn in Chicago congo
prints, images, otherness, images

from the fossilbank: Madimba.
Black Man; I'm a black man; black—
A-um-ni-pad-me-hum—
another brother gone:

"the first act of liberation
is to destroy one's cage"—
a love supreme;
a love supreme.

Images: words: language
typing the round forms; Juneteenth,
baby, we free, free at last:
black man, I'm a black man.

A garden is a manmade vision,
rectangular, weeded, shelled,
pathed, hosed, packed in,
covered with manure, pruned;

I own you; you're mine, you
mine, baby: to bear unborn things.
Double-conscious sister in the veil:
Double-conscious sister in the veil.

Black woman: America is artful
outside time, ideal outside space;
you its only machine: Madimba:
Double-conscious sister in the veil.

Michael S. Harper

MARIA K. MOOTRY

1

"Down the Whirlwind of Good Rage":

An Introduction

to Gwendolyn Brooks

Through the years, Gwendolyn Brooks has experimented with a variety of prosodic, syntactic, and narrative strategies. Her writing career has been remarkably rich in forms and ideas. Her creative practice has involved the ongoing articulation and formation of a variety of texts that express a shifting, exploratory, and ultimately performative consciousness. In terms of art, she has never been wary of "the fascination of what's difficult"; but in terms of social justice, she has always addressed a range of America's social problems. In short, at the nexus of Brooks's art lies a fundamental commitment to both the modernist aesthetics of art and the common ideal of social justice.

Nowhere is this dual commitment more apparent than in the multiplicity of voices in her works. If the reader finds echoes of T. S. Eliot and Countee Cullen in her poetry, there are also equally strong folk vernacular voices punctuating her forty-year literary career. Her three early works, *A Street in Bronzeville* (1945), *Annie Allen* (1949), and *The Bean Eaters* (1960), present a wide range of poetic forms, including blues poems, ballads, experimental free verse, quatrains, Petrarchan sonnets, and Chaucerian stanzas. Her subsequent publications, *In the Mecca* (1968), *Riot* (1969), *Family Pictures* (1971), *Beckonings* (1975), and *To Disembark* (1981), are written primarily in free verse and show her increasing concern with social issues, yet the variety of speakers continues. In fact, as the diversity of Brooks's achievement becomes apparent, our initial impression is one of a talent that does not need the unifying edge of a single, stylized voice or of a unique aesthetic with which to assert itself against tradition.

Yet Brooks's talent defines itself against the weight of tradition: She consistently utilizes the past while creating new constructs. Her variations on several traditions, several systems of values, give her poetry continuity within change, making it both difficult and original. She keeps before the reader that which is traditional at the same time that she modifies the tradition to accommodate her unique and developing sensibility.

The Afro-American legacy that Brooks has built on includes the black folk traditions represented by Paul Laurence Dunbar's lyric and dramatic poetry and by Langston Hughes's urban vernacular blues and jazz poetry, which spanned the Harlem Renaissance of the 1920s and 1930s. The modernist experimental tradition of black poets like Robert E. Hayden and Melvin B. Tolson, who flourished from the 1940s to the 1960s, also offered a contemporary formalist example. Additionally, Brooks's art was nourished by a broad spectrum of western traditions, especially by metaphysical strains of the seventeenth-century English poet John Donne, the American poet Emily Dickinson, and the early twentieth-century neometaphysical modern, T. S. Eliot.

Brooks's initiation into modernist aesthetics was formalized when, in 1941, she joined Inez Stark Boulton's poetry workshop for young black writers at Chicago's Southside Community Art Center. Stark, a former reader for the nationally influential, Chicago-based *Poetry* magazine, guided her class through modernist principles and introduced her students to major modern poets. Of Stark's influence, Brooks has written: "She gave us an education in modern poetry. I had been reading modern poetry, but I didn't know . . . what writers of the day were doing and how they were doing it."[1] Stark stressed indirection, economy, and innovation; she demanded "all the skeleton and no fat" (*Report*, p. 67). She also presented Brooks with a female role model as well as a standard of excellence for poetry.

In her autobiography, Brooks gives generous tribute to this early influence, although she denies having used "the modernists" as literary role models. In a 1969 interview with George Stavros, Brooks said she does not "even admire Pound," although she likes Eliot, particularly "Prufrock," *The Waste Land*, and "Portrait of a Lady."[2] Whether or not Brooks was influenced by these particular writers, she shares with them the consciousness of form that became the hallmark of so much poetry prized by the influential New Critics of her time. They esteemed poetry that was difficult, allusive, and obscure. Significantly, Brooks's Pulitzer Prize-winning volume, *Annie Allen*, exhibits all of the characteristics associated with modernist aesthetics. Equally significantly, Brooks expressed continued pride in her virtuoso achievement "The Anniad," a long poem that is the book's centerpiece. Twenty years after the poem was published, she commented on it: "I was fascinated by what words might do there in the poem. You can tell that it's labored, a poem that's very interested in the mysteries and magic of technique. . . . What a pleasure it was to write that poem!" (*Report*, pp. 158–59).

Part of Brooks's modernity lies in her use of dramatic modes in her poetry. Focus on character as expressed through the spoken, performative voice allows for indirection, complexity of narration, and obfuscation of poetic statement. Several of the greatest poems in American literature, including Wallace Stevens's "Sunday Morning," Pound's "Hugh Selwyn Mauberley," and Eliot's "Gerontion," are classic examples of modernist interweaving of portraiture, narration, and dramatic voice. This intermixture of modes allows the poets to demand active complicity between their reader and their poem until the full import of their poetic statement emerges as a construct put together by the reader from various indications dispersed throughout the text.[3]

If the way in which Brooks handles character is one index of her modernity and her aesthetic engagement, her choice of character has always indicated the fundamentally social context of her work, even at its most difficult. Thus, it seems necessary to distinguish between character and persona in her work. Brooks's characters are largely taken from the dispossessed, the unheroic residents of America's urban ghettos (named, by custom, "Bronzeville"). These characters dramatize a microcosm of black urban life—its struggles, its small triumphs, and its unheroic survival. By focusing on them, Brooks has been able to engage, often indirectly, some of the major social issues of her time, including war and peace, racial justice, and the plight of women. Yet this commitment to social issues is often disguised by her modernist use of personae. For example, Brooks's sonnet series, "Gay Chaps at the Bar," from her first publication, *A Street in Bronzeville,* is both a tour de force technically and an exploration of America's unequal treatment of the black soldiers during World War II. Similarly, her unusual ballads on the death of Emmett Till in her third volume, *The Bean Eaters,* offer protest subject matter in an innovative narrative form. Again, her gallery of female portraits, from the practical Hattie Scott to the "crazy woman who sings in November" instead of May, stresses varieties of heroism and antiheroism in women's responses to difficulties they confront; yet the complexity of their responses may not be fully apparent, particularly to the uninitiated reader who is unable to meet the demands placed upon him or her by Brooks's modernist use of nuance, ellipsis, and allusion.

The way in which Brooks handles her characters is only one index of her modernity. Brooks's modernity also permeates her poetry in its mixture of forms and variations on forms (ballads, sonnets, sonnet-ballads, mock-epics); in its juxtaposition of "high" and "low" styles; and in its rich prosodic texture, including the use of varied meters, creative enjambment, melisma, and indeterminate modification. The centrality of the concrete as opposed to the abstract and Brooks's skillful deployment of image and the visual line are equally important clues of her modernity. Finally, Brooks's objective rather than subjective authorial stance creates texts in which her personality seems largely effaced. In recent years, however, Brooks seems to be moving away from the objective voice of modernity to a more personal yet public voice that is, at turns, elegiac and celebratory, reminiscent of her more recent contemporaries, Robert Lowell and Theodore Roethke.

Not only is the Brooks canon complex, but her place in American literature is also equally intricate. On one level, Brooks is a word wizard, a poet's poet. On another level, she belongs to the "populist" tradition of her midwestern predecessors, Langston Hughes, Carl Sandburg, Edgar Lee Masters, and Vachel Lindsay. Leaving aside the question of aesthetics, the sociohistorical fulcrum of Brooks's art seems to be a tripartite base of regionalism, race, and gender. In terms of literature, Brooks's regionality has bifurcated roots: the populism of Sandburg, Lindsay, and Masters and the elitist "art for art's sake" tradition of Eliot, Pound, and Stevens. Historically, the early twentieth-century Midwest was the locus of a spirit of economic and social revolt manifesting itself in the sometimes coarse, sometimes tender ballads of Vachel Lindsay and the bold free verse of Carl Sandburg. Yet Brooks's specific Midwest area, Chicago, was also, significantly, the birthplace of the internationally influential *Poetry: A Magazine of Verse. Poetry* had published Sandburg's famous free-verse tribute "Chicago" in 1914. But the magazine's emphasis on experimental poetry extended to modernists like T. S. Eliot, Ezra Pound, Wallace Stevens, W. B. Yeats, and many others. Interestingly, women also figured prominently in the founding and sustenance of the magazine, including not only Inez Stark, but also co-founder Amy Lowell, and poets Harriet Monroe, Edna St. Vincent Millay, Marianne Moore, and H. D. Thus, even as a regionalist, Brooks's legacy was complex and inclusive. If in her apprenticeship years she consciously used black poet Langston Hughes as a role model for capturing the essence of "the street," her best poetry is Joycean in scope and cosmopolitan in aspiration.

Nevertheless, a sense of place lies at the center of much of Brooks's poetry and fiction. Real place names evoke vividly, if at times impressionistically, Chicago's South Side topography, including references to dance halls (Warwick, Savoy) and to the sacred collegiate paths of the University of Chicago's Midway. As examples of midwestern realism, Brooks's several publications construct a vision of Chicago's South Side comparable to Masters's *Spoon River* and Hughes's Harlem. Her starting place is often common facts, as she once explained to Illinois historian Paul M. Angle: "In my twenties when I wrote a good deal of my better-known poetry I lived on 63rd Street—at 623 East 63rd Street—and there was a good deal of life in the raw all about me . . . I wrote about what I saw and heard in the street. I lived in a small second-floor apartment at the corner; and I could look first on one side and then on the other. There was my material."[4]

In Brooks's work, a sense of place is synonymous with a sense of identity or alienation. Ineluctably intertwined with memory, fantasy, and fact, place provides the foundation for a negotiation between forces of tension and forces of support. The narrative voice mediates these forces and simultaneously clarifies and creates a community of reader and text. Thus, as we observe Satin-Legs Smith in Brooks's long mock-heroic poem, "The Sundays of Satin-Legs Smith,"[5] we discover with him the limited joys of an everyday kitchenette dweller. Satin-Legs's Sunday odyssey—down the hotel steps, out into the street, beneath Chicago's "el," into Joe's Eats and a local movie theater, and finally back to his room, all to the strain of South Side blues and ubiquitous urban noises—is an odyssey of ritualistic self-creation. It is the microcosmic dramatization of thousands of black men, uprooted for one reason or another from their southern origins, coping in the neosegregated ambience of northern ghettos.

Later, a sense of place would take on more public, even political, overtones. Thus, in the late 1960s, after she publicly announced her allegiance to the Black Arts Movement, Brooks celebrated a new vision of the South Side in poems like "The Wall," from *In the Mecca*. In this poem, Brooks establishes a factual sense of place by using a subquote from a prominent black magazine, *Ebony*, which, as Brooks notes in a quotation preceding the poem, described the Wall as: "The side wall of a typical slum building on the corner of 43rd and Langley . . . " (*WGB*, p. 414). The site evokes memories of Satin-Legs's blues-haunted sallies; however, the poem itself is a fantasy of community solidarity. With fable-like overtones, Brooks begins her poem, "A drumdrumdrum./Humbly we come./South of success and east of gloss and glass. . . . " However, in the book's title poem, "In the Mecca," Brooks's use of place, this time a huge labyrinthine apartment dwelling ironically known as the Mecca building, creates a more complex interplay of tensive and supportive forces through the juxtaposition of setting, character, and racial consciousness.

Brooks's earliest book, *A Street in Bronzeville,* evoked a celebration of urban street life that anticipates the intensely urban focus of black writers in the 1960s. From DeWitt Williams, who "drank his liquid joy" under the Chicago el at 47th Street, to Madame, the beauty parlor owner who carefully arranges her ostentatious gravesite, Brooks concentrated on unheroic commonplace South Siders: beauticians, maids, preachers—all part of the teeming segregated black northern community known all over America in the 1940s as "Bronzeville." Unlike her fellow midwesterner, Sherwood Anderson, she did not romanticize the Chicago laborer. Neither did Brooks imitate Carl Sandburg's Whitmanesque-style optimism and his peculiarly direct advocacy of the laboring man as hero and opposer of capitalist exploitation.

For Brooks, "region" ultimately meant not only the Midwest and even metropolitan Chicago but also, more specifically, southside Chicago. The most elaborate portrait of her "little postage stamp" community, reminiscent of Faulkner's Yoknapatawpha County, is found in the vividly impressionistic rendering of place in her only novel, *Maud Martha* (1953). Kitchenette apartments, cars, taverns, beauty parlors, nightclubs, and boutiques are as much the theme of Brooks's novel as are the trials and triumphs of her heroine. Brooks's clever juxtaposition of "white" areas, such as the downtown Blackstone Theatre and the University of Chicago Midway, symbolizes the urban geography of class and racial segregation that characterized our urban areas in the 1940s and 1950s. Thus as a regionalist, Brooks brought together a remarkable sense of black folk culture and American popular culture that affirmed black life and also critiqued indirectly those forces that limited black access to the American dream.

If region has played a large role in Brooks's literary development, racial consciousness, with its attendant pride, pain, and defiance, intruded very early in Brooks's poetic career. Her first serious encounter with racial prejudice at Chicago's then elitist, largely white, Hyde Park High School, led her in 1933 to submit a poem of outrage and youthful defiance to the black newspaper, the *Chicago Defender*. In the poem, she avoided explicit references to race, anticipating a strategy of indirection that would become a hallmark of her later poetry. Nevertheless, she managed to invoke God's disapproval and to portray her persona's spiritual inviolability in tones of youthful bravado: "He shall not care, his bright soul knows no bars."[6]

One aspect of her life that figures prominently in Brooks's racial themes is intraracial color conflict. This theme highlights a past tendency common in the black community of equating beauty with caucasoid features. In *Maud Martha*, the heroine's jealousy of her fairer, beautiful sister who is preferred by her doting father may be an unconscious literary reenactment of painful youthful memories that Brooks skillfully transmuted into art. The negative impact of societal and intraracial beauty standards demands intricate stratagems from Brooks's maturing heroine. Withdrawal, accommodation, compensation, and anger were possible reactions to an attitude pervasive in the black community ubiquitously expressed in the childish but cruel rhyme: "If you white, you all right/If you brown, stick around/If you black get back." In many of her poems, Brooks's characters are beset by a tortured amalgam of emotional reactions; thus, Pearl May, the persona in the "Ballad of Pearl May Lee," suffers anger and sorrow at her lover's rejection of "dark meat"; whereas the adolescent girl in "the ballad of chocolate Mabbie" withdraws after her initiation into the "truth" of color gradation in black society and finds solace in companions who look like herself; and Jessie Mitchell's mother, in the poem of the same title, seeks refuge from her daughter's contempt in memories of her own "exquisite yellow youth."

Brooks's willingness to grapple with the unpleasant theme of the "black-and-tan" conflict may seem dated to some, but it is a measure of her commitment to the realistic tradition in American literature. It also infuses her work with the cutting-edge that led to her rediscovery in the 1970s by feminist critics, who required writers to expose myths and destructive beauty norms in American culture and, thereby, transform or at least heighten America's consciousness of the dilemmas that maturing females, white or black, may suffer. The Harlem Renaissance had largely celebrated the "rainbow" of colors in its romantic racialism, but Brooks's use of the subject becomes a prescriptive component in her art. It exposed a destructive pattern of identification with majority standards by which black Americans, like other colonized peoples of color, often organized their social, cultural, and even political hierarchy along color gradation lines.[7]

However, for Brooks, racial consciousness did not always involve pain or defiance. Sometimes it involved fierce ambition. Brooks's mother, Keziah, an avid reader of the nineteenth-century black poet Paul Laurence Dunbar, very early became determined that her daughter would one day replace him as the leading black poet in America. She would become, in short, a *"lady* Dunbar."[8] That Dunbar was male and often wrote in dialect about the antebellum South did not deter Keziah. The difficulties Dunbar presented as a role model for a young, twentieth-century urban female poet, who happened to also be black, are not to be underestimated. Thus part of the dialectic of how race informs Brooks's developing creative process involves Brooks's successful appropriation of themes and techniques from black predecessors such as Dunbar, her awareness of contemporary trends, and her rejection of those conventional themes and traditional techniques that were no longer adequate to the task before her, that is, to create a contemporary "clarifying" and "defining" art.

As with Dunbar, one of the difficulties of Brooks's blackness was that it could be used to promote, to delimit, or even to devalue her work. At age eleven, Brooks had already published several poems in local newspapers; however when her first magazine publication came two years later in *American Childhood* magazine, neither the source of the publication nor the poem's title, "Eventide," indicated or stressed Brooks's racial identity.[9] When Brooks won a Midwestern Writer's Conference poetry award in 1943, and Emily Morison of Knopf invited her to submit enough poems for a book, the forty-odd poems she sent dealt with the "universal" themes of love, war, nature, and patriotism. A few dealt with "prejudice." Morison's reply was that she liked the "Negro poems" and wanted more; the result: Brooks took nineteen of her original "race" poems and wrote, post-haste, eleven off-rhyme sonnets about a group of black soldiers ("Gay Chaps at the Bar") and a "mock-epic" about a day in the life of a typical black man in *Bronzeville* ("Sundays of Satin-Legs Smith"). Thus, Brooks's early subject matter in *A Street in Bronzeville* was a response to personal experience and to her workshop influence, and also to the demands and tastes of her potential publishers.

With the appearance of *A Street in Bronzeville* by Harper and Row—assisted by the endorsement of fellow Chicago writer Richard Wright—congratulations and advice poured in from prominent former Harlem Renaissance poets, Countee Cullen, Claude McKay, and James Weldon Johnson. McKay welcomed Brooks to "the band of hard working poets who do have something to say," but cautioned that "It is a pretty rough road we have to travel, [although] much compensation is derived from the joy of being able to sing" (*Report*, p.

201). Cullen welcomed Brooks to "that too small group of *Negro poets, and to the larger group of American ones"* [emphasis mine]. Perhaps with an eye on the latter group, he added defensively, "No one can deny you your place there" (*Report*, p. 201). Within a year Cullen was dead; McKay, then living in Chicago, died three years later. So, in a sense, these Harlem Renaissance figures with their profound awareness of the difficulty of a life dedicated to poetry in America (particularly for a black poet) passed their legacies on to this young woman. James Weldon Johnson, activist, songwriter, poet, and mentor of the Renaissance, had already warned Brooks to break from old traditions and pointed her toward the modernists when he wrote in 1937: "Dear Miss Brooks. You have an unquestioned talent and feeling for poetry. Continue to write—at the same time, study carefully the work of the best modern poets—not to imitate them, but to help cultivate the highest possible standard of self-criticism" (*Report*, p. 202). The phrase "the highest possible standard" was Johnson's way of cautioning Brooks that the best black poets, even when writing on racial subjects, must compete with the best modern poets.

But, requirements of publishers aside, some critics used Brooks's racial themes to devalue her work. Louis Simpson, for example, reviewed Brooks's *Selected Poems* (1963) with the biting comment: "Although a Negro might not be able to write well without revealing her race, the writing's unimportant if being a Negro is the only subject."[10] On the surface, Brooks seemed to concur with this dictum. In one of her few early statements about the mission of a writer, Brooks herself expressed concern that because of her minority status, racial themes would be too readily accessible, often at the expense of craft. In a brief statement published in *Phylon*, she said: "The Negro poet's most urgent duty, at present, is to polish his technique, his way of presenting his truths and his beauties, that these may be more insinuating and therefore, more overwhelming."[11]

Such sentiments express the strain that Brooks felt in attempting to negotiate a fruitful relationship between race and art. Her lifelong concern for craft, however, must be placed in the context of her times. Like her contemporaries, Robert E. Hayden and Melvin B. Tolson, Brooks achieved maturity during a historical period that mingled racial pride with integrationist ethos. For these writers there was no conflict between racial identity, full development as a black writer, and finesse of form. They took no pains to "write well without revealing [their] race"; rather, their ambition was to write about race well and to master poetic forms while they gave dignity and moment to the meaning of being black in America. As Tolson commented,

"The poet is not only the purifier of language . . . but the poet is a . . . barometer in his society."[12]

A few years later, at the second Black Writer's Conference at Fisk University in 1967, the presence of dynamic young poets like Amiri Baraka (LeRoi Jones) and Haki Madhubuti (Don L. Lee) truly provided Brooks with a "barometer" for America's racial climate. Along with other members of the audience, Brooks was astonished, not because of their racial consciousness, but because of their overt stress on black solidarity and pride. Indeed, Brooks was presented with the prospect of a "surprised queenhood in the new black sun" (*Report*, p. 86). Shortly after the conference, Brooks became a nominal leader of the Chicago-based Black Arts Movement, aligning herself with Madhubuti and a coterie of black poets who espoused writing for and about blacks. Thus, in the 1960s, Brooks's literary career seemed to evolve from her earlier poetry, which sought to negotiate the demands of social awareness and the demands of craft, to one that espoused racial solidarity above the demands of art.

If critics disagree about the question of region and race in relation to Brooks's career, they have either neglected, undervalued, or misunderstood the role of gender in her art. A few early critics, such as Arthur P. Davis, noted Brooks's initial focus on women. It was not until the rise of feminist criticism in the late 1960s and 1970s, however, that Brooks's visibility as a woman writer writing about women was restored. Even then, the critical attention was flawed. White feminist critics tended to view Brooks as a superwoman and her female personae as superwomen. To them Brooks was a larger-than-life figure who completely effaced herself from her work and offered monolithic, stereotypically strong, portraits of black womanhood. Susanne Juhasz, for instance, made the following comments on Brooks's poetic vision:

> Like the white women poets of her generation, Brooks may write about women, but rarely will she include herself among them. She never achieves either the personalism or the engagement that I have identified with the "feminine" poet. Yet there is a difference between her presentation of women and that of the white women poets who are her contemporaries: in Brooks's poetry—and, indeed throughout the poetry of black women—there is a pride in womanhood that does not exist in the poetry of white women until recently. . . . *The black woman, . . . as wife and mother has been many things but never weak.* . . . Indeed! Gwendolyn Brooks, like the black women poets who have followed her,

has always expressed pride in the black woman. . . . In Brooks's poetry, the common woman emerges as strong and admirable (emphasis added).[13]

Juhasz overlooks the rage of baffled and hurt heroines like Pearl May Lee in her otherwise perceptive essay. Black feminist critics, however, who emerged from the late 1970s to the middle 1980s, emphasized Brooks's ability to explore *all* of the nuances of being a black woman in America, and, in so doing, to help in the black woman's battle against the triple jeopardy of racism, sexism, and classism.

Salvos against the simplistic Black Arts celebration of black female "queenhood" began with the 1960s essays by black women activist/scholars like Angela Davis in *The Black Scholar*. The subsequent rise of poets like Ntozake Shange, Audre Lorde, and Alice Walker in the 1970s pushed forward a new pride and self-assertion among black women writers, which developed into a "womanist" or feminist thrust in black women's art and critical theory.

With the formation of the Modern Language Association's Commission on the Status of Women in 1970, black feminist critics began an organized academic effort to address sex-biased literary standards and to reveal how inadequately many black male writers deal with black female characters. Such critics as Barbara Smith, a founding member of the commission, set about to destroy stereotypes about black women, to uncover "lost" women writers, and to initiate sensitive studies of black women writers, particularly those who focused on the black woman. By 1982, black women critics could announce unequivocally that "the political position of black women in America has been in a single word, embattled." Ironically, such a statement merely expressed discursively what Brooks had conveyed in a single poem published twenty years earlier, "the weaponed woman":

> Well, life has been a baffled vehicle
> And baffling. But She fights, and
> Has fought, according to her lights and
> The lenience of her whirling place.
>
> She fights with semi-folded arms,
> Her strong bag, and the stiff
> Frost of her face (that challenges "When" and "If.")
> And altogether she does Rather Well.[14]

Brooks's "weaponed woman" knows she is nobody's darling and is determined to be nobody's fool. One of the central complaints of the women's liberation movement, black and white, was the denial of adequate space to simply be what one wants to be. Brooks's "weaponed woman" is neither Amazon nor Sapphire; her weapons are hardly adequate to the task of confronting the massive forces of racism, sexism, and classism martialed against her. But she is naming and claiming her space, narrow though it may be. She belongs with that gallery of women from Brooks's poetry that includes Sadie and Maud, Pearl May Lee, Hattie Scott, Annie Allen, Mrs. Small, Jessie Mitchell, Mrs. S., Pepita, and scores of others. The sheer quantity of these characters indicates the persistence of Brooks's lifelong "woman-identified" vision.[15]

Writers at the forefront of the women's liberation movement could not miss the importance of Brooks's vision, even if they did not fully understand its complexity. Moving beyond stereotypical images of Mammies, Sapphires, Tragic Mulattos, and Street Women, Brooks, from the beginning of her career, had offered multidimensional images of black and white women mediated by complex narrative and descriptive strategies. The result was not only a consistent commitment to the common woman in her work but to the continued exposure of the black woman's multilayered oppression. Thus, at the center of Brooks's vision, the reader almost invariably finds some black, usually poor, largely disenfranchised but nonetheless *engaged* woman. If Richard Wright once declared that the "Negro" is America's metaphor, if Ralph Ellison posited his black "invisible man" as a metaphor of modernist alienation, then Brooks's work achieves a convincing argument that the black woman is a legitimate symbol of the human struggle for dignity, control, and meaning.

Thus, literary spokespersons for the new black feminism found in Brooks's writing the seeds of nascent black feminism. In her early writings they found a model to replace the black male "greats" who had dominated black American literature, and who, they felt, offered predominantly narrow, stereotypical portraits of black women. Through the pages of Wright, Ellison, and even James Baldwin marched a gallery of "bitches, whores, queens, and matriarchs." Opposing this narrow black literary tradition, Mary Helen Washington, for example, has praised *Maud Martha* as a model of the complexity a writer should use in writing about black women. In this story about an "ordinary" black girl growing into womanhood and wifehood, Washington, like other growing numbers of black feminist critics, found the proper respect for a black woman's importance and complexity, the insight and honesty necessary to counteract both debasement of black womanhood and false ideologically based reverences.

From her immediate family background, Brooks had obtained considerable gender-related thematic material for her poetry and novel. Beginning with her supportive and somewhat domineering mother, there were strong women in Brooks's family, particularly her mother's four sisters. These aunts included the well-married Aunt Eppie, the fun-loving Aunt Gertrude who danced the Charleston, the staunch Aunt Ella, and the "queen" Aunt Beulah, who became department chairperson at a local high school, dressed stylishly, and graduated from the University of Chicago (*Report*, pp. 53–55). These models of female power complemented the patriarchal structure of the Brooks household. From these aunts Brooks gained an enlarged sense of feminine power and persuasion that suggested an alternative to the dominant patriarchal attitudes and customs of American culture.

Despite these feminine role models, Brooks strongly identified with her father, David. She sympathized with him, for instance, when her mother criticized him for not seeking a better job during the depression years (*Report*, p. 40). Brooks created a warm almost idyllic image of a strong gentle father in her autobiography and her poetry. Little wonder that Brooks's work, for all of its "woman-identified" quality, is replete with many sympathetic portraits of black men in their quest for a masculine identity. Portraits of Satin-Legs Smith and De Witt Williams in her early work anticipate later poems dedicated to such historical figures as Malcolm X and poets like Haki Madhubuti or Etheridge Knight.

However, Brooks, who has frequently disavowed allegiance to any formal women's movement, has recently begun to acknowledge the personal sources of her women's themes and the centrality of such themes to her art. In a recent interview with critic Claudia Tate, Brooks offered the following comments on her controversial early poem, "The Ballad of Pearl May Lee": "A lot of women are observing that a good many of my poems are about women . . . I hope you sense some real rage in 'The Ballad of Pearl May Lee.' The speaker is a very enraged person. I know because I consulted myself in how I have felt. . . ."[16] Thus, forty years after her literary career began, Brooks's perception of herself and her art is still evolving. It may be a case of a "changing same" or of genuine evolution; in any case, it is further proof that her innovative creative practice demands an equally innovative, creative criticism.

Although Brooks is the only black American to have won a Pulitzer Prize for poetry and is the Illinois State Poet Laureate, her contribution to American and Afro-American literature has been invisible to most people. Before 1967, not a single one of her poems had appeared in such popular American college texts as Meyer H. Abram's *Norton Anthology*. By 1976, several of Brooks's poems were included in the revised *Norton Anthology*, but critical studies of her work were rare. In 1978, the first introductory study of her work by Harry B. Shaw offered a thematic analysis of her poems and social ideas; but to date no comprehensive book-length study of her work has been published. Thus, we felt it necessary to offer this first collection of critical essays on Brooks. In it, both established as well as more recent critics address a variety of Brooks's themes and techniques, shedding needed light on her contribution to the American and Afro-American literary traditions.

In selecting contributions for this anthology, we have largely avoided republishing recent and readily available essays, except where we felt they constituted valuable historical evidence of the progress of Brooks scholarship. In general, we were guided by three goals. One was to construct an anthology that would reflect in a chronological fashion an appreciation of the entire range of Brooks's poetic vision. A second goal was to present essays that offer insight into some of Brooks's better-known but perhaps least understood work. Third, we wanted to present analyses of neglected areas of Brooks's work, particularly *Maud Martha*, her children's poetry, and newly revealed feminist aspects of her prose and poetry.

We open the volume with Michael S. Harper's poetic tribute to Brooks, "Madimba." Harper's phrase, "A love supreme," aptly sums up the critical respect Brooks has recently received, and with his phrase "doubleconscious sister," he expresses succinctly the complexity of Brooks's artistic vision.

Next, we present general assessments, establishing Brooks's importance in American and Afro-American letters. Houston A. Baker and George E. Kent, two of Brooks's earliest and best critics, place her in a broad literary framework. Kent finds a continuing strain of "existential tensions" in Brooks's work, whereas Baker focuses on her negotiation between the "black and white American literary traditions." Kenny J. Williams, a Chicago literary historian, explores Brooks's distinction as the first Chicago poet to make a comfortable alliance between the city and poetry. William H. Hansell and Norris B. Clark offer opposing views about later phases of Brooks's career.

Hansell finds a "positive black militancy" in Brooks's 1960s poems which, he feels, ironically works toward making America fulfill its ideals; Clark, addressing Brooks's post-1968 writing, assesses the theory of a black aesthetic in relation to what he perceives as a clearcut turning point in Brooks's transitional volume, *In the Mecca*. Finally, R. Baxter Miller surveys a broad spectrum of Brooks's career and finds the overriding quality in her work to be a humanistic affirmation of the "ontological self."

In our second section, we offer a series of essays that trace Brooks's poetic vision in themes and motifs found within single volumes. Erlene Stetson sheds light on Brooks's early themes, influences, and techniques by analyzing an unpublished manuscript of thirty-three poems, *Songs After Sunset*. Stetson's identification of Elizabethan and Jacobean influences is startling and provocative. In her assessment, Donne, Milton, and Ben Johnson are important influences on Brooks's earliest work. Gary Smith provides the first critical analysis of Brooks's children's poetry, *Bronzeville Boys and Girls* and, in another essay, finds seventeenth-century metaphysical poetry a vital key to understanding Brooks's sonnet sequence, "The Children of the Poor." Next, Claudia Tate analyzes "The Anniad" as an encoded satire which, through "the mysteries and magic technique," discloses the underlying theme of womanly repressed anger. Beverly Guy-Sheftall, in her discussion of female personae in Brooks's poetry, finds both heroism and despair in the lives of *Bronzeville* women. Maria K. Mootry argues that the overriding theme in *The Bean Eaters* is a critique of American racial and gender myths inimical to individual and communal well-being. Gayl Jones, writing on Brooks's epic poem, "In the Mecca," introduces and explicates Brooks's use of voice as speech act that simultaneously reveals and creates both the individual and the community. Gladys Williams examines several of Brooks's ballads and underscores the radical innovations she made within the traditional ballad. In her essay, Hortense J. Spillers provides a good example of why Brooks's work merits close textual analysis by offering "propositions" on several of Brooks's poems. She proves that Brooks's poetry is a "tangled skein of feeling" with "power, control, and subtlety."

In our third section, we present two critical approaches to *Maud Martha*. Barbara Christian examines *Maud Martha* as a feminist novella, while Harry B. Shaw discusses the social theme of Maud's war with beauty, revealing a unifying series of martial metaphors centered around concepts of skirmish, ambush, and victory.

Obviously, our three sections cannot explore all the possibilities for explicating the complete canon of Brooks's works. Rather, we intend our volume to serve as a resource for future study and an aid to understanding Brooks's major works whenever they are studied or performed.

Notes

1. Ida Lewis, "Conversation: Gwen Brooks and Ida Lewis," *Essence* (April 1971): 27–31; reprinted in Brooks's autobiography, *Report from Part One* (Detroit: Broadside Press, 1972), pp. 167–82. Hereinafter cited in the text as *Report.*

2. George Stavros, "An Interview with Gwendolyn Brooks," *Contemporary Literature* 11 (Winter 1970): 1–19; reprinted in *Report*, pp. 147–66.

3. Here I use the language of structural analysis of literary texts, particularly as employed by Tzvetan, Todorov, Barthes, and Genette. See Robert Scholes, *Structuralism in Literature: An Introduction* (New Haven: Yale University Press, 1974), pp. 145–46 and 153.

4. Paul M. Angle, "We Asked Gwendolyn Brooks," Illinois Bell Telephone interview conducted summer 1967 in Chicago; reprinted in *Report*, pp. 131–46.

5. Gwendolyn Brooks, "The Sundays of Satin-Legs Smith," *A Street in Bronzeville* in *The World of Gwendolyn Brooks* (New York: Harper and Row, 1971), pp. 26–31. This volume reprints *A Street in Bronzeville* (1945), *Annie Allen* (1949), *Maud Martha* (1953), *The Bean Eaters* (1960), and *In the Mecca* (1968). Hereinafter cited in the text as *WGB.*

6. George E. Kent, "Gwendolyn Brooks—Portrait, in Part, of the Artist as Young Girl and Apprentice Writer," *Callaloo* 2 (Oct. 1979): 82.

7. See Frantz Fanon's penetrating study of internalized self-hatred among French speaking people of color in his classic study, *Black Skins, White Masks*, trans. Charles Lam Markmann (New York: Grove Press, 1967).

8. Joan Kufrin, "The Poem: Gwendolyn Brooks," *Uncommon Women* (Piscataway, N.J.: New Century Publishers, 1981), p. 37.

9. See Martha H. Brown, "Interview with Gwendolyn Brooks," *Great Lakes Review* 6 (Summer 1979): 48.

10. Louis Simpson, "Don't Take a Poem by the Horns," *Bookweek* 27 Oct. 1963, pp. 6, 26.

11. Gwendolyn Brooks, "Poets Who Are Negroes," *Phylon* 2 (Dec. 1950) : 312.

12. "Melvin B. Tolson, An Interview: A Poet's Odyssey," in *Anger and*

Beyond: The Negro Writers in the United States, ed. Herbert Hill (New York: Harper and Row Publishers, 1966), p. 191.

13. Suzanne Juhasz, *Naked and Fiery Forms: Modern American Poetry by Women: A New Tradition* (New York: Harper and Row, 1975), p. 154.

14. Gwendolyn Brooks, *Selected Poems* (New York: Harper and Row, 1963), p. 125.

15. See Lorraine Bethel, "This Infinity of Conscious Pain: Zora Neale Hurston and the Black Female Tradition," in *But Some of Us Are Brave*, ed. Gloria T. Hull, Patricia Bell-Scott, and Barbara Smith (New York: Feminist Press, 1982), p. 179.

16. Claudia Tate, ed., *Black Women Writers at Work* (New York: Continuum Publishing, 1983), pp. 43–44.

— **I** —

"That Mad Demi-Art":

General Assessment

2

The Achievement
of Gwendolyn Brooks

> A writer writes out of his own family background, out of his own
> immediate community, during his formative period. And he
> writes out of his own talent and his own individual vision. Now if
> he doesn't, if he tries to get away from that by bending it to some
> ideological line, then he is depriving the group if its uniqueness.
> What we need is individuals. If the white society has tried to do
> anything to us, it has tried to keep us from being individuals.[1]
>
> —*Ralph Ellison*

Gwendolyn Brooks, like W. E. B. Du Bois, seems caught between two worlds. And both she and Du Bois manifest the duality of their lives in their literary works; Du Bois wrote in a beautiful, impressionistic style set off by quotations from the world's literary masters. Brooks writes tense, complex, rhythmic verse that contains the metaphysical complexities of John Donne and the word magic of Appollinaire, Eliot, and Pound. The high style of both authors, however, is often used to explicate the condition of black Americans trapped behind a veil that separates them from the white world. What one seems to have is white style and black content—two warring ideals in one dark body.

This apparent dichotomy has produced a confusing situation for Gwendolyn Brooks. The world of white arts and letters has pointed to her with pride; it has bestowed kudos and a Pulitzer Prize. The world of black arts and letters has looked on with mixed emotion, and pride has been only one part of the mixture. There have also been troubling questions about the poet's essential "blackness," her dedication to the melioration of the black American's social conditions. The real duality appears when we realize that Gwendolyn Brooks—although praised and awarded—does not appear on the syllabi of most American literature courses, and her name seldom appears in the annual scholarly bibliographies of the academic world. It would seem she is a black writer after all, *not* an American writer. Yet when one listens to the voice of today's black-revolutionary consciousness, one often hears that Brooks's early poetry fits the white, middle-class patterns that Imamu Baraka has seen as characteristic of "Negro literature."[2]

When one turns to her canon, one finds that she has abided the questions of both camps. Etheridge Knight has perfectly captured her enduring quality in the following lines:

> O courier on Pegásus, O Daughter of Parnassus
> O Splendid woman of the purple stitch.
> When beaten and blue, despairingly we sink
> Within obfuscating mire,
> O, cradle in your bosom us, hum your lullabies
> And soothe our souls with kisses of verse
> That stir us on to search for light.
> O Mother of the world. Effulgent lover of the Sun!
> For ever speak the truth.[3]

She has the Parnassian inspiration and the earth-mother characteristics noted by the poet; her strength has come from a dedication to truth. The truth that concerns her does not amount to a facile realism or a heavy naturalism, although "realism" is the word that comes to mind when one reads a number of poems in *A Street in Bronzeville* (1945).

Poems, or segments, such as "kitchenette building," "a song in the front yard," and "the vacant lot," all support the view that the writer was intent on a realistic, even a naturalistic, portrayal of the life of lower-echelon urban dwellers:

> We are things of dry hours and the involuntary plan,
> Grayed in, and gray. "Dream" makes a giddy sound, not
>   strong
> Like "rent," "feeding a wife," "satisfying a man."[4]

> My mother, she tells me that Johnnie Mae
> Will grow up to be a bad woman.
> That George'll be taken to Jail soon or late
> (On account of last winter he sold our back gate.)
>   (*WGB*, p. 12)

> And with seeing the squat fat daughter
> Letting in the men

When majesty has gone for the day—
And letting them out again.
                    (*WGB*, p. 25)

These passages reinforce the designation of Brooks as a realist, and poems such as "The Sundays of Satin-Legs Smith," "We Real Cool," "A Lovely Love," and the volume *Annie Allen* can be added to the list. If she had insisted on a strict realism and nothing more, she could perhaps be written off as a limited poet. But she is no mere chronicler of the condition of the black American poor. Even her most vividly descriptive verses contain an element that removes them from the realm of a cramped realism. All of her characters have both ratiocinative and imaginative capabilities; they have the ability to reason, dream, muse, and remember. This ability distinguishes them from the naturalistic literary victim caught in an environmental maze. From the realm of "raw and unadorned life," Satin-Legs Smith creates his own world of bright colors, splendid attire, and soft loves in the midst of a cheap hotel's odor and decay. The heroine of "The Anniad" conjures up a dream world, covers it in silver plate, populates it with an imaginary prince, and shores up magnificent fragments against the ruins of war. And Jessie Mitchell's mother seeks refuge from envy and death in a golden past:

> She revived for the moment settled and dried-up triumphs,
> Forced perfume into old petals, pulled up the droop,
> Refueled
> Triumphant long-exhaled breaths.
> Her exquisite yellow youth. . . .
>
> (*WGB*, p. 329)

Gwendolyn Brooks's characters, in short, are infinitely human because at the core of their existence is the imaginative intellect.

Given the vision of such characters, it is impossible to agree with David Littlejohn, who wishes to view them as simplistic mouthpieces for the poet's sensibility;[5] moreover, it is not surprising that the characters' concerns transcend the ghetto life of many black Americans. They reflect the joy of childhood, the burdens and contentment of motherhood, the distortions of the war-torn psyche, the horror of blood-guiltiness, and the pains of the anti-hero confronted with a heroic ideal. Brooks's protagonists, personae, and speakers, in short, capture all of life's complexities, particularly the complexity of an industrialized age characterized by swift change, depersonalization, and war.

In "Gay Chaps at the Bar," the poet shows her concern for a theme
that has had a great influence on twentieth-century British and
American art. In one section, "my dreams, my works, must wait till
after hell," she employs the food metaphors characteristic of her
writing to express the incompleteness that accompanies war:

> I hold my honey and I store my bread
> In little jars and cabinets of my will.
> I label clearly, and each latch and lid
> I bid, Be firm till I return from hell.
> I am very hungry. I am incomplete.
>
> (WGB, p. 50)

In another section, "piano after war," she captures the mental anguish occasioned by war. The rejuvenation the speaker has felt in the
"golden rose" music feeding his "old hungers" suddenly ends:

> But suddenly, across my climbing fever
> Of proud delight—a multiplying cry.
> A cry of bitter dead men who will never
> Attend a gentle maker of musical joy.
> Then my thawed eye will go again to ice.
> And stone will shove the softness from my face.
>
> (WGB, p. 52)

In "The Anniad" and the "Appendix to the Anniad," the poet deals
once again with the chaos of arms: War destroys marriage, stifles
fertility, and turns men to creatures of "untranslatable ice." Her
work, therefore, joins the mainstream of twentieth-century poetry in
its treatment of the terrors of war, and her message comes to us
through, as I have mentioned, the imaginative intellect of characters
who evoke sympathy and identification.

War, however, is not the only theme that allies Gwendolyn Brooks
with the mainstream. One finds telling and ironical speculation in
"the preacher: ruminates behind the sermon":

> Perhaps—who knows?—He tires of looking down.
> Those eyes are never lifted. Never straight.
> Perhaps sometimes He tires of being great
> In solitude. Without a hand to hold.
>
> (WGB, p. 15)

In "Strong Men, Riding Horses," we have a Prufrockian portrait of the
anti-hero. After his confrontation with the ideals of a Western film,
the persona comments:

I am not like that. I pay rent, am addled
By illegible landlords, run, if robbers call.

What mannerisms I present, employ,
Are camouflage, and what my mouths remark
To word-wall off that broadness of the dark
Is pitiful.
I am not brave at all.

(WGB, p. 313)

In "Mrs. Small," one has a picture of the "Mr. Zeros" (or Willie Lomans) of a complex century, and in "A Bronzeville Mother Loiters in Mississippi. Meanwhile a Mississippi Mother Burns Bacon," we have an evocation of the blood-guiltiness of the white psyche in an age of dying colonialism. Brooks presents these themes with skill because she has the ability to endow each figure with a unique, individualizing vision of the world.

If they were considered in isolation, however, the characters and concerns of the verse would not mark the poet as an outstanding writer. Great poetry demands word magic, a sense of the infinite possibilities of language. In this technical realm Brooks is superb. Her ability to dislocate and mold language into complex patterns of meaning can be observed in her earliest poems and in her latest volumes—*In The Mecca* (1968), *Riot* (1969), and *Family Pictures* (1970). The first lines of "The Sundays of Satin-Legs Smith" are illustrative:

INAMORATAS, with an approbation,
Bestowed his title. Blessed his inclination.)

He wakes, unwinds, elaborately: a cat
Tawny, reluctant, royal. He is fat
And fine this morning. Definite. Reimbursed.

(WGB, p. 26)

The handling of polysyllabics is not in the least strained, and the movement is so graceful that one scarcely notices the rhymed couplets. Time and again this word magic is at work, and the poet's varying rhyme schemes lend a subtle resonance that is not found in the same abundance in the works of other acknowledged American writers. It is important to qualify this judgment, however, for while Brooks employs polysyllabics and forces words into striking combinations, she preserves colloquial rhythms. Repeatedly one is confronted by a realistic voice—not unlike that in Robert Frost's poetry—that carries one along the dim corridors of the human psyche or down the rancid halls of a decaying tenement. Brooks's colloquial narrative voice, however, is more prone to complex juxtapositions than Frost's, as a stanza from "The Anniad" illustrates:

> Doomer, though, crescendo-comes
> Prophesying hecatombs.
> Surrealist and cynical.
> Garrulous and guttural.
> Spits upon the silver leaves.
> Denigrates the dainty eves
> Dear dexterity achieves.
>   (*WGB*, pp. 85–86)

This surely differs from Frost's stanzas, and the difference resides in the poet's obvious joy in words. She fuses the most elaborate words into contexts that allow them to speak naturally or to sing beautifully her meaning.

Brooks is not indebted to Frost alone for technical influences; she also acknowledges her admiration for Langston Hughes. Although a number of her themes and techniques set her work in the twentieth-century mainstream, there are those that place it firmly in the black American literary tradition. One of her most effective techniques is a sharp, black, comic irony that is closely akin to the scorn Hughes directed at the ways of white folks throughout his life. When added to her other skills, this irony proves formidable. "The Lovers of the Poor" is unsparing in its portrayal of ineffectual, middle-age, elitist philanthropy:

> Their guild is giving money to the poor.
> The worthy poor. The very very worthy
> And beautiful poor. Perhaps just not too swarthy?
> Perhaps just not too dirty nor too dim
> Nor—passionate. In truth, what they could wish
> Is—something less than derelict or dull.
> Not staunch enough to stab, though, gaze for gaze!
> God shield them sharply from the beggar-bold!
>   (*WGB*, p. 334)

Hughes could not have hoped for better. And the same vitriol is directed at whites who seek the bizarre and exotic by "slumming" among blacks in "I love those little booths at Benvenuti's":

> But how shall they tell people they have been
> Out Bronzeville way? For all the nickels in
> Have not bought savagery or defined a "folk."

The colored people will not "clown."

The colored people arrive, sit firmly down,
Eat their Express Spaghetti, their T-bone steak,
Handling their steel and crockery with no clatter,
Laugh punily, rise, go firmly out of the door.
                                              (*WGB*, p. 111)

The poet's chiding, however, is not always in the derisive mode.
She often turns an irony of loving kindness on black Americans. "We
Real Cool" would fit easily into the canon of Hughes or Sterling
Brown:

> We real cool. We
> Left School. We
>
> Lurk late. We
> Strike straight. We
>
> Sing sin. We
> Thin gin. We
>
> Jazz June. We
> Die soon.
>   (*WGB*, p. 315)

The irony is patent, but the poet's sympathy and admiration for the
folk are no less obvious (the bold relief of "We," for example). A
sympathetic irony in dealing with the folk has characterized some of
the most outstanding works in the black American literary tradition,
from Paul Laurence Dunbar's "Jimsella" and the novels of Claude
McKay to Ralph Ellison's *Invisible Man* and the work of recent
writers such as George Cain and Louise Meriwether. All manifest a
concern with the black man living in the "promised land" of the
American city, and Brooks's *A Street in Bronzeville, Annie Allen*,
"The Bean Eaters," and "Bronzeville Woman in a Red Hat" likewise
reveal the employment of kindly laughter to veil the tears of a desperate situation. In her autobiography, *Report from Part One*, she attests
to having been in the situation and to having felt its deeper pulsa-
tions: "I lived on 63rd Street [in Chicago] . . . and there was a good
deal of life in the raw all about me. You might feel that this would be
disturbing, but it was not. It contributed to my writing progress. I
wrote about what I saw and heard in the street."[6]

Finally, there are the poems of protest. A segregated military establishment comes under attack in both "The Negro Hero" and "the
white troops had their orders but the Negroes looked like men." The

ignominies of lynching are exposed in "A Bronzeville Mother Loiters in Mississippi. Meanwhile, a Mississippi Mother Burns Bacon." And in poems like "Riders to the Blood-red Wrath" and "The Second Sermon on the Warpland," Brooks expresses the philosophy of militant resistance that has characterized the black American literary tradition from the day a black slave first sang of Pharaoh's army. The poet, in short, has spoken forcefully against the indignities suffered by black Americans in a racialistic society. Having undertaken a somewhat thorough revaluation of her role as a black poet in an era of transition, she has stated and proved her loyalty to the task of creating a new consciousness in her culture. Her shift from a major white publishing firm to an independent black one (Broadside Press) for her autobiography is an indication of her commitment to the cause of black institution-building that has been championed by a number of today's black artists. One might, however, take issue with her recent statement that she was "ignorant" until enlightened by the black activities and concerns of the 1960s. Although she is currently serving as one of the most engaged artistic guides for a culture, she is more justly described as a herald than as an uninformed convert. She has mediated the dichotomy that left Paul Laurence Dunbar (whose *Complete Poems* she read at an early age) a torn and agonized man. Of course, she had the example of Dunbar, the Harlem Renaissance writers, and others to build upon, but at times even superior talents have been incapable of employing the accomplishments of the past for their own ends. Unlike the turn-of-the-century poet and a number of Renaissance writers, Brooks has often excelled the surrounding white framework, and she has been able to see clearly beyond it to the strengths and beauties of her own unique cultural tradition.

Gwendolyn Brooks represents a singular achievement. Beset by a double consciousness, she has kept herself from being torn asunder by crafting poems that equal the best in the black and white American literary traditions. Her characters are believable, her themes manifold, and her technique superb. The critic (whether black or white) who comes to her work seeking only support for his ideology will be disappointed for, as Etheridge Knight pointed out, she has ever spoken the truth. And truth, one likes to feel, always lies beyond the boundaries of any one ideology. Perhaps Brooks's most significant achievement is her endorsement of this point of view. From her hand and fertile imagination have come volumes that transcend the dogma on either side of the American veil. In their transcendence, they are fitting representatives of an "Effulgent lover of the Sun!"

Notes

1. Ralph Ellison and James Alan McPherson, "Indivisible Man," *The Atlantic* 226 (Dec. 1970): 60.

2. Imamu Amiri Baraka (LeRoi Jones), "The Myth of a 'Negro Literature,'" *Home: Social Essays* (New York: William Morrow, 1966), pp. 105–15.

3. Etheridge Knight, "To Gwendolyn Brooks," *Poems from Prison* (Detroit: Broadside Press, 1968), p. 30.

4. Gwendolyn Brooks, "kitchenette building," *The World of Gwendolyn Brooks* (New York: Harper and Row, 1971), p. 4.

5. David Littlejohn, *Black on White: A Critical Survey of Writings by American Negroes* (New York: Viking Press, 1969), pp. 89–94.

6. Gwendolyn Brooks, *Report from Part One* (Detroit: Broadside Press, 1972), p. 133.

—— 3 ——

Aesthetic Values in the Poetry
of Gwendolyn Brooks

The aesthetic values in Gwendolyn Brooks's poetry emerge from a close and highly disciplined imitation of the properties of the objects and situations her art confronts. By imitation I mean here the creative and imaginative engagement of values, either actual or possible, in the range of circumstances stirring the artist's mind to action. If we are not overtaken by excessive rigor, we may usefully see the objects and situations under the following broad headings: existential tensions confronting any people facing human limitations and possibility; existential tensions given particularism by styles of engagement, failure, and celebration, created within black communities; and the exile rhythms of a black people still seeking to establish at-homeness in America.

Before investigating these categories, I must make some guiding observations. The categories are not self-isolating compartments, but rather conveniences for discussion; they often fuse with each other. This fusion results from Brooks's determination to present her people not as curios or exotics, but as human beings. Thus, the exile tensions of the famous poem "Negro Hero"[1] fuse with the existential; on one level the hero is simply an adventurous young man, thrilled by his own physical, mental, and spiritual resources; on another level, he is the exile possessing an unillusioned hope that his heroic risking of his life in battle will be a step toward transforming America and ending the exile status. Further, we may occasionally feel impelled to associate exile tensions with a poem that seems purely involved with the limitations or triumphs generally afforded in the human struggle.

The next observation involves the complexity of the issue of aesthetic values. It cuts across the outlined categories and affects the total body of the poetry. Brooks, in her early comments, tended to speak of beauty and truth as her aims in the creation of poetry. Her poetry reveals that such qualities are not necessarily qualities of the aesthetic object or situation, but qualities of the aesthetic experience afforded by the form when it is closely engaged. That is, the fusion of the reader with the work of art in an act of total perception is the ultimate source of the beauty and the truth. Thus, the primary aesthetic value of a given poem is in this act of *seeing,* as I have broadly defined it. Before the late 1960s, the outcome of this act of seeing was, primarily, the reader's possession of a revelation admitting a deeper human communion. The poet's turning to a more radical stance during the 1960s added a more concrete experience of *liberation* to that of *revelation.* Thus, Brooks's poetry became far more attentive to blacks as an audience than it had previously. And thus exile and quest for at-homeness in the universe move to occupy the center of the stage. But in all the works the reader must expect and engage an art that sees people as experiencing all the emotions available under the limitations of the human condition, although often without the gilded stage conventionally included to secure us in the illusion of the automatic omnipresence of human dignity. Whatever dignity and beauty arise from her people must, instead, be seized from the quality of their struggles and in their assertion of options despite imposing oppositions.

Such matters may now be more concretely illustrated and developed by our engagement of specific works of art. I have chosen these works not to rank the best poems, but rather to make use of those which, for various reasons, seem most convenient for illustration.

Let's begin, for the existential category, with "the old-marrieds," the opening poem of *A Street in Bronzeville* (1945).

> But in the crowding darkness not a word did
>   they say.
> Though the pretty-coated birds had piped so
>   lightly all the day.
> And he had seen the lovers in the little side-
>   streets.
> And she had heard the morning stories clogged
>   with sweets.
> It was quite a time for loving. It was mid-
>   night. It was May.
> But in the crowding darkness not a word did
>   they say.
>
>   (*WGB,* p. 3)

The form of the poem operates upon our aesthetic perceptions through oppositions that are both stated and implied. Ostensibly, the oppositions are the behavior of the couple in the face of conventional symbols of the time for loving. But perhaps the opposition is also in our minds, if our response is that this old couple have simply had it and are exhausted. First, the title suggests a class of people, rather than simply the sad fate of a particular couple. The images and the phrase "quite a time for loving" represent rather limited ways of conceiving loving. Therefore, the poem pushes us into other creations and comparisons—possibly into the appreciation of the rhythms of human lives that have achieved a condition wherein there is neither a special time for loving nor a need for words, and the time for loving is lifelong. The low-key presentation and the arrangement of the syntax to give apparent emphasis to the "proper" time for loving are themselves an incitement to our creative imagination.

Brooks was aware of the artistry and energetic struggle that go into the so-called ordinary lives of individuals attempting to ward off chaos and to order existence. The aesthetic registration of their achieved possibilities can be laid before us quietly but stroked permanently into the mind by various poetic devices. "Southeast corner" achieves its final lift into the mind and the feelings by a climactic sensuous image:

> The School of Beauty's a tavern now.
> The Madam is underground.
> Out at Lincoln, among the graves
> Her own is early found.
> Where the thickest, tallest monument
> Cuts grandly into the air
> The Madam lies, contentedly.
> Her fortune, too, lies there,
> Converted into cool hard steel
> And bright red velvet lining;
> While over her tan impassivity
> Shot silk is shining.
>   (WGB, p. 7)

At one level the poem would seem to fall conclusively into the category of those impressing us with the vanity of human gesture and ambition. But the images suggest powerfully that whatever worms may eventually do, Madam has had her triumph as artist. With the "tallest monument" cutting "grandly into the air," the "cool hard steel" of the casket and its "bright red velvet lining," Madam reaches the climax of her artistic ordering through the vivid touch of the last line. The image of shot silk makes a very strong impact through the poet's use of alliteration and sudden brevity of statement. If the art Madam has achieved is temporary, it is no more so than most art.

Brooks recognizes this artistry even when it is costly to higher levels of the human spirit. "The parents: people like our marriage, Maxie and Andrew" also demands attention to the final climactic image. In addition there is the contrast between the image of the people and that of their achievement.

> Clogged and soft and sloppy eyes
> Have lost the light that bites or terrifies.
>
> There are no swans and swallows any more.
> The people settled for chicken and shut the door.
>
> But one by one
> They got things done:
> Watch for porches as you pass
> And prim low fencing pinching in the grass.
>
> Pleasant custards sit behind
> The white Venetian blind.
>
>   (WGB, p. 70)

Aesthetically, the poem places a creative demand upon the reader, and one could describe at length the synchronized operation of the devices that deliver its organized energies. But I shall focus upon merely a few. Perhaps the hardest workers are the images, and one can feel their impact severally and contrastingly. "Clogged," "soft," "sloppy eyes" are notable for their vividness and unlovely suggestion of decay. The succeeding line announces the focus upon the loss of spiritual power, with the reader supplying various meanings for "bites and terrifies." Our associations with "swans" and "swallows" in the next couplet contrast with those we have for "chicken," usually nothing more than those suggesting good eating. We are moved from the symbol of the whole, "sloppy eyes," to the whole that it represents, "the people," that is, this married couple. And the poet forces the reader to answer the question: "shut the door" on what? Once the question has been answered, the next four lines offer dramatic contrast between loss and achievement by simply describing the couple's achievement ironically in the language with which we and the neighbors would ordinarily praise them. The fourth line of this group is notable for additional registration of the general theme: reduction of vitality. The last two lines contain the images of blandness in a triumphantly rising tone, and force a contrast between this blandness and the surging but lost human spirit represented by the "light that bites or terrifies" and by the grace, beauty, and other qualities associated with swans and swallows.

Thus, the poem, in a very brief compass, involves itself in large issues regarding the human condition and the pathos of human choices. Still, there is a respect for the couple as artists. That is, they create a form that brings order and value, however pedestrian, to existence. The reader who has fused with the art construct should feel a beauty emerging from the precision of the form in producing the shock of recognition. Intelligence, feelings, psychic responses, and emotions are aroused through the encounter with a variety of devices. Special note should be taken of simple but mind-bending imagery, formal eloquence of language contrasting with the colloquial; sharp and functional packaging and delivery of thought and feeling through rhymed couplets; and alteration of pace in various lines to produce appropriate tones.

I have mentioned poems that obviously afford an element of beauty in the act of perception. "The murder," however, offers a different challenge. The first verse is suggestive.

> This is where poor Percy died,
> Short of the age of one.
> His brother Brucie, with a grin,
> Burned him up for fun.
> (WGB, p. 22)

Three stanzas render Percy's probable responses as he dies, and the final one returns the murderer Brucie to the cocoon of childhood innocence. The aesthetic effects are horror, wonder, and awe, as the artistic construct registers the feeling of the shortness of the distance between childhood innocence and monstrosity. The poem's beginning notes the innocent delight of both boys in the fire, but near the end identifies the monstrosity sometimes lurking behind innocence.

> No doubt, poor shrieking Percy died
> Loving Brucie still,
> Who could, with clean and open eye,
> Thoughtfully kill.

Note the juxtapositions of words embodying both innocence and temporary entrance into monstrosity.

The foregoing may suggest the aesthetic field of the poems in the existential category, but it can hardly indicate the range and the rather large number of Brooks's poems that fall into this classification. Such splendid works as the following should be included: several war sonnets registering the struggle of the human spirit against the destructiveness of war (*A Street in Bronzeville*); "the birth in a narrow room," "do not be afraid of no," " 'Life for my child is simple, and is good,' " "the children of the poor" (*Annie Allen*); "Strong Men, Riding Horses" and "A Lovely Love" (*The Bean Eaters*); various children's poems;[2] several pieces in the "New Poems" section of *Selected Poems;*[3] and several poems in such later works as *Riot* and *Beckonings.*[4] These poems reveal the continuity of the poet's art with the rest of existence, and, in their aesthetic values, represent a considerable articulation of varied postures involved in the human experience: the awe-inspiring entrance of the human being into potentially complex existence ("the birth in a narrow room"); the uneasy struggle to retain beauty in the face of war (the war sonnets of "Gay Chaps at the Bar"); the self-validating quality of love without conventional stagings ("A Lovely Love"); various aspects of love in sundry poems; the complex emotions involved in motherhood ("the children of the poor" and other poems); the organization of one's being in the face of life's enticements to self-betrayal ("do not be afraid of no"); and so on. That the foregoing poems in what I have called the simply existential category are inspired by Brooks's intense confrontation with black life is, for the era before the 1960s, both an aesthetic and a political gesture. That is, they achieve her determination to reveal blacks' participation in the varied complexities of existence, not as curios but simply as people struggling to bear their weight in the universe.

Poems in the next category are primarily concerned with the daily round of existence in ordinary lives but marked by their representation of distinctive black styles. Actually, the poet is strongest in effecting aesthetic values, not in joining the styles to the existential, but to exile rhythms, as will be seen later. The foregoing principle tends to apply also to black writers in general, the most important exceptions being numerous poems of Langston Hughes and Sterling A. Brown. Margaret Walker might be included, with special reference to her poem "Lineage," in which the rendering of the strength and life-drive of ancestors evokes a sense of deep historical rhythms. Such poems seem to require, if they are not to be superficial or stereotypical, transference of value from specific black folk forms (spirituals, blues, ballads, for example), or from images and symbols that continually vibrate with suggestions of historical strivings, or from a few evocative devices that a poet may hit upon.

Brooks's most outstanding attempts in relation to folk forms, I think, are the popular "of De Witt Williams on his way to Lincoln Cemetery" and "Queen of the Blues," both included in *A Street in*

Bronzeville. The aesthetic value of "of De Witt Williams . . . " resides in the bold celebration of the ordinary life as represented by a boy who did nothing more than migrate to the North, gain his measure of enjoyment of the fruits of existence, and pass on to the great beyond. The symbols to which the reader responds are those representing hangout places and typical resources for joy. But ultimate celebration is suggested by a refrain that implies that this "ordinary" existence is also graced by the grand exit described in the spiritual: "Swing low swing low sweet sweet chariot./Nothing but a plain black boy."

"Queen of the Blues" has delightful images and expressions from the blues singer's tough life in the urban night, but it seems to me less successful aesthetically. The speaker emphasizes the emotions of compassion and pathos, and regards Mame, the queen of the blues, as embracing a life of shame opened to her by the lack of conventional restraints. The queen's story is the conventional one, without devices for a fresh facelifting of the artistic construct. The ultimate problem is that the poem lacks aesthetic distance from the values of the speaker-poet. "Steam Song" is a more recent poem that seems to stand sturdily in its own space.

> That Song it sing the sweetness
> like a good Song can
> and make a woman want to
> run out and find her man
>
> Ain got no pretty mansion
> Ain got no ruby ring.
> My many is my only
> necessary thing.
>
> That Song boils up my blood
> like a good Song can
> It make this woman want to
> run out and find her man.
>   (*Beckonings*, p. 8)

In a number of poems, the poet satirizes the presentations of the hip style, but the strongest treatment of the style appears in critical conjunction with exile rhythms in "The Sundays of Satin-Legs Smith" (*A Street in Bronzeville*). Besides the foregoing types of poems, Brooks has others that evoke identification of poetic style with blackness, often by a single word or phrase or through voice tones and familiar images that would be seen as involving blacks.

"A song in the front yard" clearly concerns the tensions between the style of black respectability and the more spontaneous life of the less respectable. To the black reader, the name Johnnie Mae would suggest the racial identity of the subjects. Names and the label "thin brown mouse" for the colleged Maud in "Sadie and Maud" make the identification of the respectable and wilder styles racially clear, but the zing of style is suggested by such expression as "Sadie was one of the livingest chits/In all the land." Aesthetically, in these light-hearted poems from *A Street in Bronzeville,* the poet poses in tension the values of the ordered existence and those of the less restrained.

Another aspect of black style is represented by the Hattie Scott poems, portraits of the coping spirit of an ordinary domestic worker. They present incisive portrayals of her responses to existence in relationship to work, love, beauty, and man-woman associations. Their aesthetic value resides in artistic constructs that register a day-to-day heroism. In the first of this series, "the end of the day," Hattie identifies herself with the sun: "But the sun and me's the same, could be:/Cap the job, then to hell with it." In the second, "the date," she is grumblingly ready to transcend the oppressive gestures of her domestic employer by boldly departing for her evening on the town with her date: "I'm leavin'. Got somethin' interestin' on my mind./Don't mean night school." In the third ("at the hairdresser's"), she triumphs over her difficulties with the competing girls of long and wind-blown hair. The last two verses illustrate the poet's mastery of her character's voice tones.

> Got Madam C. J. Walker's first.
> Got Poro Grower next.
> Ain't none of 'em worked with me, Min.
> But I ain't vexed.
>
> Long hair's out of style anyhow, ain't it?
> Now it's tie it up high with curls.
> So gimme an upsweep, Minnie.
> I'll show them girls.
>
> (*WGB*, p. 37)

The fourth and fifth poems strike the hard, folk, cynical note, with Hattie picturing the brevity with which her lover will mourn her passing and the violence with which she would have repelled the whipping that her friend, Moe Belle Jackson, so humbly accepted from her husband. In such later volumes as *Annie Allen* (1949) and *The Bean Eaters* (1960), Brooks continued such explorations but tended to edge them with satire or humor. Style portraits appear, too, in *In the Mecca,* but they derive some of their impact from being in a setting created by exile rhythms. Although the exile rhythms are not always directly presented in other later works dealing with individual black styles and incorporation of African ones (Family Pictures, 1970; Beckonings, 1975), they are sufficiently registered by other poems within the book to provide a carry-over impact.

In approaching the final category of the poems, those dealing with exile rhythms, I wish to repeat that the word "exile" means here a people experiencing resistance to their desire for at-homeness in the universe of their native land and seeking firm establishment of it. Brooks's mode for communicating these exile tensions before the 1960s differs from that of the late 1960s through the 1970s. Rightly, this difference in mode raises the question of audience, because audience is a central shaping factor in the selection and registration of aesthetic values.

To avoid the superficial commentary by which one usually explores the question of audience and for brevity's sake, I must express the situation pragmatically. As sometimes theorized, the artist, moved by something called "the human condition," pauses in the arrangement of rhythms to inquire, Who's out there listening? Before the 1960s, those declaring their attention to Brooks would be a large number of whites and a small number of blacks. The whites' answer would express interest in the universal and a disinclination to read about problems. From many, there would also be unstated premises or doubts regarding the blacks' humanity outside special exotic categories. Thus the question, Is your work about Negroness or about the human condition? would suggest unstated premises. By the time of World War II, within the answer of the small number of blacks reading black poetry or any poetry, would also be the expression of interest in the universal, but without the qualifications or unstated premises or doubts regarding blacks' humanity. Perhaps the titles of articles appearing in a 1950 issue of the magazine Phylon, which was devoted to the theme "The Negro in Literature: The Current Scene," sufficiently suggest the thrusts of blacks' interest: Gwendolyn Brooks, "Poets Who Are Negro"; Lewis G. Chandler, "A Major Problem of Negro Authors in Their March Toward Belle Lettres"; Thomas Jarrett, "Toward Unfettered Creativity"; and others. Critical articles or reviews reflected happiness when they could assure the reading public that the artistic construct transcended racial categories and racial protest. But, somewhat paradoxically, they also insisted upon the art construct's informative role by asserting that the black artist was telling us what it meant to be a Negro.

Gwendolyn Brooks and writers from Gustavus Vassa to the present, however, were not simply molded by the foregoing expectations.

The fact that when we do read earlier black works we emerge with a strong sense of profit shows that most serious artists forcefully made their own integrity an important element of their works. Richard Wright's letter to his editor Edward C. Aswell urging publication of Brooks's first book, *A Street in Bronzeville*, illustrates the point. Says Wright regarding the poems:

> They are hard and real, right out of the central core of Black Belt Negro life in urban areas. . . . There is no self-pity here, nor a striving for effects. She takes hold of reality as it is and renders it faithfully. [The next sentence is bracketed, evidently by Wright's editor, or another Harper's editor.] There is not so much an exhibiting of Negro life to whites in these poems as there is an honest human reaction to the pain that lurks so colorfully in the Black Belt. A quiet but hidden malice runs through most of them.[5]

Much of the remainder of the letter stresses the poems' integrity as well as the artist's, along with a plea that she be helped at all costs.

Perhaps I can suggest the complexity of audience and its impact upon the rendering of aesthetic values by pointing out the following. The response of the artist to the audience before the 1960s—and her own convictions—produced signals and rhythms representing an intricate and complex imaging and revelation of black experience. After the mid-1960s, the response of the larger black audience to the question, Who's listening out there? was, loudly, We are, and we want everything which will move our condition. Responding from the heart, the poet infused images and symbols into the art construct that emphasized liberation rather than representation and revelation only. The trademark of all her poetry, however, is a firm registration of existential rhythms operating in tension with all other emphases. I now turn to samples representing exile rhythms in works from both before and after the mid-1960s.

In order to deal with so important and extensive a body of poetry, I shall have to add some shorthand techniques to my method. First, the exile rhythms may arise from either interracial or intraracial prejudice. Second, qualities of the objects of art (the blacks and accompanying situations) may be broadly characterized as follows: the spirit downed or reduced but not defeated ("kitchenette building" and others in *A Street in Bronzeville*); the spirit corrupted ("Jessie Mitchell's Mother" in *The Bean Eaters*); the spirit's movement into isolation after assertion of human value ("the ballad of chocolate Mabbie," "Ballad of Pearl May Lee," "The Sundays of Satin-Legs Smith" in *A Street in Bronzeville*); the spirit stoically holding on

despite assault ("The Last Quatrain of the Ballad of Emmett Till" in
The Bean Eaters; "To a Winter Squirrel" in *In the Mecca*); and the
largely individual or special group spirit in the act of heroic assertion
("Negro Hero" and "the white troops had their orders but the Negroes
looked like men" in *A Street in Bronzeville;* "The Ballad of Rudolph
Reed" in *The Bean Eaters;* various personalities in "In the Mecca" in
the book of the same title). *In the Mecca* (1968) is transitional. The
long poem "In the Mecca" represents a transition to the focus upon
liberation. Because the poems in the section "After Mecca" are a
movement toward liberation values, I leave them for the second part
of this discussion.

Still another group of poems represents blacks in the act of perception of whites, in which whites or their patterns of behavior also
become art objects. Representing blacks and the poet as self-con-
tained and cultivated observers are such poems as "Beverly Hills,
Chicago," "I love those little booths at Benvenuti's," "downtown
vaudeville," "'Men of careful turns, haters of forks in the road,'" all
in *Annie Allen;* "A Bronzeville Mother Loiters in Mississippi. Meanwhile, a Mississippi Mother Burns Bacon" and "The Chicago *Defender* Sends a Man to Little Rock" in *The Bean Eaters.* Perhaps "The
Sundays of Satin-Legs Smith" should also be mentioned among the
foregoing group; although the portrait of the black character dominates that poem, the real cool black observer makes her first appearance in it. To many of today's readers the foregoing poems are
likely to be seen as containers of polite protest. But whites experienced considerable bite from most of them; the poet was queried
about why she was bitter, and why she was "forsaking lyricism for
polemics." The reason for their impact is not hard to discover. The
narrator speaks not as one whose wounds and howls can be addressed
by a single moment of pity, but as one for the most part containing
pain and speaking as the equal capable of staring eye for eye and
delivering rapier thrusts.

The more bitter and more dramatically slashing poems of this
group are "Negro Hero" (*A Street in Bronzeville*), "Bronzeville
Woman in a Red Hat" and "The Lovers of the Poor" (*The Bean
Eaters*). (Other categories, such as that of heroic assertion, also contain bitterly slashing poems.) These poems address issues of dignity
and brotherhood. In the short epic, "In the Mecca," as distinguished
from the book that contains it, the appearance of personalities bent
upon revolutionary change signals the approaching end to the formerly implied hope for change through intergroup cooperation.

"Kitchenette building" renders its sense of the reduction of the spirit of a people, crowded and impoverished in urban housing, mainly by the impact of contrasting images of concrete struggle for existence with those representing aspirations and dreams. Most obvious are the overripe odors of the struggle to maintain minimal dignity for body and spirit as contrasted with the level of life suggested by the music of an aria. But in addition there is the contrast between colors: the grayed life of the people versus the "white and violet" of aspiration and dream. The poem, however, should be compared with "when you have forgotten Sunday: the love story" in which the married couple creatively manage a triumph of the human spirit over circumstances.

As noted earlier, "The Sundays of Satin-Legs Smith" joins the exile rhythms with an enactment and a criticism of hip black style. The tendency of some readers is to ignore the criticism and merely to enjoy the nostalgic recollection of Smith's representation of a colorful period. The poem celebrates his powerful assertion of a sense of the beautiful through clothes, a highly styled behavior that permits withdrawal to self-gratifying indulgences including the absolute value he places upon sex. But it comes down hard on the shortcomings of Smith and the addressed white observer whose oppression has reduced the reach for beauty and evoked a response of grotesqueness. The public voice makes the situation clear, and the poet's private voice, with compassion, underlines the criticism of Smith.

> People are so in need, in need of help.
> People want so much that they do not know.
>
> Below the tinkling trade of little coins
> The gold impulse not possible to show
> Or spend. Promise piled over and betrayed.
> (*WGB*, p. 28)

Full rendering of Smith's artistry is accompanied by some of the complex irony with which the poem abounds. In the following passage, the extraordinary management of tone renders both the rhythms of Smith's triumphant gestures and a suggestion of his limitations.

> These kneaded limbs receive the kiss of silk.
> Then they receive the brave and beautiful
> Embrace of some of that equivocal wool.
> He looks into his mirror, loves himself—
> The neat curve here; the angularity

> That is appropriate at just its place;
> The technique of a variegated grace.
> (*WGB*, p. 28)

Later, the poet's tone is direct in characterizing Smith's limitations: "The pasts of his ancestors lean against/Him. Crowd him. Fog out his identity." And finally, the lyric ending of the poem ironically enforces the reader's realization of Smith's failure as artist of his existence. The reach for the absolute is usually thought of as a reach for the supreme spirit of the universe: Smith's is for the most physical sensations of sex only:

> *Her body is like new brown bread*
> *Under the Woolworth mignonette.*
> *Her body is a honey bowl*
> *Whose waiting honey is deep and hot.*
> *Her body is like summer earth,*
> *Receptive, soft, and absolute . . .*
> (*WGB*, p. 31)

Note the effect of the mixture of images and the repetition of "her body." Still, Smith, in his rituals of expression, which are really rituals of isolation from the richer elements of existence, "Judges he walks most powerfully alone,/That everything is—simply what it is."

"Satin-Legs" is an excellent example of a poem in which the poet seems to work fully all the rhythms and significance applicable to the human space occupied by her subject. Although technically the poem runs a contrast between white expectations and black reality, the reader's realization that all images of highest aspiration are in white terms is unsettling: Grieg, Tschaikovsky, "the shapely tender drift of Brahms."

No such issue arises with respect to other categories or in other poems with the same theme of the character's movement into isolation. "The ballad of chocolate Mabbie," a poem in which the heroine is pushed into spiritual isolation by intraracial prejudice against dark skin, drives home its pathos by the simple lines "Mabbie on Mabbie with hush in the heart./Mabbie on Mabbie to be." Among the heroic poems, the poise of the black soldiers in "the white troops had their orders" remains as an undisturbed image. Long after one has experienced the poem, the "Negro hero" of the piece by that title remains memorable for several reasons: the sophisticated use of sound values, the achievement of various speech tones by the speaker, rich imagery that serves ironic purposes, wit, and the tension between the existential self of the hero and his role as soldier. The title character of "The Ballad of Rudolph Reed" is made memorable by the metaphor of "oakening" as he lays down his life in defiance of the whites who would destroy his family and home. His wife also stands out coura-geously in the final lines:

> Small Mabel whimpered all night long,
> For calling herself the cause.
> Her oak-eyed mother did no thing
> But change the bloody gauze.
>
> (*WGB*, p. 362)

In "To a Winter Squirrel," a poem in which a victimized young woman admires the resources of the squirrel and considers her own limitations, the image of the woman's spirit is driven home in the second verse: "Merdice/of murdered heart and docked sarcastic soul,/Merdice/the bolted nomad, on a winter noon/cooks guts; and sits in gas. . . . " The squirrel lives in its meaning for Merdice: "She thinks you are a mountain and a star, unbaffleable;/with sentient twitch and scurry" (*WGB*, p. 407).

The poems in which the emphasis is upon blacks perceiving whites, from the point of view of the artist's intentions, offer no serious problems in the expression of bitter criticism. Such poems are intentionally a bitter satire upon white pretensions. Problems occur in the more restrained poems when the black observer becomes too cool, too detached, too oblivious of the immediately historical pres-sures in a jet-speed trip to the universal, or too pleading. Those fully achieved aesthetically, I would suggest, are three poems from *Annie Allen*. "Beverly Hills, Chicago," presents a portrait of blacks abashed by the contrast between their poverty and the material comfort and grace of white styles of living; "I love those little booths," describes whites disappointed in their expectations of the exotic behavior of blacks; and "downtown vaudeville," presents the superciliousness of whites confronting the art of a black performer.

On the other hand, "Men of Careful Turns" (*Annie Allen*), a poem attacking the idea of gradualism in race relations, loses dignity as the observer-narrator pleads to be included in the regular round of human communion. "A Bronzeville Mother" (*The Bean Eaters*) has pleased many because of the poet's stance of considering a white woman, who was the source of the lynching of an early adolescent black boy, simply as mother. In doing so, the poet ignores the grotesque histor-ical conditions that the heroine would have to work through before exemplifying the humanity with which she is endowed. "The Chicago *Defender"* (*The Bean Eaters*) also leaps over historical rhythms in order to get as quickly as possible to the universal—and thus sidesteps the nasty rhythms in the experience of attempting to integrate the schools in Little Rock, Arkansas.

The long poem "In the Mecca" gathers up the evidence of the exile status of blacks in order to balance it against the older hopes for resolution through simple human awareness. Hopes cannot rise on the scale provided by the poem. The story creating the framework of "In the Mecca" is that of Mrs. Sally returning to her numerous family from galling domestic work to discover finally her youngest child murdered by a warped man named Jamaica Eddie. With the other stories and portraits occasioned by the encounters with occupants of the huge Mecca apartment building, Mrs. Sally enforces the sense of a lost people in a lost or abandoned universe. Yet in many there are hidden beauty, tragic rhythms, charm, an awareness of profound human values. The voices of thwarted or simply hidden or confused lives are accompanied by those seeking clarity and others giving images of violent revolution. Usually the poet's voice is simply for humanness. The images of all people in this universe are incisive, hard, concrete. The apartment area and building are themselves concrete and definite in their symbolism. Indeed, so much power has been generated that a justifiable complaint, aesthetically speaking, is that it cannot be contained by the poem's ending: a beautiful dirge for the murdered Pepita, which allows for a termination on the notes of pathos and compassion. The poet Alfred, one of the poem's speakers, seems closer to the right ending note:

> something, something in Mecca
> continues to call! Substanceless; yet like
>   mountains,
> like rivers and oceans too; and like trees
> with wind whistling through them. And steadily
> an essential sanity, black and electric,
> builds to a reportage and redemption.
>   A hot estrangement.
>   A material collapse
> that is Construction.
>
> (*WGB*, p. 403)

The next poems are involved not with representation or revelation only, but with the values of liberation. Leaving to others elaborate political pronouncements, elaborate get-whitey strategies, and freewheeling suggestions of violence, Brooks seized largely upon cultivation of group and intragroup self-appreciation, togetherness, creativity, endurance, wisdom, and faith, for the liberation values to be pushed. Here her first examples of strong achievement are those involving the portrayal of personalities (Merdice of "To a Winter Squirrel," the anonymous boy of "Boy Breaking Glass" in *In the Mecca*) and such heroes as Medgar Evers and Malcolm X. These poems allowed for the exercise of the artistic reflexes that Brooks had been cultivating over the years, the results of which are frequently poems whose linguistic subtleties would confuse the mass audience of blacks she found it mandatory to reach. Note the second verse of "Medgar Evers."

> Old styles, old tempos, all the engagement of
> the day—the sedate, the regulated fray—
> the antique light, the Moral rose, old gusts,
> tight whistlings from the past, the mothballs
> in the Love at last our man foreswore.
>
> (*WGB*, p. 410)

Or these lines in "Malcolm X": "a sorcery devout and vertical/ beguiled the world." Here the poems are well conceived, achieved, and finished, nonetheless. And I'm not always sure of the judgment we make regarding what a mass audience can understand—especially a people who made so much out of complex biblical books. But it is clear that the path to the people requires watchfulness regarding self-conscious literary formalisms.

Whereas the foregoing poems are achieved, those about the street gang and its members sometimes suggest the need for a longer stage of conceptualization or another kind of execution. Many hoped that street gangs, with their presumed ability to see through establishment values, would turn to love and liberation values in behalf of their communities, but the historical record will probably show that, given the nature of street gangs, such turnings are not easily to be anticipated. In "Gang Girls" (*In the Mecca*), the poet engaged gang realities closely, and found the girls to be captive souls whose sacrifice was great. The poet reveals the situation, but neither indicates responsible parties nor makes a relationship with liberation.

Brooks's next three pamphlet-like books began to be more suggestive regarding the aesthetics of her newer approach to audience. The title poem of *Riot* (1969) suggests a movement toward a more straight-line simplicity, although words continue to work for complex suggestion. The other poems in the volume maintain the simplicity of the first poem, and one of them, "An Aspect of Love, Alive in the Ice and Fire," has the majestic finish which one experiences with the earlier work. *Family Pictures* (1970)[6] and *Beckonings* (1975) confirm that simplicity, a hardworking but less complex diction, and further negotiations with folk forms and their values increasingly form a part of her emerging system. Besides the difficulty posed by the necessity to change old artistic habits, the poet faced a rather fluid political situation and the changing responses of blacks to it. The titles of the three little books are significant regarding such changes. *Family Pictures* suggests at-homeness among friends, but *Beckonings* suggests that the poet must now point to the areas where values must be developed and maintained. This role is likely to make the development of the poet's newer aesthetic an even greater struggle, because it frequently demands artistic constructs that are admonitory, hortatory, and prophetic—roles that threaten to become enveloped in abstract terms. We have seen, however, that Brooks's great gift is the concrete. And the poems of *Beckonings* show that she is aware of such threats and is preparing to meet them.

It is difficult to be more than tentative about the liberation poems. But the will and commitment that created the earlier poems will also probably effect its triumph in this category. How great a triumph? Only the future can tell.

Notes

1. Gwendolyn Brooks, *The World of Gwendolyn Brooks* (New York: Harper and Row, 1971), pp. 32–34. Hereinafter cited in the text as *WGB*.

2. *Bronzeville Boys and Girls* (New York: Harper and Row, 1956); *Aloneness* (Detroit: Broadside Press, 1971); and *The Tiger Who Wore White Gloves* (Chicago: Third World Press, 1974).

3. *Selected Poems* (New York: Harper and Row, 1963).

4. *Riot* (Detroit: Broadside Press, 1969); *Beckonings* (Detroit: Broadside Press, 1975).

5. Richard Wright to Edward C. Aswell, 18 Sept. 1944, in Gwendolyn Brooks File, Harper and Row, New York, N.Y.

6. *Family Pictures* (Detroit: Broadside Press, 1970).

4

The World of Satin-Legs, Mrs. Sallie, and the Blackstone Rangers: The Restricted Chicago of Gwendolyn Brooks

On August 15, 1967, less than a year before the riot that was to rock Chicago and make it a symbol for the nation's shame, the city's elite were invited to the Civic Center Plaza to witness the unveiling of Picasso's gift to the city. By this time Gwendolyn Brooks had already become an acknowledged leader of the literary community. There were other poets in Chicago, but none was better known. Her work— *A Street in Bronzeville* (1945), *Annie Allen* (1949), for which she had received a Pulitzer Prize in 1950, the novel *Maud Martha* (1953), and *The Bean Eaters* (1960)—had turned national attention to the city once again. For a place whose commitment to culture was often questioned, Brooks was the resident and visible manifestation of Art; hence, it came as no surprise that she was among the political, social, and cultural dignitaries who gathered in the Civic Center Plaza to see the gigantic sculpture that was an enigma to many.

There had been much discussion about Picasso's gift. Some said it was a seated woman, others claimed it was an unidentifiable bird poised for flight. One or two suggested that it was really a representation of the artist's Afghan hound. Still others dismissed it as just a pile of Corten steel and thought it was an ultimate joke on Chicago. Nonetheless, for this momentous event marking the first such public art in the city's business district, the celebrated Chicago Symphony Orchestra played, and Gwendolyn Brooks recited her commemorative ode, "The Chicago Picasso," which opens with the lines:

Does man love Art? Man visits Art, but squirms.
Art hurts. Art urges voyages—
and it is easier to stay at home,
the nice beer ready.[1]

As thousands visited the plaza to see "the thing" or "the Picasso" (what it was called depended upon the viewer's orientation), the city's newspapers heralded the occasion for days with articles and photographs.

On August 27, 1967, less than two weeks later, another dedication to art took place in the city. It was also "a first," but the political, social, and cultural dignitaries were not present. Brooks had told them earlier that "art urges voyages—/and it is easier to stay at home." They did. Indeed, the corner of 43rd Street and Langley Avenue, in the heart of the black South Side ghetto, was not a place to visit until an election year. Some of the absent dignitaries undoubtedly convinced themselves that a crude mural on the outside wall of a dilapidated slum building had no significance. Others may have secretly thought the painting nothing more than glorified graffiti, and South Side buildings were commonly decorated in such a manner. Called "The Wall of Respect," the mural depicted the heroes and struggles of an oppressed race. Clearly William Walker, its principal designer, was not Picasso, nor were the twenty-one artists who joined with him and the 43rd Street Community Organization; but together they began the "mural movement" in the city and were forerunners of many such joint artistic and community efforts. For that day Brooks wrote "The Wall."

A drumdrumdrum.
Humbly we come.
South of success and east of gloss and glass are
sandals;
flowercloth;
grave hoops of wood or gold, pendant
from black ears, brown ears, reddish-brown
and ivory ears;

black boy-men.
Black
boy-men on roofs fist out "Black Power!" Val,
a little black stampede
in African
images of brass and flowerswirl,
fists out "Black Power!"—tightens pretty eyes,

leans back on mothercountry and is tract,
is treatise through her perfect and tight teeth.

Women in wool hair chant their poetry.

Phil Cohran gives us messages and music
made of developed bone and polished and honed cult.
It is the Hour of tribe and of vibration,
the day-long Hour. It is the Hour
of ringing, rouse, of ferment-festival.

On Forty-third and Langley
black furnaces resent ancient
legislatures
of ploy and scruple and practical gelatin.
They keep the fever in,
fondle the fever.

All
worship the Wall.

I mount the rattling wood. Walter
says, "She is good." Says, "She
our Sister is." In front of me
hundreds of faces, red-brown, brown, black, ivory,
yield me hot trust, their year and their Announcement
that they are ready to rile the high-flung ground.
Behind me, Paint.
Heroes.
No child has defiled
the Heroes of this Wall this serious Appointment
this still wing
this Scald this Flute this heavy Light this Hinge.

An emphasis is paroled.
The old decapitations are revised,
the dispossessions beakless.

And we sing.

(*WGB*, pp. 414–15)

A few may have visited the mural out of curiosity, but the city's newspapers duly ignored the event.

"The Chicago Picasso" and "The Wall" illustrate how completely Gwendolyn Brooks faced the dilemma of a divided Chicago. Accepted and praised by the city's elite, she nonetheless gave voice to the inarticulate of her urban community and assured posterity to the would-be losers. Yet within the framework of Chicago's literature, she is philosophically and aesthetically part of a tradition that had its beginning in the early city.

Long before other writers were willing to admit the urban mystique into the realm of literature, the Chicago novelists had examined the role of the city. During the latter part of the nineteenth century and into the twentieth, writers as diverse as E. P. Roe, Henry Blake Fuller, Robert Herrick, Frank Norris, Theodore Dreiser, and Sherwood Anderson had shown the extent to which a city could condition the lives of its inhabitants. In so doing, they made the sense of place a major part of their work, and readers were always aware of the powerful city looming behind the reactions of the characters. Although they had appeared earlier in fiction, cities were frequently used as either a background to prove the evil consequences of industrialism or as a setting for an action that was not particularly related to the locale. Beginning with the journalists and continuing through the novelists, Chicago's writers claimed that the city was a mighty force that not only had to have a language that would best transmit its meaning, but also—of even greater importance—implied that readers would have to cast aside the old moralities in order to understand the significance of the city in American life.[2]

Adapting the principles of Darwin to their fictional world, the early writers explored the national myth of success, and agreed that the American dream was really rooted in an economic system that accepted (often reluctantly to be sure) the businessman as the ultimate hero. While those who succumbed to the promises of the city were often pathetic, even the successful were not exempt from urban control. Unquestionably a realism that often bordered on naturalism (a technique still not quite respectable in the East) was considered the most effective medium for such literature. From this period came some city-based stories and characters that were destined to alter the American novel.

William Dean Howells, the high priest of the American critical establishment, praised the perceptions of Chicago's writers. Furthermore, he singled out the so-called democratic elements of the city's literature as "the really valuable contributions of the West, and of Chicago in which the West has come to consciousness." In fact, he declared "the democracy which was the faith of New England became the life of the West and now is the Western voice in our literary art."[3] Somewhat later H. L. Mencken was to call the city "the literary capital of the United States" and stated "all literary movements that have youth in them and a fresh point of view" are products of Chicago, "the most civilized city in America." He observed: "Find me a writer who is indubitably American and who has something new and interesting to say and who says it with an air, and nine times out of ten . . . he has some sort of connection with the abbatoir by the lake—that he was bred there or got his start there, or passed through there during the days when he was tender."[4]

While the nineteenth-century journalists had made much of human interest stories that featured tales of the city's downtrodden and the major novelists had examined the lives of businessmen, it was not until the early years of the twentieth century that there was the rise of a protest literature. In 1905 Clarence Darrow (perhaps a better lawyer than novelist) had exposed a judicial system that favored the privileged in *An Eye for an Eye*. The following year Upton Sinclair portrayed an immigrant family who journeyed to Chicago in search of the promised American dream only to find a nightmare of unrelieved filth and corruption that finally led to the degradation of the human spirit. *The Jungle* forced readers to see another side of urban America. A fictionalized version of the Haymarket Affair appeared in 1908. *The Bomb* by Frank Harris stresses the city's antipathy toward alien groups and demonstrates the gulf between the haves and the have-nots, between capital and labor. Because many of these early protests did not treat anger artistically, the polemical nature of the works often intruded upon their aesthetic experience.

Studies of Chicago eventually must take into consideration the peculiar regionalism within the city. Like its actual counterpart, literary Chicago is divided into three areas although for a number of years writers minimized the distinctions between the south, north, and west divisions. Readers, of course, were aware that the early fictional titan lived on South Michigan or South Prairie or South Drexel while later ones lived on the north side; but much action transpired in downtown commercial structures, where such elusives as "the power" or "the spirit" of the city were stressed. Finally, the "sides" of Chicago were too prominent to be ignored; the work of James T. Farrell, Nelson Algren, Richard Wright, and Meyer Levin gave another form to the urban novel. The city was now defined in terms of specific ethnic neighborhoods. Thus, in addition to various elements of protest are the memorable portraits of Farrell's southside Irish, Wright's Black Belt, Algren's Polish communities of the northwest, and Levin's Jewish sections on West Twelfth Street.

If Chicago's novelists (first through tales of the dominant business elite, then through protest fiction and chronicles of urban neighborhoods that Blanche Gelfant has called "ecological novels")[5] were strangely influenced by the city, the poets seemed to offer a rejection of such an effect. Consequently, the realism of Chicago's fiction is not initially seen in the city's poetry. For instance, William Vaughn Moody—perhaps one of the most outstanding of the early poets—was untouched by the regional tradition. Later, when Harriet Monroe published Carl Sandburg's "Chicago" in *Poetry*, the work was scorned by the highly respected *Dial*, which announced: "The typographical arrangement of this jargon creates a suspicion that it is to be taken seriously as some form of poetry, and that suspicion is confirmed by the fact that it stands in the forefront of the latest issue of a futile little periodical described as a 'magazine of verse.'"[6] What obviously bothered the editors of the *Dial* was Sandburg's reliance upon a stark realism when many in the national literary establishment preferred the glow of the romantic tradition in poetry.

Although not as antagonistic as the *Dial* but fearing that the idea of Chicago as "the hog butcher of the world" would become a dominant poetic image, Charles G. Blanden and Minna Mathison issued *The Chicago Anthology: A Collection of Verse from the Work of Chicago Poets* in 1916. Of the 176 poems in the volume, only two specifically are related to the urban experience, with four somewhat remotely attached to the region. The commemorative poems to Theodore Thomas, David Swing, and Maurice Browne are of Chicago only insofar as their subjects were part of the city's life. In the anthology's introduction, Llewellyn Jones—the outstanding critic of the Chicago Renaissance—took issue with the popularity of Sandburg's singular poetic portrait of the city. He argued "the realists are uttering a dangerous half truth when they tell us that the poet must write about what he sees with the corporeal eye. The only thing the poet . . . can write about is his own soul—and this applies just as much to the dramatic poet as to the lyric singer." As if to answer any objection concerning the lack of social realism in the volume, Jones avowed that the poems presented "were just as much inspired by Chicago as if they had been written concerning the stockyards."[7]

That Sandburg's *Chicago Poems* should have also appeared during the same year as *The Chicago Anthology* is perhaps one of those coincidences of publishing history. Generally, however, Chicago's poets—even those who subscribed to the tenets of freedom associated with the work of Walt Whitman—were not sure about the use of their city. Lacking the confidence of the prose writers, they were content to write about European scenes and those abstractions that are considered to be the purview of poetry, apparently believing that a rendition of the city in poetic form would somehow destroy the "artistry" and the acceptability of their work.

For many years the history of poetry in Chicago was best told not only through *Poetry: A Magazine of Verse*, but also through the multitude of poetry discussion groups in the city. While the Chicago Renaissance had placed great emphasis upon literary freedom as had the literary pages of the daily newspapers, there was an uneasy alliance between the city and poetry. When regional elements were used, poetry tended to express the "midwestern spirit" as in the work of Edgar Lee Masters and Vachel Lindsay. Cast in the mold of Sandburg, some of Sherwood Anderson's verse in *Mid-American Chants* (1918) attempted to deal with the city; but generally, the poets— unlike the storytellers who produced a Chicago novel—seldom created much that was rooted in the actuality of the urban experience. Thus, Gwendolyn Brooks became one of the first poets in Chicago to produce a significant body of urban poetry as she followed some of the patterns of the city's novelists and transferred the urban concerns of the Harlem Renaissance to her city.

In 1945, five years after Richard Wright's native son intruded upon the consciousness of the American reading public, Gwendolyn Brooks's examination of an unnamed street in Bronzeville appeared. In a series of poems she explored both the hope and the hopelessness of a people caught in the maelstrom of an uncaring city. Her Chicago was the South Side Black Belt (affectionately called "Bronzeville" by some of its inhabitants[8] and referred to as the "Black Metropolis" by social scientists), which had developed through the years and which began to fade with the construction of huge public housing complexes. In a measure, its initial growth was affected by the Washington-Du Bois controversy. Among the early community leaders were integrationists and separatists, each group maintaining its way would lead to the achievement of first-class citizenship. At the same time, black Chicago was as much a product of the American dream as other ethnic communities in the city. Despite failures and disappointments, there were many visible evidences of success.

It was clear, however, by the opening of World War I that the animosity of the white population had reached such proportions that it seemed the best response was to make certain that self-sufficiency would not be sacrificed in a search for an integrated society. In spite of the debilitating effects of the race riot of 1919, the 1920s saw continued migrations into the city. For a period in its history, Chicago was the destination of Negroes who felt that the city offered a place where their dreams could be realized. Old residents still tell tales about the days when it was said: "If you can't make it in Chicago, you can't make it anywhere." That some did make it was used as proof of the efficacy of the American dream.

The roster of the successful reads like a who's who of black America. These men and women demonstrated that the city held promises at least for some. There was a thriving business district (a portion of which has recently been nominated as one of the city's historic districts). Centered near 35th and State streets, this area—really the core of Black Metropolis—was the locale not only of the Binga State Bank but also of the Douglas National Bank, which was the first black bank to receive a national charter. Black entrepreneurs who built commercial structures included not only Jesse Binga and Anthony Overton but also Joseph Jordan, who provided offices for the Pyramid Building and Loan Association. One could find the offices of the city's first black architect, Walter T. Bailey, in the district as well as various newspaper offices and real estate firms. Radiating from this center were Frank Gillespie's Liberty Life Insurance Company and the world-famous Olivet Baptist Church, which had been established in 1850. Eventually boasting a membership of ten thousand, it had moved to 31st Street and South Parkway in 1918 and provided many services for the new Chicagoans. Equally impressive were the successfuls' showplace homes that lined the major thoroughfares. (That many of the houses had been abandoned in the inevitable "white flight" was seldom mentioned.) With such a concentration of capital, people, and power, it is not surprising that the political organization of black Chicago was the envy of other cities.

And so it was that many blacks crowded into the Illinois Central Railroad and were literally disgorged at the old Twelfth Street Station unceremoniously called "Uncle Tom's Cabin" by less charitable Chicagoans. From that terminal, they crowded into the city's South Side buildings and abandoned West Side houses, all of which had been partitioned to bring the greatest dollar per square foot for the least amount of space. Others managed to do a little better with their housing, but jobs were not plentiful; and all of them were victimized by both black and white Chicago. Among the migrants were David and Keziah Brooks with their small daughter, Gwendolyn. They were fortunate to find one of those unimpressive balloon-frame construction houses for which Chicago is known. Like those of other newcomers to the city, their dreams for the future were dashed by the realities of their present. Mrs. Brooks had been a teacher in Kansas. Mr. Brooks, a former student at Fisk University, had wanted to be a doctor; but once settled in Chicago, he had to accept various odd jobs to sustain his family. Writing of those days, Keziah Brooks said: "Since both my husband and I had always believed welfare was only for sick and elderly people, we had never considered being on relief, regardless of conditions. Therefore, the Depression had an adverse effect on our lives."[9] Yet, despite economic privations, family life was loving, disciplined, and supportive for the young child.

Other families, however, became discouraged as they discovered that the promise of the city had been merely a mirage that had lured them from their former homes. The postwar years soon led to the disillusionment of the depression. By the 1930s and 1940s, the heirs to the American dream had become the disenchanted and the dispossessed. A generation had been produced that no longer had faith in itself. Many of its members were frustrated by a place that apparently offered no way out. Even the role models in the community were scattered and did not seem as commanding as they once had been. Urban renewal, derisively called "Negro removal," had destroyed much of the best of the Black Metropolis.

The urban world that Gwendolyn Brooks examines in her work is fundamentally the universe of the city's South Side ghetto after years of benign neglect. This is not "the city triumphant." Hers is not a city of the successful whose stories were used to prove the actuality of the promise of the good life. This is not the Chicago of the elite, not the city of spectacular boulevards and buildings. This is a city of back streets and alleys, of kitchenettes and vacant lots. The American dream no longer mattered to the people whose lives had so consistently been empty that they often were not aware of its nightmarish quality. Brooks's Bronzeville is symbolic of the impersonality of the overcrowded ghetto generally ignored by white Chicagoans caught in the daily activities of their own lives. Few, of course, realized that existing behind the facades of the multitude of kitchenette buildings were some ordinary people leading ordinary lives not daring to dream their dreams. Locked into a community that was isolated psychologically and physically from the rest of the city, they were among the forgotten of Chicago. In the end, Brooks's restricted Chicago is a place of despair and loneliness where even God, faith, and the more soothing aspects of religion seldom penetrate. Yet, her work is not antireligious. The miracle of life is expressed not in some philosophical manifesto but in the very fact that her people—in spite of everything—can exist from day to day.

While she writes of the ordinary lives of the dispossessed (hardly the traditional subject for poetry), her poems become extraordinary and made rich not only through deft handling of language, but also by her variety of forms. Ironically, her mother predicted that her daughter would be "the *lady* Paul Laurence Dunbar."[10] Undoubtedly her mother was interested in the public and popular poet, but few ever realized the extent to which he experimented with form. Although perhaps not as avant garde in his time as Whitman, Dunbar utilized various stanza patterns and rhyme schemes. His study of English poetry and the American local colorists convinced him that the poetic instinct had to be accompanied by an understanding of the relationship between form and function. That he often used traditional patterns should not blind readers to the number of instances when he did not. Brooks has also made it clear that poetry is more than instinct. She studied the work of other poets, participated in workshops, and learned much from other writers. If her subjects are generally controlled by what she observed of the life of Bronzeville, her verse patterns run the gamut from the expected to the avant garde. Couplets, tercets, and quatrains combine with variations of the rhyme royal and the sonnet ultimately to move to a free verse that frequently utilizes one- or two-word lines. Brooks demonstrates the versatility of Dunbar and the subsequent poets of both the Chicago Movement and the Harlem Renaissance.

Rejection of a slavish fidelity to historic and conventional patterns has always been one of the marks of innovative poets. Even when they could not do it, the literati of the Chicago Renaissance insisted that poets should be as true to themselves as to their craft without an undue regard for the niceties of human behavior or for the past. The obligation to tell "the truth" placed emphasis upon reality as the poets understood it. Margery Currey, Eunice Tietjens, Alice Corbin Henderson, Margaret Anderson, and Harriet Monroe were among those who realized that the times called for a redefinition of Art. (It is perhaps unfortunate that the more devout black aestheticians equate artistic freedom with a denial of what they consider to be "white" forms without understanding the history of literary protests.) Essentially Brooks achieved the independence that was much-admired among the Renaissance participants. While she employs dramatic monologues and narratives—especially the ballad—with extreme care, her lyrics bring a new interpretation to the form in a setting where life rarely "sings." Probably the test of her versatility is best displayed in long poems such as "In the Mecca," where the form is altered to match the various speakers. Furthermore, even before Brooks became closely associated with the more recent group of black poets, her work exhibited the sharpness, the brevity, the heavy rhythms and independence from historic forms that characterize their work. At the same time, if one considers the extent of her public performances and popularity, she did indeed become the *"lady* Dunbar." Few modern poets have succeeded more in bringing poetry to the people.

Thus in many ways several literary movements seemed to converge in Brooks. Like the early novelists of Chicago, she tacitly accepted the notion of the city's power. She has also acknowledged that she saw in the work of Langston Hughes "that writing about the ordinary aspects of black life was important."[11] The economy of language that marked, for example, Sandburg's "Fog" and the celebration of jazz rhythms that one finds in Langston Hughes seem to meet in Brooks's study of the seven urban pool players in "We Real Cool." Blyden Jackson has spoken perceptively of her increased usage of language compression.

> Her craftsmanship is careful. [She] belongs to the school of writers who do not believe in wasting a single word. Selection and significance—one can divine in her diction how she has brooded over them, how every word has been chosen with due regard for the several functions it may be called upon to perform in the dispensation of a poem. But the brooding goes deep and it affects not only words. The words must be put together. And the principle of dire economy which governs her choice of diction disciplines severely all of her poetic maneuvers. Terseness, a judicious understatement combined with pregnant ellipses, often guides the reader into an adventure which permits a revelation of Miss Brooks' capacity for sensitive interpretations of the human comedy.[12]

In addition to a superb sense of language, Gwendolyn Brooks has a clear vision that permits her to observe her people in a particular setting that articulates a consciousness of the relationship between *place* and *life*. No reader of urban literature can ever again be satisfied with such simplistic assumptions that begin with *"the city is."* Arthur P. Davis has called Brooks "the poet of the unheroic." He has noted that "for her the modern world [is] *unheroic.*" Her people "lack bigness; we are little creatures contented with little things and little moments," but Davis says "she understands and sympathizes with our littleness."[13] Yet, despite her acute sense of observation that readily sees the many ironies of her characters and their lives, Brooks never pokes fun at them. In fact, many of her people even seem suspended in time, place, and history. Thus she has the ability to endow simple facts with complex meanings, and the importance of her work ultimately rests in the wealth of interpretations that result from her view of urban life.

Perhaps Brooks's characters are not a memorable lot if considered individually, but collectively they display the pathos and frustrations of modern life in a restricted neighborhood. Many of the people of her universe are unnamed and are as anonymous as their drab lives. Among them are the silent "old marrieds," the mother contemplating the meaning of abortion, the hunchback girl looking forward to death, pretty men who are useless, and disappointed women including the plain black girls for whom life means little. Others, like the "explorer," are futilely searching for a "still spot in the noise" or are in the process of making discoveries such as the reporter from the *Chicago Defender.* Although the persona of "Strong Men, Riding Horses" seems obtuse, the reader is able to understand the difference between the heroics of a televised western and the reality of ghetto life. "A Man of the Middle Class" recognizes that his imitation of others has produced nothing but emptiness, and the old woman of "A Sunset of the City" questions whether the answer for a life where she is "no longer looked at with lechery or love" is "to leap and die." All of these unnamed characters are urban figures who exist in an environment that does not actively conspire against them; the city simply does not care. That many of them live in kitchenette buildings where dreams "fight with fried potatoes/And yesterday's garbage ripening in the hall" adds to a general sense of hopelessness. If such people as the dead owner of a beauty school—whose "fortune" is "converted into hard steel" and buried with her—assume a universality, those who are identified by name are also prototypes. On the surface, Mrs. Martin who escapes from her personal shame by moving "to the low west side of town," weary "Hattie Scott" who has little to anticipate, the harried Mrs. Small, "sweet Annie," "poor Percy"—the one-year-old killed by "his brother Brucie"—and even Matthew Cole who lives on Lafayette Street where "the red fat roaches . . . stroll/unafraid up his wall" seem so particularized; yet in the end they somehow transcend the insignificance of the episodes related about them.

The urban world of Satin-Legs Smith is a circumscribed universe. One of his greatest joys is his collection of highly styled outlandish clothes in "the innards of [his] closet," which Brooks describes as "a vault"

> Whose glory is not diamonds, not pearls,
> Not silver plate with just enough dull shine.
> But wonder-suits in yellow and in wine,

Sarcastic green and zebra-striped cobalt.
All drapes. With shoulder padding that is wide
And cocky and determined as his pride;
Ballooning pants that taper off to ends
Scheduled to choke precisely.
                              Here are hats
Like bright umbrellas; and hysterical ties
Like narrow banners for some gathering war.
                              (*WGB*, pp. 27–28)

Essentially his life is limited to his Sundays. After the ritual of selecting an outfit, he preens, struts down the street, and passes time at the movies where he can live vicariously through others; but even here his race intrudes upon his perceptions. Hence, he joins in "boo[ing]/the hero's kiss, and . . . the heroine/Whose ivory and yellow it is sin/For his eye to eat of." Like Wright's Bigger Thomas, Satin-Legs relies on a celluloid world to add some excitement in his life. Later he and his girl of the moment have dinner at "Joe's Eats," where "you get your fish or chicken on meat platters./With coleslaw, macaroni, candied sweets,/Coffee and apple pie."

Ludicrous though he seems, however, he is not a comic figure.

The pasts of his ancestors lean against
Him. Crowd him. Fog out his identity.
Hundreds of hungers mingle with his own,
Hundreds of voices advise so dexterously
He quite considers his reactions his,
Judges he walks most powerfully alone,
That everything is—simply what is.
                              (*WGB*, p. 30)

Satin-Legs obviously exists from day to day, looking forward to the repetitive pattern of his leisure time. He does not question his barren life. In fact, he may not even know that it is empty. Confined to a restricted neighborhood, unmindful of any opportunities, he has to snatch what little pleasure he can. One wonders if the wistful persona of "a song in the front yard" (*WGB*, p. 12) will grow up to be another version of Satin-Legs. There seems to be an absence of role models in Brooks's Bronzeville; at any rate, after her mother cautions that Johnnie Mae "will grow up to be a bad woman," the lonesome speaker says: "I'd like to be a bad woman, too,/And wear the brave stockings of night-black lace/And strut down the streets with paint on my face." That she—like Satin-Legs—is black and a victim of the ghetto is ultimately inconsequential. They are also victims of their respective searches for "a good time today."

In the Mecca (1968) presents one of Brooks's clearest portraits of the discarded people who get the scraps and leftovers of life. Mrs. Sallie Smith is the central figure of the title poem. The irony and tragedy of her life are made more complete by her residence in the apartment building named the Mecca. An actual structure built in 1891 during the period when Chicago was considered to be the innovative architectural capital of the world, and located a short distance from the famous Prairie Avenue (Chicago's original "gold coast"), the Mecca was an early example of a multifamily dwelling for the wealthy. Apartments were still rare in the United States, and no luxury was spared in the execution of this structure. Designed by George Edbrooke, who had already become famous for his ability to utilize aesthetically large spaces, and built by the D. H. Burnham Company, the Mecca made use of the atrium long before modern architects understood this classical method of bringing the outdoors inside. Its central courtyards topped by skylights were poetic combinations in space of iron grillwork and glass. Decorated with plush carpeting and working fountains, these enclosed courts were fitting entranceways to the elaborate apartments of the elite who lived in the much-discussed Mecca. During the Columbian Exposition of 1893 it was one of the places in the city that visitors wanted to see. (Later it was still a tourist attraction, but not because of its beauty.)

Because the city's wealthy began to move to the north side at the turn of the century, the building—which is now seldom mentioned in official documents—did not have a long heyday. Even Burnham's major biographers exclude his involvement with the building for, like Frank Lloyd Wright's Francis Apartments (also located in what became the heart of the Black Belt), the Mecca became a symbol for the colossal failure of at least one aspect of urban life. For those who trace the history of a city through the rise and fall of its buildings, how poignant must have been the degeneration of the Mecca from the stunning showplace for the elite to an overcrowded tenement for thousands of dispossessed blacks. Estimates of the number of people who lived in the building ranged from three to nine thousand. Nobody seemed to know for certain, and no one apparently cared. But the Mecca's great hulk warned a city of its failure to come to terms with change and reminded a group of urban isolates that they had been consigned to the bowels of the city. Razed in 1952, the Mecca remains in memory as a symbol of absolute urban blight.

Given, then, the history and the nature of the Mecca, it is telling that Brooks should have begun her long narrative poem with a line that sounds almost biblical: "Now the way of the Mecca was on this wise." On one level the work chronicles the plight of Mrs. Sallie who, weary after a long day's work, looks forward to climbing to her apartment in search of "marvelous rest." Her symbolic rise will lead to nothing more exciting than preparing an uninspired dinner for her family. In the midst of her task, however, she discovers that her daughter, Pepita, is missing. Thus, instead of the rest she so richly deserves, it is necessary to search for Pepita. Her own anxiety reinforces the underlying violence of place. It is made even more terrible through understated descriptions of the once-magnificent building.

While the pathos of Mrs. Sallie's search is very real, the poem serves as a means by which Brooks examines other fragmented lives of the tenants of the overcrowded Mecca. There is, for example, Alfred who is a teacher but longs to be a writer. There is also Don Lee, the poet, who has already denied the America of comfort and unreachable dreams. He does not wish to see "a various America."

> Don Lee wants
> a new nation
> under nothing . . .
> wants
> new art and anthem; will
> want a new music screaming in the sun.
> (*WGB*, pp. 393–94)

Amos, still another tenant, says a prayer for America:

> "Bathe her in her beautiful blood.
> A long blood bath will wash her pure . . .
> Slap the false sweetness from that face.
> Great-nailed boots
> must kick her prostrate, heel-grind that soft breast,
> outrage her saucy pride . . .
> Let her lie there, panting and wild, her pain
> red . . .
> With nothing to do but think, think
> of how she was so long grand,
> flogging her dark one with her own hand,
> watching in meek amusement while he bled.
> Then shall she rise, recover.
> Never to forget."
> (*WGB*, pp. 394–95)

Along the same philosophical lines, Way-Out Morgan, a gun collector, "listens to Blackness stern and blunt and beautiful." As he recalls southern and northern injustices, he "predicts the Day of

Debt-pay shall begin." The militants in the building are balanced by such pathetic creatures as "great-great Gram [who] hobbles, fumbles at the knob,/[and] mumbles, 'I ain't seen no Pepita.'" But the query about the lost one brings to her mind life in a slave cabin where "we six-uns curled/in corners of the dirt, and closed our eyes,/and went to sleep—or listened to the rain/fall inside, felt the drops/big on our noses." As the search for Pepita continues and the reader is introduced to various characters, one becomes aware that these people are trapped not only by their dreams of urban life, but also by the Mecca itself.

Gwendolyn Brooks captures in a series of sketches and brilliantly executed lines the pervasive misery of the place. During the days when restrictive covenants prevailed in Chicago, the Black Belt represented the same diversity that one finds in the apartment building. There are those who—like Mrs. Sallie—pathetically display the desperate acceptance of what the city offers simply because they are powerless before overwhelming and little-understood forces. Some speak of a violence that is to come, but they seem more consumed by rhetoric than action and are equally pathetic. Then there are those who prey upon the residents, such as Prophet Williams who has "an office" in the Mecca, and Jamaican Edward, the murderer of Pepita.

Following the title poem are others gathered under the heading "After Mecca," and they include not only the odes to the Picasso sculpture and Wall of Respect but also a three-part poem "The Blackstone Rangers," devoted to the highly organized South Side gang whose "country is a Nation on no map." That black Chicago is often victimized by "black crime" is a reality that does not need sensational news accounts to document. The turning upon one's own is the price, as Brooks suggests, that must be paid for the sense of futility that often accompanies urban life. For example, at the end of "Beverly Hills, Chicago," the personae look longingly at the nice houses in the white neighborhood; afterwards "when we speak to each other our voices are a little gruff." This sense of inadequacy can, of course, lead to more overt actions. While black Chicago was being terrorized by the Blackstone P. Nation, Gwendolyn Brooks and others were attempting to work with some of the members of the gang on the supposition that they had artistic statments that needed to be heard. Her poem, then, recognizes the potential for violence in Bronzeville while it celebrates some of the leaders of the Rangers.

Much, of course, has been made of the alleged "conversion" of Gwendolyn Brooks to black nationalism. She herself probably gave more credence to the meaning of the 1967 Second Black Writers Conference at Fisk University than it really deserved.[14] Changing one's hair style and refusing certain amenities from a white reading public, while perhaps significant political statements, are ultimately far more cosmetic than substantive. From the beginning of her work Brooks was well aware that racism was a powerful consideration in the American experience, and protest has served as a cornerstone of her poetic world. It has varied from gentle observation to bitter invective. She did not need anyone to remind her of conditions in the black ghetto nor to help her understand the depth of the effects of prejudice—not only on the victims, but also on the perpetrators. Like her predecessors from the slave poets to those of the Harlem Renaissance, she took note of the strange dichotomy between American practices and American rhetoric. Consequently, the distillation of the urban experience is coupled by a racial fire that indicates that Brooks has always been able to channel the injustices of racism into a poetic experience.

During the early days of World War II, Dorie Miller became one of the first military heroes for black America. Every school child in Chicago knew the story of the man who had been forced by his race to be a cook in the Navy rather than a fighting man; yet, when his ship was attacked, he left his post in the kitchen. In the dramatic monologue "Negro Hero," which recounts his deeds, the persona observes he "had to kick their law into their teeth in order to save them." Increasingly, the demands of loyalty to a flawed democracy tax the real meaning of patriotism.

The intellectualizing that appears to inform "men of careful turns, haters of forks in the road" at the end of *Annie Allen* is abandoned in "The Ballad of Rudolph Reed," which appears in *The Bean Eaters*. The hero of the tale is simply a man who works hard and who wants his family to have a house where the plaster will remain on the walls and where they "may never hear the roaches/Falling like fat rain." When he finds the house of his dreams, he fails to notice the displeasure of his white neighbors. Even when the rock-throwing begins, he is prepared to ignore it until one of his small daughters is injured.

> Then up did rise our Rudolph Reed
> And pressed the hand of his wife,
> And went to the door with a thirty-four
> And a beastly butcher knife.

He ran like a mad thing into the night.
And the words in his mouth were stinking.
By the time he had hurt his first white man
He was no longer thinking.

By the time he had hurt his fourth white man
Rudolph Reed was dead.
His neighbors gathered and kicked his corpse.
"Nigger—" his neighbors said.

(*WGB*, p. 362)

The simple desire for decent housing takes on some of the aspects of "the impossible dream" in a city once governed by restrictive covenants, and where, in "Beverly Hills, Chicago," Brooks notes that "even the leaves fall down in lovelier patterns here." Clearly "The Ballad of Rudolph Reed" is a response to the prolonged Trumbull Park housing riots of the 1950s but is—unfortunately—as applicable today as it was then. (In 1984 a family was forced to move from a modest house in a white Chicago neighborhood when the house was attacked and the garage burned.)

The efforts of some whites to alleviate suffering in the slums result in the pathetically humorous presentation of the ladies from the Betterment League, who in "The Lovers of the Poor" visit an over-crowded slum building that proves to be "entirely too much for them." These suburban ladies belong to a "guild" that "is giving money to the poor./The worthy poor/The very very worthy/And beautiful poor." But there is nothing beautiful about the experience.

The stench; the urine, cabbage, and dead beans,
Dead porridges of dusty assorted grains,
The old smoke, *heavy* diapers, and, they're told,
Something called chitterlings. The darkness. Drawn
Darkness, or dirty light. The soil that stirs.
The soil that looks the soil of centuries.
And for that matter the *general* oldness. Old
Wood. Old marble. Old tile. Old old old.

(*WGB*, p. 334)

Then in a masterful stroke of description, Brooks explains:

Not homekind Oldness! Not Lake Forest, Glencoe.
Nothing is sturdy, nothing is majestic,
There is no quiet drama, no rubbed glaze, no
Unkillable infirmity of such
A tasteful turn as lately they have left,

Glencoe, Lake Forest, and to which their cars
Must presently restore them. . . .

(*WGB*, p. 334)

If the North in general, and Chicago in particular, are imagined to represent hope for a better life, "Of DeWitt Williams on His Way to Lincoln Cemetery" dispels the notion. Although DeWitt was "born in Alabama./Bred in Illinois./He was nothing but a/Plain black boy." One of Gwendolyn Brooks's best analyses of race in America tangentially deals with another "plain black boy." Titled, "A Bronzeville Mother Loiters in Mississippi. Meanwhile, a Mississippi Mother Burns Bacon" and told by the white woman who caused the murder of the young Chicagoan Emmett Till, the poem is an excellent study of the violence and warped mentalities that perpetuate certain types of racial confrontations. Like all occasional poetry, this one is restricted by the limitations of the event; but like the best of such poetry, it rises above the specificity of the moment. The reader becomes quite aware of the helplessness of victims of racial violence, including the women whose "honor" is allegedly protected by brutish and loutish men. The reporter in "The Chicago *Defender* Sends a Man to Little Rock" observes that his editor wants the story of the violence of Little Rock, but the journalist discovers that there is no *big story* in that small Arkansas town. In fact, the people of Little Rock are simply "like people everywhere," and he concludes "the loveliest lynchee was our Lord."

Whether or not one agrees with Arthur P. Davis, who suggested that Brooks has "gone 'black'" and "with the new blackness has come an increase in the obscurity of much of her verse,"[15] the fact remains that the author of *A Street in Bronzeville* is the same Brooks of *Riot*. Appearing in 1969, the work "[arose] from the disturbances in Chicago after the assassination of King in 1968," and it recounts various aspects of a growing impatience with American racism. The title poem, which—on some levels—could be considered as a companion to "The Ballad of Rudolph Reed," chronicles the life and death of one of the white elite of the city. John Cabot does not understand the meaning of the riot. The spirit of Chicago is evoked by a juxtaposition of such place names as "Lake Bluff," the gallery of "Richard Gray," and "Maxim's" with other allusions to the city. Cabot tries to make a distinction between "the Negroes [who] were coming down the street" and the "two Dainty Negroes in Winnetka." Without ever understanding the real issue, he pleads at the end, "Lord!/Forgive these nigguhs that know not what/they do" as he goes "down in the smoke and fire/and broken glass and blood." Once again, Chicago provides the setting for a universal theme.

While her characters are clearly victims in varying degrees of white racism in the city, they are also victims of black racism. (One can perhaps make the case that the latter is a byproduct of the former.) Similar to that of other Afro-American writers, the work of Gwendolyn Brooks frequently touches upon "the color line." Instead of focusing upon the "tragic mulatto," a favorite character in American literature, she turns her attention to the dark-skinned girl, much in the tradition of Wallace Thurman's *The Blacker the Berry*. This focus seems to date her work, but by transferring her explorations to a midwestern city of the mid-twentieth century, Brooks suggests the pervasiveness of "the color-line" issue, although the overt anger of Thurman is absent. Instead, there is the emptiness produced by a situation over which the character has no control. There is the heartbreak of "chocolate Mabbie" and the animosity between a light-skinned mother and her dark daughter in "Jessie Mitchell's Mother." But like Satin-Legs, these girls never rise above being the ordinary figures that they are. There is not the pride of the Harlem Renaissance or the later nationalists, rather many of the poems on the subject present characters who are distinguished merely by their plainness, who are not endowed with the majesty that some poets have ascribed to blackness.

Maud Martha treats the life of a young black girl in an environment where color consciousness is an overriding concern. Not only does she learn—as did Bigger Thomas—that there are city streets that divide the races, but also that within her own community she must cope with the fact that she is "dark." Life in the ghetto is made even more difficult by this fact. In "The Life of Lincoln West," which appears in *Family Pictures* (1970), the poet examines the pathetic early life of another child who is subjected to mistreatment. "His father could not bear the sight of him," and "his mother [who] high-piled her pretty dyed hair" was simply tolerant.

> One day, while he was yet seven,
> a thing happened. In the down-town movies
> with his mother a white
> man in the seat beside him whispered
>
> . . . .
>
> "THERE! That's the kind I've been wanting
> to show you! One of the best
> examples of the specie. Not like

those diluted Negroes you see so much of on
the streets these days, but the
real thing.

Black, ugly, and odd. You
can see the savagery. The blunt
blankness. That is the real
thing."[16]

Despite his mother's reaction, little Lincoln West is happy for the
first time. To be "the real thing" eased his uncomprehending discomfort. In *Annie Allen*, Brooks reminds her character in an observation
that acknowledges the extensiveness of a color-conscious society:

Stand off, daughter of the dusk,
And do not wince when the bronzy lads
Hurry to cream-yellow shining.
It is plausible. The sun is a lode.

True, there is silver under
The veils of darkness.
But few care to dig in the night
For the possible treasure of stars.
(*WGB*, p. 121)

Arthur P. Davis has suggested that in "her pieces on color prejudice . . . the language is simple and strong, and the passion even
stronger." He concludes: "We get the impression that Gwendolyn
Brooks has somehow stepped into the picture and, forgetting her
usual restraint, expressed intense personal feeling."[17]

Although Chicago's Black Belt underlies her work, Brooks forces her
readers to go beyond the limited world of Satin-Legs, beyond Mrs.
Sallie's desperate search, even beyond the horrors of the Mecca,
beyond the fear engendered by the Blackstone Rangers who haunted
the city's streets with the ever-present threat of violence, and beyond
the self-hatred that emerged in the ghetto. The city conditions, but
never controls, her vision. At the same time, she joins such writers as
Countee Cullen, Claude McKay, James T. Farrell, and Richard
Wright in being able to treat protest aesthetically without artistic
compromise. Consequently, her work transcends both region and
race. Despite the current tendency of some critics to politicize her
work, Blyden Jackson has wisely noted: "Miss Brooks is one of those
artists of whom it can truthfully be said that things like sex and race,
important as they are, in the ultimate of ultimates, appear in her

work only to be sublimated into insights and revelations of universal application."[18]

Gwendolyn Brooks finds no easy solution for the problems of modern life, and she does not offer—as do some urban observers—organized religion as a panacea for her characters. There is not even a cult leader to soothe the harried figures. The fact that "One wants a Teller in a time like this" acknowledges a need for guidance because "one's not a man, one's not a woman grown./To bear enormous business all alone." She continues:

> One cannot walk this winding street with pride,
> Straight-shouldered, tranquil-eyed,
> Knowing one knows for sure the way back home.
> One wonders if one has a home.
>
> One is not certain if or why or how.
> One wants a Teller now:—
> (WGB, p. 116)

But the Teller, when it appears, ranges ambiguously from a maternal spirit through interpreters of God; such a figure seems so elusive.

In "firstly inclined to take what is told" the persona expresses a willingness to accept "the narcotic milk of peace for men/Who find Thy beautiful center and relate/Thy round command, Thy grand, Thy mystic good." But God seems so far away from the world of Bronzeville. Finally, in "'God works in a mysterious way,'" the persona commands God to come out of hiding.

> If Thou be more than hate or atmosphere
> Step forth in splendor, mortify our wolves.
> Or we assume a sovereignty ourselves.
> (WGB, p. 56)

But the reader knows the powerless people huddled together in an equally powerless place can never assume "sovereignty." If this is their tragedy, it is also—in a measure—representative of the tragedy of an existence in which men and women are constantly in conflict.

But lest God be blamed, the poet suggests in a projection of the Second Coming that when the Son of God came down, He planned "to clean the earth/of the dirtiness of war." In answer to the query concerning the failure to bring peace and goodwill to all people, "In Emanuel's Nightmare: Another Coming of Christ" declares:

> His power did not fail. It was that, simply,
> He found how much the people wanted war.
> How much it was their creed, and their good joy.

And what they lived for. He had not the heart
To take away their chief sweet delectation.

Thus, in the end,

God's Son went home. Among us it is whispered
He cried the tears of men.

Feeling, in fact,
We have no need of peace.

(*WGB*, p. 369)

Eventually Brooks considers the spiritual barrenness of modern life in such works as the three "sermons" dealing with the "warpland" that Bernard Duffey sees as "having much in common with a sense of waste land."[19]

Even before becoming the Poet Laureate of Illinois, Gwendolyn Brooks did much to make her community aware of the importance of poetry as well as of the creators of it. Whether or not one agrees with her claim that a black poet's "quiet walk down the street is a speech to the people, is a rebuke, is a plea, is a school,"[20] the fact remains that she has been able to create an urban school of poetry out of her observations of a restricted Chicago. When asked by Paul Angle about the role of the city in her life as a writer, she responded that Chicago "nourishes." She added: "It was better for me to have grown up in Chicago because in my writing I am proud to feature people and their concerns—their troubles as well as their joys. The city is the place to observe man *en masse* and in his infinite variety."[21] If, however, her restricted Chicago and ghetto characters seem too limited to speak to a wide audience, her comment in 1967 is especially cogent. "The universal wears contemporary clothing very well."[22] While Gwendolyn Brooks essentially views a particular place, her city is symbolic not only of every black ghetto whether in Boston, New York, Philadelphia, or Los Angeles, but also of the isolation wrought by modern life. In rising above the specificity of locale and through her examination of the inner recesses of some tortured human souls, she demonstrates the universality that we have come to expect of great writers.

Notes

1. Gwendolyn Brooks, *The World of Gwendolyn Brooks* (New York: Harper and Row, 1971), p. 412. Hereinafter cited in the text as *WGB*.

2. See Kenny J. Williams, *In the City of Men: Another Story of Chicago* (Nashville: Townsend Press, 1974) and *Prairie Voices: A Literary History of Chicago from the Frontier to 1893* (Nashville: Townsend Press, 1980). Compare Clarence Andrews, *Chicago in Story* (Iowa City: Midwest Heritage Publishing, 1982).

3. William Dean Howells, "Certain of the Chicago School of Fiction," *North American Review* 176 (May 1903): 734–46.

4. H. L. Mencken, *Chicago Tribune*, 28 Oct. 1917. See also Mencken's "The Literary Capital of the United States," London *Nation*, 17 April 1920.

5. Blanche Gelfant, *The American City Novel* (Norman: University of Oklahoma Press, 1954), pp. 175–227.

6. *Dial*, 16 March 1914.

7. Llewellyn Jones, Introduction to *The Chicago Anthology: A Collection of Verse from the Work of Chicago Poets*, ed. Charles G. Blanden and Minna Mathison (Chicago: Roadside Press, 1916), pp. 12–14.

8. Gwendolyn Brooks, *Report from Part One* (Detroit: Broadside Press, 1972), p. 160. Hereinafter cited in the text as *Report.*

9. Joan Kufrin, "Our Miss Brooks," *Chicago Tribune Magazine*, 28 March 1982, p. 10.

10. Brooks, *Report*, p. 56.

11. Ibid., p. 170.

12. "From One 'New Negro' to Another, 1923–1972," in *Black Poetry in America: Two Essays in Historical Interpretation*, ed. Blyden Jackson and Louis Rubin, Jr. (Baton Rouge: Louisiana State University Press, 1974), p. 84.

13. Arthur P. Davis, "Gwendolyn Brooks: Poet of the Unheroic," *College Language Association Journal* 7 (Dec. 1963): 114.

14. Brooks, *Report*, pp. 83–86, and her Introduction to *Jump Bad: A New Chicago Anthology* (Detroit: Broadside Press, 1971), pp. 11–12.

15. Arthur P. Davis, *From the Dark Tower: Afro-American Writers, 1900–1960* (Washington, D.C.: Howard University Press, 1974), p. 186.

16. Gwendolyn Brooks, *Family Pictures* (Detroit: Broadside Press, 1970), pp. 11–12.

17. Davis, *Dark Tower*, p. 188. See also his "The Black-and-Tan Motif in the Poetry of Gwendolyn Brooks," *College Language Association Journal* 6 (Dec. 1962): 90–97.

18. Jackson and Rubin, "From One 'New Negro' to Another," p. 82.

19. Bernard Duffey, *Poetry in America: Expression and Its Values in the Times of Bryant, Whitman, and Pound* (Durham, N.C.: Duke University Press, 1978), p. 253.

20. Gwendolyn Brooks, Foreword to Langston Hughes, *New Negro Poets: USA* (Bloomington: Indiana University Press, 1964), p. 13.

21. Brooks, *Report*, p. 135.

22. Ibid., p. 146.

WILLIAM H. HANSELL

5

The Poet-Militant and Foreshadowings of a Black Mystique: Poems in the Second Period of Gwendolyn Brooks

Gwendolyn Brooks, in a 1976 interview at the University of Wisconsin-La Crosse, said that her work falls into three periods that correspond to "changes" in her perspective.[1] A study of her work seems to reveal strong grounds for agreement with that view. My criteria for making the division derive from changes in Brooks's portrayal of the role of the poet and of the function of art. From the earlier concern with the personal experiences of her characters in her first period, she gradually adopts attitudes that foreshadow a mystique of blackness. In the second period, this mystique of blackness is suggested by Brooks's commitment to the idea that art has a political function; she advocates militancy for both poet and layman. Moreover, she dramatically portrays the black poet's role in a revolution of ideas intended to bring about a rededication to American ideals.

A significant theme in the poems of the second period is Brooks's belief that an artist's immediate environment is what the artist knows best and must deal with if he or she is to retain integrity and authenticity, and more especially with her belief that the most valid and meaningful art has direct relevance to the lives of the people from which it arises. Because Afro-Americans everywhere in this country, as much in urban ghettoes as in southern farm communities, were in a ferment of political activity, Brooks responded to this influence by increasingly introducing politics into her work. Events, as Brooks said herself in 1969, caused her to see new things: "Many things I'm seeing now I was absolutely blind to before. . . ."[2]

The "New Poems" section of *Selected Poems*[3] is truly transitional in that it contains poems in her earlier manner and poems that forcefully state her new concern with the artist as political militant; and for the purposes of this discussion as well as to sharpen the contrast, I have grouped the poems accordingly. Poems typical of her earlier work will be discussed first. "Old people working (garden, car)" (*SP*, p. 125), for example, is closer to her earlier concern with the personal experiences of her characters. It portrays an elderly couple who have only very slight awareness of anything beyond their immediate concerns. These two preserve their dignity, despite the trivial tasks required of them, by making their labor an expression of their love and gesture of defiance:

> Old people working. Making a gift of garden.
> Or washing a car, so some one else may ride.
> A note of alliance, an eloquence of pride.
> A way of greeting or sally to the world.

Their "garden," their "gift" of beauty and love, is their welcome or challenge to the world. The couple have little enough to work with, and the physical product of their work is for "some one else," but the spiritual capacity that generated the work and is sustained by it belongs to the couple alone. Other "New Poems" dealing with subjects and themes similar to her earlier work are "To Be in Love" (*SP*, pp. 120–21) and several very short poems in the subsection titled "A Catch of Shy Fish."

A somewhat ambiguous poem about two artists, "Spaulding and Francois," (*SP*, pp. 126–27), contrasts the "Art-loves" of artists to the demands of their audience. The artists who speak in the poem long to portray "Things Ethereal," "spiritual laughter," "the happiness/Of angels," but, as the final section states,

> . . . the People
> Will not let us alone; will not credit, condone
> Art-loves that shun
> Them (moderate Christians rotting in the sun.)

Obviously, from the artists' point of view, what the people want seems contemptible, "moderate Christians rotting in the sun" is a description full of contempt. Taken on its own, "Spaulding and Francois" seems a conventional artistic outcry against the demands of an insensitive, unimaginative, even materialistic audience. Yet, in view of Brooks's constant concern with commonplace individuals and experience, it is difficult to reject the feeling that the artists, in their abstraction and otherworldliness, are also being mocked. In any case, it is certain from other poems in the "New Poems" section that Brooks remains very much committed to the idea that the commonplace and practical are legitimate, and perhaps necessary, concerns of the artist.

"Big Bessie throws her son into the street" seems to have as its primary theme the necessity of dealing with reality, with actual conditions, as opposed to indulging oneself in the contemplation of beauty. The mother, "Big Bessie," commands her son to give up his "beautiful disease," which seems to be like the desire of "Spaulding and Francois" to contemplate "the happiness/Of angels." Big Bessie's son is not told that he must totally abandon all concern with beauty and with dreams ("candles in the eyes"); he is told those things "are not enough." Her command to him, therefore, is to engage life directly, to "Go down the street." As Brooks portrays the situation, the son could represent an individual who would prefer to remain aloof from practical affairs. His mother's urging is that he must participate. By extension, Brooks affirms in this poem her belief that individuals must take a vital and direct role in affairs.

Poems dedicated to Robert Frost and Langston Hughes imply a similar artistic attitude. In "Of Robert Frost," Brooks stresses his capacity for balancing the desire, to borrow from another poem, for "Things Ethereal" with the demands of "the common blood." More abstractly stated, her comment on Frost seems to emphasize his success at balancing contraries. Brooks's tribute to Langston Hughes stresses different qualities. She celebrates his love of life and his contribution to racial pride, but she also stresses Hughes's apparent belief that art should not be an end in itself when the times demand a different kind of activity. Rather, as Brooks describes those times in the final lines of the poem, it is clear that the function of a poet like Hughes, as "helmsman, hatchet, headlight," is to direct events and provide whatever weapons are necessary.

"Riders to the Blood-Red Wrath" is perhaps the most explicit portrayal of Brooks's new sense that the political militant and the poet who writes about militant themes share identical roles. Each brings closer the time when authentic "Democracy and Christianity" will prevail. The poet seems as much an actor, a participant, as the militant in the street.[4] In this longest of the "New Poems," a woman narrator declares that her illicit sexual relations with a man show that she is "waiving all witness" with conventional attitudes toward love. She dismisses objections of the tradition-minded, because she evidently believes her own behavior is appropriate. By breaking with "ancestral seemliness" and shamelessly believing in this new "excess," she affirms a new style of life that cuts her and her lover off from those who dwell in the past and who fear the future. The girl's new allegiance is to those who confront reality and who militantly participate in the effort to bring about the Afro-American's full participation in American life. The newness of the narrator's values, I believe, lies primarily in her belief that authentic American ideals have never significantly determined behavior. There has been only pretense both on the part of whites and of blacks.

The second section of "Riders" makes it immediately evident that this "renegade" behavior is not simply a rejection of conventional sexual mores. The narrator announces:

> The National Anthem vampires at the blood.
> I am a uniform. Not brusque. I bray
> Through blur and blunder in a little voice!
>   (*SP*, pp. 115–16)

Metaphorically the narrator states that American ideals have permeated her being and now drive her to protest against national practices. Her protest, although seemingly insignificant, is nonetheless "a tender grandeur" that must no longer be concealed:

> Under macabres, stratagem and fair
> Fine smiles upon the face of holocaust,
> My scream! unedited, unfrivolous.
>   (*SP*, p. 116)

We are told that the woman has suffered intensely from the suppression of the desire for vengeance, and that her self-control prevented her from accepting rewards she felt deserving of:

> . . . meriting the gold, I
> Have sewn my guns inside my burning lips.

In the third section of the poem it would appear that, despite her restraint, the narrator suspects her pain and rage may have been prematurely detected. "Did they detect my parleys and replies?" she asks, and then relates the events that might have revealed her true feelings:

> My Revolution pushed his twin the mare,
> The she-thing with the soft eyes that conspire
> To lull off men, before him everywhere.
>   (*SP*, p. 116)

Apparently personifying overt actions as male, and the necessary disguises she has employed as female, the narrator tells us that the "she-thing" (black submissiveness as well as the narrator's feminine submissiveness?) has beguiled "them," beguiled and misled those she is rebelling against. Her disguise "in mottles of submission" has both concealed her true nature and uncovered "sedition" in the enemy.

The narrator remains confident, moreover, that the enemies are ignorant of certain qualities in her character, as of her ability to endure and to contain her rage but not to feed on it.

> They do not see how deftly I endure.
> Deep down the whirlwind of good rage I store
> Commemorations in an utter thrall.
> Although I need not eat them any more.
>
> (*SP*, p. 116)

The narrator, and Afro-Americans generally, have not been reduced to feeding only on their grief and rage, literally, are not consumed with bitterness. The lines also state that the rage is good because it is justifiable; it is rage aroused by undemocratic and un-Christian practices that violate American ideals.

With section five and the explicit references to the African and slave heritage, the narrator clearly begins to speak for the entire race and reveals a major inspirational source for the decision to break with discredited practices. She is sustained by an ancient tradition neither passive nor pacific. Africa provides a testimony to a rich cultural past of wealth and power, a testimony to a warlike heritage.

After Africa, the narrative introduces events that led to enslavement in America, especially the "middle passage" during which the captors and captives established inextricable bonds. Then the period of slavery is recalled, and memories of the cruelty and labor revived. The Afro-American's entire condition, the narrator states, was artifice, the creation of the master.

Continuing, the narrator reads in the racial experience a lesson of international significance:

> But my detention and my massive stain,
> And my distortion and my Calvary
> I grind into a little light lorgnette
> Most sly: to read man's inhumanity.
>
> (*SP*, p. 117)

The "little light lorgnette" seems to be the poet-narrator's phrase for her poetry, which disguises its true revolutionary intentions. She goes on to reveal her awareness that "she" (her race) has not been the only victim of war and injustice:

> And I remark my Matter is not all.
> Man's chopped in China, in India indented.
> From Israel what's Arab is resented.
> Europe candies custody and war.

Recognizing that suffering and persecution observe no racial or national boundaries, the narrator announces her love and her duty to "esteem" all Men:

> Behind my exposé
> I formalize my pit: "*I* shall cite,
> Star, and esteem all that which is of woman,
> Human and hardly human."
>
> (*SP*, p. 118)

"Hardly" here seems to mean "inhuman" rather than "barely"; but Brooks seems to have meant that she loves even those responsible for slavery and other inhumanities.

Having pledged her faith in all humankind, the narrator now announces her mission. Her rejection of past evils and her affirmation of universal ideals that have failed to sufficiently effect practices mark her effort as a rebirth and rededication: "Democracy and Christianity/Recommence with me."

Although the black experience is the immediate provocation, and its relationship to inhumanities everywhere the general one responsible for inspiring the narrator to a rededication, it is important to observe that the ideals are American ideals. In later poems, for example, in all three "Sermons," "In the Mecca," and *Riot*, the rededication will be to "blackness" or "black integrity," rather than, as explicitly stated here, "Democracy and Christianity." The Afro-American's "continuing Calvary," in any event, is no longer to be a passive victim, or object of charity or good intentions, but to be the militant, perhaps violent, agent in the attempt to achieve liberty and love for all:

> And I ride ride I ride on to the end—
> Where glowers my continuing Calvary.
> I,
> My fellows, and those canny consorts of
> Our spread hands in this contretemps-for-love
> Ride into wrath, wraith and menagerie.
>
> (*SP*, p. 118)

Those who are fully dedicated to "this contretemps-for-love" and those who are simply "canny consorts," perhaps meaning the opportunists, nonetheless contribute.

The positive significance of black militancy as here portrayed cannot be overstressed. Brotherhood, equality, and love are the impelling forces. Despite whatever furious resistance, and without confidence of victory, as the final lines state, the black citizen is dedicated to a mission of truly initiating the rule of democracy and Christianity: "To fail, to flourish, to wither or to win./We lurch, distribute, we extend, begin."

Therefore, beyond "Good rage," the Afro-American is sustained by the African heritage, by the acknowledgement, however painful, that the fate of the white and black races is irrevocably linked, by the recognition that blacks have ties with all peoples subjected to persecution and oppression—thus are linked to all humankind—by the realization that the black preserves the highest values and ideals, which in this poem are combined under the rubric "Democracy and Christianity," and finally, by the conviction that it is the Afro-American's mission to try, with whatever allies he or she finds, to bring these ideals into practice. Although "Riders" portrays a black militant dedicated to American ideals, the importance Brooks ascribes to the "warrior" heritage, to the strength and former greatness of African forebears, and to the lessons learned during slavery and afterwards foreshadows a black mystique.

Two uncollected poems of Gwendolyn Brooks, which were published in a period between the *Selected Poems* and *In the Mecca*, further illustrate developments already noted in "Riders to the Blood-Red Wrath" and can be included with work of her second period.

"The Sight of the Horizon" repeats the determination and qualified optimism of "'Riders to the Blood-Red Wrath,'" but there is much less emphasis on the potential for violence in the struggle. In fact, the poem seems primarily concerned with asking what course can be trusted to carry blacks most directly to the long-denied goal of freedom from racism and oppression. Brooks does not appear to advocate any particular strategy; her insistence is that the effort be predicated on achieving total participation. It is the only "Horizon," the only "Garden," which will at the same time redeem both blacks and America.

Alluding broadly to the history of postponed equality, the first stanza states the continuing uncertainty over the course to be taken.

> After such mocks—what Motive?
> What certain Spur? (To find

> Among all nervous rebels that bewitch
> The melancholy capitals of the mind.)

But if the strategy to follow is doubtful, shadowed by "melancholy" possibilities, the goals seem attainable and fairly certain. These are the fulfillment of an ideal and the attainment of a vital necessity for life. There is something more, too. I believe the third and fourth lines just quoted state the narrator's awareness that traditional attitudes must change. Black people, in this sense, can no longer accept the identity and role determined by "white" society.

> The Sight of the Horizon.
> Possession of our breath:
> Possession of our vagrant vision: even
> The legendary mammoth of our death.

Of course, the lines might also suggest Brooks's awareness that if "possession" of the vision is demanded, the consequence could be fatal reprisals. Just as in "Riders," however, the imperative seems to be "To wither or to win."

The last two stanzas of "The Sight of the Horizon" state clearly that nothing short of full achievement of their vision will satisfy Afro-Americans. An America free of racism and oppression, therefore a society for the first time fully American in practice, is the goal. The twofold aspect of the black person's mission is thus carried over from "Riders," because as blacks enter fully into their proper share, America for the first time fulfills its ideals.

> We seek no clue of green.
> We seek a Garden: trees,
> The light, the cry, the conscience of the grass.
> In this most social of all centuries.
> We seek informal sun.
> A harvest of hurrah.
> We seek our center and our radius.
> Profound redemption. And America.

The second uncollected poem from Brooks's middle period comes the closest to accepting the necessity of violence to "repair . . . a ripped, revolted land" and make possible love and unity between men in this country. "In the Time of Detachment, in the Time of Cold" is a tributary poem to Abraham Lincoln and was included as the first of seven dedicatory pieces by various authors in *A Portion of That Field*.[5] In tone and theme it is closer to "Riders to the Blood-Red Wrath" than to "The Sight of the Horizon." Lincoln is addressed as the only one who can lead the way in a gravely troubled time.

The opening lines invoke "the good man" who could still act as the "renouncer" of the present time's "Grave grave legalities of hate. . . ." The narrator describing the contemporary situation, with its betrayals ("bogus roses") and violence against advocates of equality and justice ("demondom") speaks not for a race, but for all Americans. Lincoln is beseeched to restore the unity and love in a "ripped, revolted land." But because the unity may not easily be achieved, Lincoln's spirit is invoked, finally, as the possible inspiration for violent changes in ideas and attitudes:

> Singe! smite! beguile our own bewilderments away.
> Teach barterers the money of your star!
> Or
> Retrieve our trade from out the bad bazaar.
>
> In the time of detachment, in the time of cold, in this time
> Tutor our difficult sunlight. Rouse our rhyme.

The allusion to the biblical episode in which Christ performed the single act of violence in his recorded life is very appropriate in this context. He drove money-lenders from the Temple, charging they corrupted the law and holy places; Lincoln, of course, accepted the use of violent means to halt what he believed was an erroneous and harmful misinterpretation of the Constitution. It is also interesting to note that the final phrase, "Rouse our rhyme," seems intended to imply that "rhyme," poetry, is an appropriate form for the expression of militant and idealistic political attitudes. Rhyme is here the proper accompaniment of whatever actions are necessary to restore America to its ideals. The poet, then, complements the work of the politician-statesman.

The "New Poems" in *Selected Poems*, therefore, are most notable for their portrayal of black artists as the militant leaders in the effort to accomplish a revolution in white attitudes toward blacks. From the tribute to Hughes, to the courage of Big Bessie, and to the narrator of "Riders to the Blood-Red Wrath"—these essentially resolve the conflict of the artist in choosing between abstract beauty and practical good in favor of the latter. The first evidence of Brooks's acceptance of a mystique of blackness is revealed, I believe, in her portrayal of the black artist's special role as literally that of remaking America in the image of what formerly had been merely professed ideals. Perhaps Brooks is saying that the black artist is suited to such an apocalyptic function because blacks have chiefly been victims and seldom offenders. For example, the narrator of "Riders" states that the Afro-American's cooperation in the distortion of American ideals has been a disguise, a self-protective mask. The works of the second period announce that the masks, which were often as destructive as they were protective, are coming off in order to end tacit cooperation in "demondom" and to allow Afro-Americans full participation, even leadership, in the work of taking America closer to its ideals.

Notes

1. Works of the first period are *A Street in Bronzeville* (1945), *Annie Allen* (1949), and *The Bean Eaters* (1960). The second period is represented by the "New Poems" section of *Selected Poems* (1963) and by two uncollected poems, "The Sight of the Horizon" (1963) and "In the Time of Detachment, in the Time of Cold" (1965). The third phase in her development is marked by her most recent collections: *In the Mecca* (1969), *Riot* (1969), *Family Pictures* (1970), and *Beckonings* (1975).

2. George Stavros, "An Interview with Gwendolyn Brooks," *Contemporary Literature* 11 (Winter 1970): 5.

3. Gwendolyn Brooks, *Selected Poems* (New York: Harper and Row, 1963), pp. 113–27. Hereinafter cited in the text as *SP*.

4. Without any specific reference to Gwendolyn Brooks, Larry Neal, a poet and essayist, has declared the same identity of roles.

5. *A Portion of That Field* (Urbana: University of Illinois Press, 1967), pp. 1–2.

NORRIS B. CLARK

— **6** —

Gwendolyn Brooks
and a Black Aesthetic

> I am absolutely free of what any white
> critic might say because I feel that
> it's going to be amazing if any of them
> understand the true significance of
> the struggle that's going on . . .
> what they [critics and writers] want for
> me and what I want for myself now
> are just two different things.[1]
>
> —*Gwendolyn Brooks*

The political and social forces that coalesced during the 1950s and 1960s intensified the sense of "unity in struggle" among most black Americans and had dramatic effects upon the evolution of a black aesthetic during the 1960s and early 1970s. The *zeitgeist* of civil rights, black power, black nationalism, black cultural nationalism, and the more liberal attitudes among whites increased the desires of some black writers to establish a communal identity independent of white America.

Establishing credence for a black aesthetic hypothetically was to serve a threefold purpose: (1) it was to provide black writers with another alternative to secure positive identities as black writers; (2) it was to create political and social alternatives for the black community; and (3) it was to answer, in a provocative context, what Frederick Stern has called "Questions concerning the relationship between literature and society, between the life experiences of social human beings and the art that they produce."[2] Although a black aesthetic has not been defined in any precise way, it was, according to Addison Gayle, Jr., conceived as "a corrective—a means of helping black people out of the polluted mainstreams of Americanism. . . . "[3] Because of his or her historical position in America at the time, the black artist adhering to a black aesthetic was engaged in a war with America and the "mainstreams" of artistic criteria.[4] The artist was in rebellion against the aesthetics of "whiteness" and what it has meant historically to whites and blacks. Those black artists who strove toward a black aesthetic were responsible for creating new aesthetic criteria. As such, they were following the ideology of race first, then art. In its broadest context, a black aesthetic has been conceived by some black writers as one that supports, regardless of literary ability, any black artist who speaks honestly to and about black people.[5] It was also a rejection of the traditional assumptions of art for an espousal of the rhetoric of black nationalism.

In addition to the two groups of "aesthetically unconventional" advocates of a black aesthetic—those who viewed art as anti-intellec-tual or as political—are black artists who, although serious about raising the consciousness of the black masses, were more concerned with aesthetic expression in art. Artists such as Gwendolyn Brooks, Clarence Major, Ron Milner, and Ishmael Reed did not view the black aesthetic movement as propagandistic or racism-in-reverse. They, like Julian Mayfield, Toni Morrison, Michael S. Harper, William Harris, William Melvin Kelley, Ron Welburn, or Albert Young, real-ized that political persuasion (propaganda), rhetorical inanities, "Black English," or a strict adherence to a political dogma would be insufficient to promote the aesthetic qualities of art. They realized that "simple protest and anger are not enough and rhetoric will not be useful in masking the inadequacies of literary craftsmanship."[6]

Those black artists, especially Gwendolyn Brooks, functioned within and around a nationalistic concept of a black aesthetic; they have been as dedicated to raising the level of black consciousness as the black cultural nationalists. Rather than create artifacts from a political or racial perspective, they sought to establish a positive black identity and to reorder racial consciousness through serious exploration and rediscovery of the black community's unique cultur-al heritage: its own particular beauty, its rich and varied oral tradi-tion, its private joys and agonies, as well as its communal "trials and tribulations." They believe, as other black aesthetic advocates, that there is an aesthetic difference that stems from a particular racial and historical context in Africa and America. "Whether or not we believe blacks are born separate, or should achieve separateness, there is no question that separateness has been thrust upon them."[7] By creating around and out of this separate existence, heretofore serious advocates of a new black consciousness created an art that is not peculiarly black; rather, it is more particularly related to an existence in a multicolored world and exhorts others to share in the exhalations of the beauty of blackness. "The black arts movement has reached a new level of commitment and sophistication; its focus is no longer protest against white America, but should [be an] embracement and celebration of the black experience."[8]

The black artist who was concerned with the plight of blacks in the United States and concerned with trying to encourage and develop valid black artistic expressions was faithfully portraying the innermost thoughts and feelings of black people—their excitement, romance, suffering, and frustration. That kind of artist created art, not as art per se, but an art that is meaningful to black people. Following the tradition of black American writing while adding new refinements, artists like Morrison, Brooks, and Reed added integrity to the Black Arts Movement. Moreover, they challenged the basic premise of aesthetic criteria. They raised questions about the relationship between "art and politics" rather than "politics and arts." Their ideological emphasis was on art rather than on polemics or racial rhetoric. Their writings depicted the experiences of black Americans in the medium of black language, which is:

> direct, creative, intelligent communication between black people based on a shared reality, awareness, understanding which generates interaction; it . . . places premium on imagistic renderings and concretizations of abstractions, poetic usages . . . idiosyncracies—those individualized stylistic nuances . . . which, nevertheless hit "home" and evoke truth; it is an idiom of integrated insight, a knowledge emanating from a juxtaposition of feeling and fact. . . .[9]

To create for black persons by drawing upon their historical, sociological, and psychological experiences as black people in white America and in a manner that was honest and truthful to human experiences was the goal of serious black artists who aesthetically re-created the black American experience. However, capturing black experiences in a medium that communicates only to blacks did not establish a black aesthetic; rather, such artistic expression promised to establish an aesthetic that is meaningful to black people and thus meaningful to other humans.

The evolution of the poetry of Gwendolyn Brooks from an egocentric orientation to an ethnocentric one is directly related to her advocacy of a black aesthetic and to the shifting aesthetic criteria in modern America. "For one thing, the whole concept of what 'good poetry' is is changing today, thank goodness . . . I'm just a black poet, and I write about what I see, what interests me, and I'm seeing new things."10

Although she has always written poetry concerned with the black American experience, one that inheres the diversity and complexity of being black and especially being female, her poetics have primarily undergone thematic developments. Her emphasis has shifted from a private, internal, and exclusive assessment of the identity crises of twentieth-century persons to a communal, external, and inclusive assessment of the black communal experience. That change not only corresponds to the fluctuating social, political, and ideological positions of the national black American communities during the sixties and seventies, but it also correlates with the evolution of aesthetic humanism's fundamental concerns about the nature of reality, our relationship to it and its vast variety.

> The principle of unification asks that any one aesthetic theory reckon with the fact that each of us has his own areas of aesthetic responsiveness, antipathy and indifference. Some of us have capacities for many of the dimensions of aesthetic experience (e.g., the appreciation of the comic, the whimsical, beauty, the sublime); and some have few. Some of us have found that with the passing of the years there has been a change and, perhaps, an increase in our own loci of aesthetic appreciation, in our capacities for these various types of aesthetic experience, and in the degree to which we prize the aesthetic. A change in the rule of the aesthetic in our lives almost certainly accompanies a change in our world view—i.e., our perspective on reality and our interpretation of the human spirit.11

Brooks's latest poetry, *Riot* (1969), *Family Pictures* (1970), *Aloneness* (1971), and *Beckonings* (1975), clearly incorporates a pronounced humanistic concern for a collective black America as well as accepting a black aesthetic ideology in terms of aesthetic relativism. Her transitional text *In the Mecca* (1968) clearly advocates and represents a turning point in her conception of art and of a black aesthetic, an artistic position in which she continues to use language as "our most faithful and indispensable picture of human experiences, of the world and its events, of thoughts and life. . . . "12 It is a position that remains attentive to the needs and the energetic struggle of the oppressed, as all writers of a black aesthetic persuasion maintain.

Gwendolyn Brooks's poetry, as black aestheticians have advocated, has always been committed to depicting the "simple" lives of black Americans in the medium of black language, black rituals, black experiences; it has always been reflective of the multiple values inherent in the black community. Brooks's earliest poetry, for which she is most noted in academia, *A Street in Bronzeville* (1945), *Annie Allen* (1949), *The Bean Eaters* (1960), and *Selected Poems* (1963), equally depicts, as does her latest poetry, the basic uncertainty of black people living amid the physical turbulence and psychic tensions of American society—the whirlwind of stasis within flux of twentieth-century America. One merely needs to look at Brooks's "The Sundays of Satin-Legs Smith" or "Gay Chaps at the Bar" to see her concern for the dilemma of the oppressed minorities' identity struggle. As George E. Kent points out in "The Poetry of Gwendolyn Brooks," her most recent way of expressing black tensions is a "natural and organic progression and growth inspired by the turmoil of the 1960s, which provided further extension of herself and her vision, and approach to community. . . . "[13] As Brooks herself has stated, her present focus is: "to develop a style that will appeal to black people in taverns, black people in gutters, schools, offices, factories, prisons, the consulate; I wish to reach black people in pulpits, black people in mines, on farms, on thrones. My newish voice will not be an imitation of the contemporary young black voice, which I so admire, but an extending adaptation of today's Gwendolyn Brooks' voice."[14]

Critics suggest that Brooks's poetry, whether an extension of herself as an artist or as a black artist, can be divided into three groups: (1) *A Street in Bronzeville* and *Annie Allen*, primarily devoted to craft and exhibit an "objective and exquisite detachment" from the lives or emotions of individuals; (2) *The Bean Eaters, Selected Poems,* and *In the Mecca*, also devoted to craft but exhibit a strong awareness of black social concerns; and (3) *Riot, Family Pictures, Aloneness,*and *Beckonings*, less devoted to craft and more concerned about pronounced statements on a black mystique, the necessity of riots (violence), and black unity. Those categories can also be characterized in political language as traditional, prerevolutionary, and revolutionary; or in the language of sociologists as accommodationists, integrationists, and black nationalists; or in racial language as white, colored, and black. Regardless of how one chooses to classify Brooks's poetry, if one must, her corpus remains as an undeniable statement about the condition humane. More precisely, it is a statement about the myriad black American experiences as it communicates the feeling of brotherhood and love. In each phase, arbitrarily defined or not, Brooks has clearly been committed to, as black aesthetic advocates desire, black people.

Although the central theme of Gwendolyn Brooks's poems does

not essentially change—to reveal the black person's presence and participation in the complexities of life—as her changing sensibility about the objectives of art evolves, the formal poetic techniques used to create art "to mean something, [that] will be something that a reader may touch"[15] remain "technically proficient."[16] A different emphasis between the thematic content of her earlier poems—self, motherhood, tenements, war heroes, racial ambivalence, joblessness, pretensions, poverty, religion—and her later "black" poems—a black aesthetic, black unity, black consciousness, contemporary black heroes, overt racism, riots—is noticeable. Yet, her poetry still continues to characterize not only the subtleties of racial tensions and to exhibit an intense and brilliant craftsmanship, a propriety of language in ordinary speech, but it also maintains the traditional reliance on rhetorical devices that elicit ambiguity, irony, paradox, tension and contrast—a "finely turned phrase"—as in "Young Africans."

> Knowing where wheels and people are,
> Knowing where whips and screams are,
> Knowing where deaths are, where the kind kills are.
>
> As for that other kind of kindness
> If there is milk it must be mindful.
> The milk of human kindness must be mindful
> As wily wines.[17]

It should constantly be remembered that "she knows the ways in which Shakespeare, Spenser, Milton, Donne, Keats, Wordsworth juxtaposed intense emotion . . . creating patterns of pull and push among its elements . . . the ways in which moderns like Pound, Eliot, Yeats and Frost break traditional poetic patterns."[18] Brooks's varied use of the traditional formal elements of poetry: rhyme, meter, couplets, quatrains, sonnet forms, ballad forms, elegies, mock epics, figures of elocution—anaphora, assonance, dissonance, enumeration, gradation, isocola, prolepsis; combined with folk elements derived from the black community: jazz and blues rhythms, black speech patterns (only determined by idiom)—slurred rhymes, slant rhyme, sprung syntax, jarring locution—and black folk heroes give Brooks a distinction as a unique modern black poet. She continuously "dislocates language and molds words into complex patterns of meaning . . . ,"[19] as in "fume of pig foot," "wrapped richly, in right linen and right wool," or "careening tinnily down the nights/across my years and arteries." Her formal concerns with poetry—to avoid clichés, to balance modern influences with intuitional phrasing, to unify rhythm with tonal effect, to discover and to create order, to avoid imitation, to use traditional forms as well as nontraditional forms, to use colloquial speech, rhyme, quick rhyme, to "blacken" English—give Gwendolyn Brooks a distinction among the ranks of contemporary modern American writers and among the ranks of most black American writers, especially advocates of a black aesthetic.

Clearly, Brooks's poetic sensibility, as a poet or as a black poet, is both modernist and traditionalist in style, form, language, and theme, rather than political. Not only does she combine in her poetic artifacts the formal, European, and American traditions, but she also infuses them with her point of view, that which any artist must do, and makes them uniquely American, modern, and black. Unlike many of the poets of a black aesthetic ideology, Brooks displays a unique individualism in her work that is devoid of racial polemic or black rhetoric. Despite her present attentiveness to a black audience and her conscious linguistic strategies, as in "My Name is Red Hot. Yo Name Ain Doodley Squat," she is neither a protest poet nor a practitioner of a popular cultural aesthetic. Whether her poems are of a dramatic nature or a narrative nature as in "'The Boy Died in My Alley'" or "The Life of Lincoln West," respectively, or of song or elegy as in "Steam Song" or "Elegy in a Rainbow," respectively, or not associated directly with "blackness" as in "Horses Graze," Brooks remains a poet first, one who expresses her blackness through art. She does not, as Houston Baker suggests, have a white style and black content.[20]

Brooks's continuous use of nontraditional technical elements, black English, or idioms of the street indicate that Brooks's poetic style is not white, rather it is black American—one which incorporates poetic techniques from a dual heritage. One should also keep in mind that some black Americans do not speak in the idiom or linguistic structure of black English. Indeed, W. E. B. Du Bois's assessment of a dual consciousness is what Brooks's poetry has always been about: "this longing to attain self-conscious [person]hood, to merge his double self into a better and truer self. In this merging he wishes neither of the older selves to be lost."[21]

Although Brooks's poetry is modern, American, and black, some critics think her latest poetry has lost its "universality" because it deals with social themes or exhibits a conscious concern for the political, social, and economic circumstances that stultify the lives of black people. One critic, Daniel Jaffee, condescendingly objected to Brooks's definition of her art as black poetry rather than poetry: "The label 'black poetry' cheapens the achievement of Gwendolyn Brooks.

It recommends that race matters more than artistic vocation or individual voice."[22] Despite an opinion that Brooks's achievements are cheapened because of race, such critical sensibility points not to the dilemma of her changing concept of poetry, but to the inherent dilemma of artistic evaluations that do not view race as a significant aspect of aesthetic, social, and moral judgments. To uncritically assume that "black" cheapens art denies, a priori, unbiased aesthetic evaluation, artistic integrity to black art forms and the artist, consciously or subconsciously. Moreover, such views minimize the notion that literary style is the bridge that unifies the artistic sensibility, literature, and the cultural environment into a dynamic historical and social experience. It further stigmatizes and stereotypes that which is deliberately, and potentially beautifully, created in an historically accurate and representative manner. In addition, it denies validity to Brooks's black consciousness or poetic voice as well as her magnificent poetic sensibility that has always given credence to race as significant and thus important as thematic material: "In the black experience everything is important just as it is in the white experience."[23] Brooks's statement resonates with Roy Harvey Pearce's assessment that literature shares the characteristics of its culture in language, social expressions, and concerns. It also shares the patterns of sound, syntax, event, and meaning within the reader's experience, including the reader's experience of linguistics and literary conventions.

As George Kent suggests, Gwendolyn Brooks's "dilemma" points to the dilemma of all black artists. On the one hand, critics want to acknowledge that artifacts transcend race, while on the other paradoxically emphasizing that an art construct tells or shows the reader what it has meant to be a black American.[24] As Brooks has stated, emphasized from *In the Mecca* to *Beckonings*, her art is to be more committed not only to recreating artistically the lives of black people, but also to using technical devices that permit black people to see reflections of themselves and to feel the dynamics of those reflections in her poetry. Brooks's recent artistic sensibility and criteria for art are akin to those to which many advocates of a black aesthetic adhere: to speak as a black, about blacks, to blacks.[25] It also adheres to what Susanne K. Langer advocated in 1953:

> A poem always creates the symbol of a feeling, not by recalling objects which would elicit the feeling, but by weaving a pattern of words— words charged with meaning, and colored by literary associations— akin to the dynamic pattern of the feeling (the word "feeling" here

covers more than a "state"; for feeling is a process, and may have not only successive phases, but several simultaneous developments; it is complex and its articulations are elusive).[26]

Although Brooks's *The Bean Eaters* indicates a thematic change from general themes such as personal aspiration, motherhood, marriage, dreams, isolation, and birth, *In the Mecca* (1968) is Brooks's transitional text. *The Bean Eaters* illustrates that her increased social awareness began with "A Bronzeville Mother Loiters in Mississippi. Meanwhile a Mississippi Mother Burns Bacon," "The Last Quatrain of the Ballad of Emmett Till," and "The Chicago *Defender* Sends a Man to Little Rock" or the exquisite and subtle condemnation of racism in sonnet form, "Gay Chaps at the Bar." In contrast to those earlier poems, in *In the Mecca* Brooks makes explicit statements about how blacks should think, the ideology of Negritude, a black aesthetic, and black power. In essence, those "political" statements evolve from her reawakened and redirected artistic consciousness and reflect the black cultural milieu of the 1960s and 1970s. Even though there is an emphasis on "blackness," Brooks, importantly, continues to explore the universal qualities—social and psychological—of blacks, as they *survive* in an interracial and intraracial society. *In the Mecca* isn't solely about black nationalism or a black aesthetic; rather, it is primarily a testimony to the undisputed fact that black persons are not curios, that they do have values, that there is dignity among the uncertainties of their lives. *In the Mecca* is actually a tribute to black existence, one that avoids castigating "Whitey" to emphasize liberation of those ordinary lives that blossom and wilt among "hock[s] of ham," "hopes as heresy," "roaches and gray rats." For Brooks as indicated by *In the Mecca*, "Life sits or blazes in this Mecca./And thereby— tenable./And thereby beautiful."

In the Mecca also clearly indicates, via the character of Don Lee, who "wants a new nation . . . new art and anthem,"[27] Brooks's leanings toward a black aesthetic as suggested by Haki Madhubuti (Don L. Lee), whom Brooks regarded as a stimulus for a new renaissance.[28] Yet the true significance of *In the Mecca* is not so much Brooks's advocacy of a black aesthetic or Alfred's ability to finally act (rebel) or Pepita's ignoble death—"a little woman lies in dust with roaches" (*Mecca*, p. 21). The true aesthetic significance, thematically, is that the black lives, whether Way-out Morgan's, Alfred's, Darkara's, or Pepita's, are meaningful and reflect an "ultimate reality" in formal juxtaposition to expectations. It symbolically repre-

sents the existential dilemma of twentieth-century humankind—
the province of art and especially the province of "black art." People
living or dying in the Mecca exhibit the existential tensions confronting any people with human limitations and possiblity.[29] That epic
poem reflects our madness, our helplessness, our pain and feelings of
rejection. It represents the universal nature of oppression, self-im-
posed or externally imposed. Not to know and cherish the tragedy of
our own lives is not to know the joy of being here.

Gwendolyn Brooks's later poetry after *In the Mecca* also does not
only reflect a specific black aesthetic in which all black persons are
"beauti-ful"; rather her art, from advocating militant resistance in
"Riders to the Blood-Red Wrath" (1963) to wishing "jewels of black
love" in "A Black Wedding Song," thematically suggests a range of
"ways"—"The Ways of the Mecca are in this Wise"—in which
blacks can, should, and do respond to oppression. Although there is a
stronger sense of a black nationalist perspective in "Boys. Black.,"[30]
it is one that extends the black nationalist perspective of action as
suggested by Alfred's role in *In the Mecca* rather than scathe white
America. Clearly, unlike the poetry of many young black writers of
the sixties, especially those whom Arthur P. Davis regards as the
poets of "black hate," Brooks's poetry is neither irrational nor propagandistic. She does not use devices such as incendiary polemics,
militant slogans, four-letter expletives, fused words, slashed words,
or phonetic spellings. Instead there is a clear use of language with
some hip talk, some street talk and idiom to make her poetry less
"obscurantis" to blacks in an attempt to advocate a sense of communal and individual responsibility for the spiritual and physical death
of blacks as in "The Boy Died in My Alley."

> I joined the Wild and Killed him
> with knowledgeable unknowing.
> I saw where he was going,
> I saw him crossed. And seeing
> I did not take him down.
> (*Beckonings*, p. 5)

In essence, Gwendolyn Brooks's thematic concerns, the tense and
complex dimensions of living through the paths of petty destinies,
have changed but have not eliminated an acceptance of those who
choose to live and to love differently. Unlike the more radical black
aesthetic poets, she does not condemn the "Intellectual Audience" as
Nikki Giovanni has done, or equate Negroes with repulsive beasts as
does Welton Smith in "The Nigga Section," or curse white people, as

in Carolyn Rodgers's "The Last M. F." Brooks's later works, *Riot,
Aloneness, Family Pictures,* and *Beckonings,* instead, emphasize a
need for black unity by using "the exile rhythms of a Black people
still seeking to establish at-homeness in America,"[31] but not to the
exclusion of universal themes and subjects such as "brotherly love,"
literary critics, heroes, music, love between man and woman, false
ideals, friendship, beautiful black blues. Nor like the more radical or
political black poets of the sixties and early seventies such as Imamu
Baraka, Sonia Sanchez, the "radical" phase of Nikki Giovanni, Welton Smith, or other black aesthetic advocates does Brooks create
racist, propagandistic, and taciturn poems that advocate violence as
therapeutic (Fanon's dictum), exhort whites to bring about equality,
castigate or demean others. Instead, she depicts black realities without brutally frank language via her black voice, a voice that emanates
a conscious humanistic concern for others. Similar to "great masters," Brooks's poetry does not tell us that there is evil, corruption,
oppression, futility, or racism; rather, she shows us the tragedy and
its relationship to individuals in hopes that we may learn a moral
insight from the juxtaposition of beauty and horror, death in life as in
"The Life of Lincoln West."

Brooks's unique voice in her latest poetry is one that not only
ideologically varies from a narrowly defined black aesthetic, but also
thematically deviates from its total reliance on obscure African references or Africa as a source of inspiration or upon a doctrine of how to
live, as in Ron Karenga's Kawaida Doctrine, or a pro-Muslim religious
orientation as some black aestheticians advocate:[32]

> Blackness
> is a going to essences and to unifyings.
> "MY NAME IS AFRIKA!"
> Well, every fella's a Foreign Country.
> This Foreign Country speaks to you.
> *(FP,* p. 15)

Not surprisingly, Brooks's voice which contrasts the American ideals
and practices—W. E. B. Du Bois's "Veil Metaphor"—especially the
insensitivity and ignorance of whites toward blacks, as in *Riot,* is not
filled with private symbolism or biting satire. Rather, self-identity in
Brooks's poems leads to group-identity. She does not, as Baraka has
done, only focus on a black nationalist, black Muslim, black power,
or blacker-than-black perspective. Rather, her voice is one that re-
creates the feelings and thoughts of the unheard, as riots do,[33] rather
than merely languish in a black aesthetic of polemics devoid of

lyricism. Even though Brooks's poetry calls for a black dignity and a black pride, erstwhile symbolized by Africa, she acknowledges that blacks "know so little of that long leap languid land [Africa]" and suggests that enacting "our inward law"—unity (community, family) among black Americans—is more important than any external reliances upon a leader, a god or God(s) or the heat of "easy griefs that fool and fuel nothing" (*Beckonings*, pp. 15–16). Her attempt to create black unity is not to establish a bond among third-world peoples but to establish a bond between those oppressed black Americans who "are defining their own Roof. . . ." Consequently, her content is not only specifically American but is, more so than many writers of a black aesthetic persuasion, also reflective of the attitudes, aspirations, and concerns of black Americans as they *historically* have been confronted with the denial of American ideals, racism, and pathos of human choice.

Unlike the black writers of polemics and propaganda or the rhetoricians of hate and violence, Brooks doesn't attempt to impose her personal philosophy upon others; she does not demean or denigrate blacks whose psychological mechanism to survive leads them to be "Toms" or race traitors. (In fact, some critics have questioned her attitudes or personal voice as not being strong enough on issues such as abortion.) Brooks's poetry remains one of love and affirmation, one that accepts some hate and perhaps some violence as necessary without condemning or castigating those who have been pawns to interracial and intraracial forces. Adequately reflecting the hopes and aspirations of the black community, Brooks displays a love for her brothers and sisters regardless of psychosocial or socioeconomic position. In doing so, she clearly embraces "blackness" and the values of liberation, and thus the values of all humanity. That quality, despite an emphasis on embracing blacks first, is one that is universal in literature of self-affirmation and self-identity; the universal is revealed through the particular. As her sensitivity to the spirit of social revolution emanates from her sense of "love," Brooks advocates a sense of self-love and compassion while reflecting the tensions of her time period, a tension due to racial oppression: "On the street we smile./We go/in different directions/down the imperturbable street" (*Riot*, p. 22).

Thematically and imagistically, Brooks's poetry after *In the Mecca* reflects a social sensibility that incorporates, as her earlier work has done, especially war poems, the expressive and mimetic aspects of a black experience rather than an arbitrary, political black aesthetic. An art form that has aesthetic qualities related to the black experience should, by definition, incorporate a sense of what it is like to face life's multitude of complexities as a person affected by racial values (Afrocentric and Eurocentric) pertaining to the black communities. Regardless of the ideological or social position the writer has, the genre should render that representation in a manner that is most particular, although not necessarily unique, to an existence as a person confronted with the issues of "blackness." This is not meant to imply that the central theme must be about blackness; rather it is to suggest that the world view that the art conveys, in theme as well as in image and structure, should provide a sense of what it is like to see historically, culturally, and psychologically through the eyes of a black person. The tensions of living as a black person—whether in blackness or whiteness—should be illustrated and discernible. To that end, Brooks's poetry extends. If one considers her multidimensional themes combined with her conscious attempt to fuse the traditional with the colloquial or common, it is evident that Brooks's later poetry is not thematically "more black" than her earlier poetry. Her poetry, despite her diminished reliance upon formal diction, continues to be an expression of her craftsmanship as well as an expression of her black voice as expressed in 1950. "Every Negro poet has 'something to say.' Simply because he is a Negro he cannot escape having important things to say."[34]

The technical proficiency with which Brooks creates those meaningful lives, whether heroic, mock heroic, or parody, is what poetry is about. It is to that specific end, exposing the truth of human existence in forms meaningful to the black community, that Brooks's poetry leads. Despite the extension of Gwendolyn Brooks's poetry to a new black consciousness of the late 1960s and 1970s, her formal devices remain as alive in her later poetry as they are in her earlier poetry.[35] She does continue to pay attention to craft, to the neat turn of phrase: "Now the way of the Mecca was on this wise," "as her underfed haunches jerk jazz," or "In the precincts of a nightmare all contrary. . . ." She "blackens English": "That Song it sing the sweetness/like a good Song can, . . ." (*Beckonings*, p. 8), "Unhalt hands" (*Beckonings*, p. 13), or uses extensive alliteration: "These merely peer and purr/and pass the passion over" (*Riot*, p. 18). She continues to infuse the traditional standard American English not only with her intuitional phrasing and coinage of words, but also with the "common folk phrasing" as exhibited in songs and folk sermons. In doing so, Brooks's poetry is more reflective of aesthetic relativism while maintaining some elements of traditional "white" culture as in "Que tu es grossier!" or "death in the afternoon." That relativism related to the black experience can be observed in her use of black folk heroes, or in "The Wall," a poem in which art for art's sake is not a valid concept whereas the wall allows celebration and commitment (i.e., it is communal and functional as "Negritude" advocates). Specific references are made to black literary heroes as in "Five Men Against the Theme, 'My Name is Red Hot. Yo Name ain Doodley Squat,'" or musical heroes as in "Steam Song" (Al Green) or "The Young Men Run" (Melvin Van Peebles). Combined with the sounds and sense of sermons, jazz, blues, and double entendre, these references help to bring ghetto life alive and to enhance the significance of an idea and its "metaphysical function" as in "Elegy in a Rainbow." In addition, Brooks continues to exhibit irony, a complex sense of reality, a sensitivity to traditional line and beats, metered as well as in free verse. She juxtaposes lines that appear to move rapidly with those that tend to slow the reader down, as in "The Boy Died in My Alley." Furthermore, she uses sudden contrasts or repetition to make each word bear the full measure of weight and suggestion. "I don't want to stop a concern with words doing good jobs. . . . "[36] Whether extravagant overstatement or understatement as in "A Poem to Peanut," all of those elements not only exist in black literature, but have always been a part of Brooks's concept of polishing her technique.

Unlike all of the racial polemicists of the 1970s whose poetry significantly fails to unify form and content, Brooks's poetry does, in fact, achieve a fastidious balance between the cognitive and the emotive aspects of a black person's existence and poetic form. Yet that balance is most available to those who accept, as she always has, the vision of blacks, their values for living and "blooming the noise and whip of the whirlwind," (Mecca, p. 54) and the fact that blacks are human and worthy of being poetic themes. It is out of that whirlwind breezing over the "warpland" that Brooks succeeds in depicting universal human fulfillment: exploring the problem of dolls and dynamite, self-love and communal love, hope, and fear, peace and violence, affirmation and destruction, resurrection and death. In all of Brooks's poetry, unlike what is in much of the poetry of a political black aesthetic, the underlying idea is that she, as artist, is engaged in "preachment" (and reporting) rather than polemics. She earnestly advocates abandoning old social ideas about blacks to celebrate the black experience and black character in its oxymoronic evolution, a "clear delirium," and in its substancelessness which contains an essential sanity that nourishes ("I like that word nourish.")[37] man's reason for being. To those who would examine the metaphysical and stylistic implications of Brooks's later poetry, they will find its "underpinning aesthetic is social and subjective,"[38] albeit black first.

Although the forms of Gwendolyn Brooks's poetry contribute to and enhance an understanding of the content—move it from the simple, mundane, and colloquial to a complex, eternal, and universal—her recent poetry does achieve aesthetic beauty and historical truth. It fails functionally in her terms only. Her latest objective: "I want to write poetry that will appeal to many, many blacks, not just the blacks who go to college but also those who have their customary habitat in taverns and the street. . . . "[39] is not, as she acknowledges, achieved because it doesn't reach those "taverneers." Brooks acknowledges her failure of *Riot*—"It's too meditative"—and *Beckonings* has a dual impulse (a self-analytic commentary on the nature of her own poetry). She also states that only two love poems (songs), "When you've forgotten Sunday" and "Steam Song," can be well received in tavern readings.[40] Similar to some of the "Broadside poets," as well as other black writers who desire to write for the black masses—as Walt Whitman and Ralph Waldo Emerson had also advocated—Gwendolyn Brooks falsely assumes that her task is to create art for those who don't appreciate formal art. As with most poetry, even that which infuses informal folk elements with formal literary elements, undereducated or subeducated persons—those to whom the fourth-to-sixth-grade reading level of newspapers appeals—cannot or choose not to be subjected to it. Rarely do they appreciate the subtlety and interrelationships of finely turned phrases or understand, reflectively or meditatively, the appeal of formal alliteration and repetition to a complex meaning or abstract idea. The unsophisticated generally expresses an emotional understanding or appreciation of rhythm or meter by nodding or tapping his or her foot; the sophisticated generally searches, from an objective distance, for rhetorical and metrical relationships or correlations to history, psychology, religion, or culture. Ironically, it is precisely because Brooks's poetry fails to appeal to the black masses that it appeals aesthetically to the "blacks who go to college" as well as those *littérateurs* who can and will reflect upon the "sound and sense" of a poetic artifact. As Brooks's biographer, George Kent, suggests, she should not be concerned about writing for those in the taverns. Those with a formal educational (not intellectual) background are generally the ones who appreciate the forms as well as the content of art. Regardless of whether the content is preachment, polemic, propaganda, or "purely" aesthetic, what "formal" artists have to say about the condition of humankind, and how they say it, is different from what the masses generally want to hear, read, or sense. Similarly, relying upon the approval of the masses to validate art, especially black art as black aestheticians advocated, is not only antithetical to the formal literature that Brooks writes, but also places an unrealistic expectation upon the masses. "To be perfectly frank, a serious literate black public does not exist within our national group so that we writers, editors, and critics have had to make definitions in a vacuum among ourselves."[41]

The aesthetic success of Gwendolyn Brooks's later poetry, and her sense of its failure, reflects the historical literary dilemma of cognitively and emotively appreciating the truth and beauty of a black experience and art per se. To create art reductively, only for one group, limits the art; to create art without letting it organically or ontologically exist limits the number of persons who have the faculties with which to appreciate it. Formal art can never be truly functional; folk art is always functional. To infuse, as Gwendolyn Brooks has, the informal with the formal, in a medium designed to be formal, subsumes the informal component, especially when it evolves from a self-conscious literary formalism. Thus attempting to reach those in taverns, the origins of some folk traditions, alters and negates the ontological component of art. It necessarily extends it beyond the folk to the formal by making it solely functional in a "literary" sense. What Brooks does with words, forms, and content—not consciously imitating anyone—is the essence of the aesthetic imagination unifying disparate elements into a coherent whole—structurally, semantically, and phonetically. As a spokesperson of the black masses, Brooks is literally different from those for whom she writes; consequently, she is the "seer and the sayer," the Emersonian poet, who articulates the needs, ideas, and aspirations of others. In doing so, she can only create, to make clear in terms she knows and understands, her perception of the raw material. Her quest, then, is to create works of an aesthetic nature and of a "black origin"—whether critics appreciate it or not. To do so, as she has, is not "to be content with offering raw materials. The Negro poet's most urgent duty, at present, is to polish his technique, his way of presenting his truths and beauties, that those may be more insinuating, and therefore, more overwhelming."[42]

Notes

1. Phyl Garland, "Gwendolyn Brooks: Poet Laureate," *Ebony* 23 (July 1968): 56.

2. Frederick C. Stern, "Black Lit., White Crit?," *College English* 26 (March 1974): 637.

3. Addison Gayle, Jr., "Introduction to *The Black Aesthetic* (New York: Doubleday, 1972), p. xxii.

4. Ibid., p. xxiii.

5. Stephen Henderson, *Understanding the New Black Poetry* (New York: William Morrow, 1973), p. 7.

6. Herbert Hill, Introduction to *Anger and Beyond: The Negro Writer in the United States* (New York: Harper and Row, 1966), p. xxii.

7. Ted Wilentz, ed., *Natural Process* (New York: Hill and Wang, 1970), p. viii.

8. Ron Welburn, "Black Art," *New York Times Book Review*, 14 Feb. 1971, p. 20.

9. Sarah Webster Fabio, "Who Speaks Negro?" *Black World* 16 (Dec. 1966): 57.

10. Gwendolyn Brooks, "An Interview with Gwendolyn Brooks," conducted by George Stavros, 28 March 1969, in *Contemporary Literature* 11 (Winter 1970): 3–5.

11. Susanne K. Langer, *Philosophy in a New Key* (New York: Charles Scribner's Sons, 1951), p. 76.

12. Mary Carman Rose, "Aesthetic Creativity and Aesthetic Theory," *British Journal of Aesthetics* 16 (1975): 7.

13. George E. Kent, "The Poetry of Gwendolyn Brooks, Part I," *Black World* 20 (Sept. 1971): 31.

14. Haki R. Madhubuti, "Black Books Bulletin Interviews Gwen Brooks," *Black Books Bulletin* 2 (Spring 1974): 28.

15. Stavros, "An Interview," p. 2.

16. George Kent, "Poetry of Brooks I," pp. 32–36. Also see Gloria T. Hull, "A Note on the Poetic Technique of Gwendolyn Brooks," *College Language Association Journal* 19 (Dec. 1975): 280–85, and D. H. Melhem, "Gwendolyn Brooks: The Heroic Voice of Prophecy," *Studies in Black Literature* 8 (Spring 1977): 1–3.

17. Gwendolyn Brooks, *Family Pictures* (Detroit: Broadside Press, 1970), p. 18. Hereinafter cited in text as *FP*.

18. Gladys Margaret Williams, "Gwendolyn Brooks' Way with the Sonnet," *College Language Association Journal* 26 (Dec. 1982): 216.

19. Houston A. Baker, "The Achievement of Gwendolyn Brooks," *College Language Association Journal* 16 (Sept. 1972): 28.

20. Ibid., p. 23.

21. W. E. B. Du Bois, *The Souls of Black Folks* (Greenwich, Conn.: Fawcett, 1961), p. 17.

22. Daniel Jaffee, "Gwendolyn Brooks: An Appreciation from the White Suburbs," quoted in Marva Riley Furman, "Gwendolyn Brooks: The Unconditioned Poet," *College Language Association Journal* 17 (Sept. 1973): 9.

23. Brooks, "An Interview," p. 19.

24. George E. Kent, "Aesthetic Values in the Poetry of Gwendolyn Brooks," in *Black American Literature and Humanism*, ed. R. Baxter Miller (Lexington: University Press of Kentucky, 1981), p. 85.

25. Gwendolyn Brooks, Introduction to *Jump Bad: A New Chicago Anthology* (Detroit: Broadside Press, 1971), p. 12.

26. Susanne K. Langer, *Feeling and Form* (New York: Charles Scribner's Sons, 1953), p. 230.

27. Gwendolyn Brooks, *In the Mecca* (New York: Harper and Row, 1968), p. 18. Hereinafter cited in the text as *Mecca*.

28. Gwendolyn Brooks, *A Capsule Course in Black Poetry Writing* (Detroit: Broadside Press, 1975), p. 7.

29. Note the political, religious, social, cultural reverberations of the term "Mecca" and its antithetical relationship to American society. *In the Mecca* also provides a perspective that illuminates the problem of aesthetic historical paradox.

30. Gwendolyn Brooks, *Beckonings* (Detroit: Broadside Press, 1975), pp. 15–16. Hereinafter cited in the text as *Beckonings*.

31. Kent, "Aesthetic Values," p. 75.

32. Although Brooks acknowledges Africa as a source of inspiration, she does not rely upon Africa any more than other concepts of blackness.

33. Gwendolyn Brooks's epigraph to *Riot* (Detroit: Broadside Press, 1969), p. 5. Hereinafter cited in text as *Riot*. "A Riot is the language of the unheard."—Martin Luther King

34. Gwendolyn Brooks, "Poets Who Are Negroes," *Phylon* 11 (Dec. 1950): 312.

35. George Kent, "The Poetry of Gwendolyn Brooks, Part II," *Black World* 20 (Oct. 1971): 36–48, 68–71.

36. Stavros, "Interview," p. 6.

37. Gwendolyn Brooks, "Update on Part One: An Interview with Gwendolyn Brooks," conducted by Gloria T. Hull and Posey Gallagher, *College Language Association Journal* 21 (Sept. 1977): 32.

38. R. Baxter Miller, " 'Does Man Love Art?': The Humanistic Aesthetic of Gwendolyn Brooks," in *Black American Literature and Humanism*, p. 107.

39. Brooks, "Update on Part One," p. 19.

40. Hull and Gallagher, "Interview," pp. 21–23. One should also seriously question William Hansell's assessment of Brooks's "The Wall." "Brooks' poem functions just as the wall does. The people see themselves in it and are

inspired." "Aestheticism Versus Political Militance," *College Language Association Journal* 17 (Sept. 1973): 15.

41. Don L. Lee (Haki R. Madhubuti), "Black Writers and Critics: Developing a Critical Process without Readers," *The Black Scholar: Journal of Black Studies and Research* 10 (Nov/Dec. 1978): 38.

42. Brooks, "Poets Who Are Negroes," p. 312.

R. BAXTER MILLER

— 7 —

"Does Man Love Art?":
The Humanistic Aesthetic
of Gwendolyn Brooks

Humanism has long characterized the poetry of Gwendolyn Brooks. Since *A Street in Bronzeville* (1945) she has varied the forms of Shakespearean and Petrarchan sonnets; especially since *The Bean Eaters* (1960) she has experimented with free verse and social theme. For more than thirty years she has excelled in the skills of alliteration, balance, plosive, and rhetorical question. Against a background of light and dark, her techniques reveal a deeply human struggle. Her world evokes death, history, pain, sickness, identity, and life; her personae seek the grace and vision of personal style. Although her forms vary, her poems generally impose order upon "the flood of chaos."[1] Are the creations ambivalent? Does form sublimate the personality as well as reveal it? Did Keats correctly desire "negative capability" and discern Shakespeare's greatness?

Appreciation of the paradox gives poetry power and meaning. Humanism is the personally cultural medium for seeking and defining knowledge, ethical value, and aesthetics. Through subjectivity the living writer inspires the inanimate poem. Conversation anthropocentrically signifies the speaker. Written language, rather, implies first, an autonomous narrator and second, a historical author. Humanism is the instrument for creating and interpreting signs. The method opposes society to self, environment to heredity, death to life, horizontality to verticality, formalism (science) to myth-making, and barbarism to civilization. By humanism, characters experience choice, empathy, love, style, identity, and need. Humanism represents both the relative and the absolute, and Brooks portrays the tension between the two (her whirlwind) where one struggles for stasis within flux.

Her attempts place western art forms and artists in a black folk perspective. At different times her speakers refer to baroque and rococo styles in architecture and to traditional musicians—Saint Saëns, Brahms, Grieg, or Tschaikovsky. Pablo Picasso appears at least once in her poetry. But these images have counterparts. Satin-Legs Smith and a black youth rioting in the streets are common people. Even Langston Hughes becomes an ironic means for rehumanizing what F. R. Leavis has called the Great Tradition. By demonstrating the inseparability of objective and subjective art, Brooks frees the tradition from itself. Her formal style creates a poetic world in which a folk view contrasts with an elite one, although class differences obscure a common bond. Here one culture's destruction is another culture's creation, so there is a need to redefine culture itself.

Brooks's personae live somewhere between determinism and personal choice. The artist signifies the reader, his or her human relative; the artist represents history and collectivity as well as creative process. Using this framework to portray both narrator and artist as hero and heroine, the poet verifies the importance of his or her personal struggle. Here I describe Brooks's humanistic aesthetic. First, she charts its fall from meaning to meaninglessness in early and more stylized poems such as "The Sundays of Satin-Legs Smith" and "still do I keep my look, my identity . . ." (*A Street in Bronzeville*, 1945); second, she develops the aesthetic through a middle stage characterized by distance, alienation, and continued questioning in the second sonnet of *Annie Allen* (1949); third, she forcibly reaffirms the principle in freer forms such as "Langston Hughes" (*Selected Poems*, 1963), or "Boy Breaking Glass" and "The Chicago Picasso" (*In the Mecca*, 1968).[2]

"Satin-Legs" (*WGB*, pp. 26–31) posed early the existential question that was to concern Brooks for more than thirty years. As with later poems, such as number XV in *Annie Allen* and "Second Sermon on the Warpland" in *Mecca*, it sets style and imagination against a deterministic reality and asks if they can prevail. In *Annie* the answer is maybe; in "Second Sermon," a presupposed yes; in "Satin-Legs," no. "Satin-Legs" can be conveniently divided into three parts. The first (lines 1–42) describes a folk character who rises from bed and gets dressed one morning in black Chicago. Some sweet scents ironically suggest his royalty and contrast sharply with his impoverished environment. The resulting tensions indirectly show the relative beauty of roses, dandelions, and garbage. The second part (lines 43–74) illustrates a common journey by narrator and reader into Satin-Legs's closet, a metaphor of man. Here the wide shoulder padding representing Satin-Legs's sculpture and art contrasts with the baroque and rococo styles, European forms of the seventeenth and eighteenth centuries. In the third part (lines 75–158), ear and eye imagery reveal Satin-Legs's unawareness of the world about him, as clothing helps to suggest human deprivation. The narrative movement leads first from the speaker's original antagonism toward her listener ("you") to a light epic concerning Satin-Legs's wardrobe. Following the disappearance of "you" from the poem, the narrator finally views Satin-Legs from a lonely detachment. Ironically this last section juxtaposes blues with the European classics of the late nineteenth century and simultaneously shows that cultural values are relative.[3] In a final irony, Satin-Legs ends each Sunday sleeping with a different prostitute.[4]

The human dimension in the first part, more narrowly confined, first depends upon animal imagery (Satin-Legs, the elaborate cat), then upon the metaphor of life's drama (getting dressed), and last upon the irony characterizing social code ("prim precautions"). An oxymoron communicates Satin-Legs's confusion ("clear delirium"), yet the phrase clarifies a double consciousness working in the poem where the narrator's thinking occasionally merges with that of Satin-Legs. Whereas his perspective is generally muddled, hers is usually clear. Applying some theories of Noam Chomsky, Lévi-Strauss, and Jacques Derrida stimulates two questions.[5] First, what unifies Satin-Legs with his narrator? Second, what does the narrator share with the listener, whom George Kent (in his essay) calls white? Unconsciously Satin-Legs wants to re-search[6] his limited life and his deferred human potential in order to redefine life's meaning. At first he temporarily succeeds when the narrator's words reveal his consciousness: "life must be aromatic./There must be scent, somehow there must be some."[7] His clothing style and cologne merely translate beauty into different kinds of imagery, either visual or olfactory. Conceptions of art, ideal in nature, are universal; but their manifestations, their concrete realities, differ. With a playful tone, the narrator begins her journey, which leads through aloofness and sarcasm to sympathetic judgment. En route she ironically opposes the cultural transformations of humanity to humanity itself.

The final two stanzas in the first part firmly establish the opposition. Would the "you," the narrator questions, "deny" Satin-Legs his scent of lavender and pine? What substitute would the listener provide? In a recent article on Brooks's *In the Mecca*, I observe that Brooks alludes to the Biblical passage in which God speaks to his afflicted servant Job out of the whirlwind.[8] The observation pertains here because the same chapter ends with God's inquiring, "Who provideth for the raven his food?" (Job 38:41). Whereas in "Satin-Legs" the narrator asks the listener if he or she can be God, the speaker in "Second Sermon" secularizes God's command: "Live and go out./Define and/medicate the whirlwind." An overall difference separates Satin-Legs, who needs an external definition for his life, from the speaker who in "Second Sermon" both demonstrates and demands self-definition.

Coming after 1967, "Second Sermon" characterized a later period when Brooks's concern for a white audience lessened, and her voice became more definite. "Satin-Legs," in contrast, shows a more intropective and questioning tone. Should Smith have flowers, the speaker asks, good geraniums, formal chrysanthemums, magnificent poinsettias and beautiful roses "in the best/Of taste and straight tradition?" While bolstering the narrator's sensitivity, the images prepare for the inquiry as to whether a common humanity can exist: "But you forget, or did you ever know,/His heritage of cabbage and pigtails. . . ." Here the poem implies some questions. Is oppression both synchronic and diachronic? When does one's perception shift from momentary to universal time? How do race and class transform the perception? For the speaker such unstated queries are secondary because the listener's desire for knowledge must precede their being asked. After the narrator describes Smith as being flowerless, except for a feather in his lapel, she relates dandelions to death. But for whom?

> You [the reader] might as well—
> Unless you care to set the world a-boil
> And do a lot of equalizing things,
> Remove a little ermine, say, from kings,
> Shake hands with paupers and appoint them men,
> For instance—certainly you might as well
> Leave him [Smith] his lotion, lavender and oil.
>   (*WGB*, p. 27)

For Brooks's narrator and the reader, to "shake hands with paupers and appoint them men" is to perceive that worth and happiness are human rights, not social privileges. And the poem's listener must accept the responsibility required by the understanding in order to participate fully in the aesthetic experience.

The second part of "Satin Legs" educates the reader by representing
Smith as humanity's icon and its need to create art. Form, as a motif,
unifies Smith's clothes style as described in the first part with the
literary styles of the sixteenth and seventeenth centuries, as well as
with the architectural styles of the seventeenth and eighteenth centuries. "Let us" signals the simultaneous entry by the narrator and
the reader into the "innards" of Smith's closet, a journey not into his
wardrobe alone but into the human heart. His closet, a vault, lacks
those diamonds, pearls, and silver plate that characterize the modern
upper class. When addressed earlier to a speaker's coy mistress, Andrew Marvell's lines imply a more genteel tone: "Thy beauty shall no
more be found,/Nor, in thy marble vault, small sound/My echoing
song. . . . "9 Brooks subtly parodies Anglo-American poetry, for to
transpose "vault" from the pastoral world to the urban one is to
retrace Anglo-American and African literature to their anthropomor-
phic center. In her only direct intrusion, the narrator interrupts:
"People are so in need, in need of help./People want so much that
they do not know." By their directness, the lines bridge the aesthetic
distance that separates Satin-Legs from his speaker. Yet the closure
accentuates human time, the rupture between the flawed medium of
language and the mythic ideal which evokes language. Language can
only signify myth, and the discrepancy between the two represents
the difference between the real and the ideal. Paradoxically the poem
becomes a linguistic object that divides Smith from his narrator; its
language separates its reader from both, even while simultaneously
involving the reader. The aesthetic experience becomes grotesque for
the same reason Smith's wardrobe finally does. The weakness of all
art forms and styles lies in their absolute objectification, because
only humanness can invest art with meaning.

By contrasting black folk style with traditional style, the last three
stanzas of the second part illustrate the theme. Dressed in silk and
wool, Smith looks self-lovingly into his mirror, "The neat curve here;
the angularity/That is appropriate at just its place;/The technique of
a variegated grace." In expanding the range of characterization,
Brooks re-searches the tradition of Anglo-American poetry and finds
an ontological justification for freeing the tradition from itself. Her
means is still parody, but this time the writer parodied is less Marvell
than Shakespeare. Written more than three centuries before, the
bard's fifty-fifth sonnet associates a lover's affections with marble
and stone. By intensity, however, love outshines and outlasts these
substances: "When wasteful war shall statues overturn,/And broils
root out the work of masonry,/Nor Mars his sword nor war's quick

fire shall burn/The living record of your memory." Brooks, by contrast, writes about Smith: "Perhaps you would prefer to this a fine/ Value of marble, complicated stone./Would have him think with horror of baroque,/Rococo. You forget and you forget." The Shakespearean-type literary form here prepares for Brooks's later description of architectural design. Baroque represents the elaborate and ornate forms of the seventeenth century, whereas rococo signifies the curved, fanciful, and spiralled forms of the eighteenth. Brooks, however, replaces these styles in the wide pattern of human creativity where Smith belongs. For twentieth-century America, her narrator shows, western humanism's foundation in the Italian and English Renaissance is paradoxical, for even Shakespeare spoke about the "living record," a testimony not of empirical history but of personal engagement. Brooks's Smith is pathetically blameworthy because he has style without the living memory. But a true imagination must fuse the aesthetic object with life.

The third part of the poem, the journey into the world, shows that Smith lacks a true imagination. At Joe's Eats, he dines with a different prostitute each Sunday.[10] He is not, as George Kent observes, the artist of his existence. Obsessed with sex, he has come to accept the distinction between subjective and objective reality. Having first admired him, the narrator now stands more distantly away. Determinism has overcome the personal flamboyancy that opposed it. Heroic Man, who organizes by art, has deteriorated into Absurd Man, who stands apart from it.[11] Smith and the narrator exchange places; her irony and her judgment become more severe.

The dramatic reversal, as Artistotle calls it, is slow. When Smith dances down the steps, his movement, an art form, reminds the reader of Smith's getting dressed earlier. But basking in sunlight and drinking coffee at breakfast merely obscure his lost awareness: "He hears and does not hear/The alarm clock meddling in somebody's sleep;/ . . . /An indignant robin's resolute donation. . . . /He sees and does not see the broken windows." The robin unhappily sings its song, as Smith "designed" his "reign" before. Its song symbolically typifies the human assertion that develops first from poem XV in *Annie Allen*, next through the short poems "Langston Hughes" and "Big Bessie throws her son into the street" in *Selected Poems*, finally in "Second Sermon" in *In the Mecca*. In both of the latter volumes, Big Bessie appears at the end because she typologically combines infirmness with endurance.

Smith, however, lacks Big Bessie's complex vision. Although he is the narrator's means for revealing many styles, he cannot recognize that his own flair conceals his sordid environment. He overlooks the wear of a little girl's ribbons and the certain hole that underlies a little boy's neat patch. Socially blind, he ignores the women who return from church to their homes on Sunday. Perceiving them clearly would help him to illuminate his own identity, because their lives illustrate the inseparability of determinism and personal choice. Their social conditions have partially governed whether their service is to God, to those well-off people requiring domestics, or to men's carnality.

Verbal play contributes to an overall structure in which music now replaces architecture, although both media demonstrate cultural subjectivity. Smith loiters in the street, where he hears "The Lonesome Blues, the Long-lost Blues." In imagining Saint-Saëns, Grieg, Tschaikovsky, and Brahms, the speaker asks, "could he love them?" The four composers represent France (Western Europe), Norway (Northern Europe), Russia (Eastern Europe), and Germany (Central Europe). When considered together they form almost a graphic structure of the Continent. All lived in the nineteenth century, and, among the three, only Grieg (who died in 1907) lived into the twentieth. Why does the poem show temporal stasis here when the second part showed a progression from the sixteenth century to the eighteenth? Trying to resolve his historical identity, for Smith, compels first an explanation of his cultural self. His musical aesthetic must include spankings by his mother, forgotten hatreds, devotions, father's dreams, sister's prostitutions, old meals, and deprivations. At the movies Smith boos the hero and heroine because the latter is a blonde. Rehumanizing the movie's iconography means modifying the cultural values that the Renaissance articulated even before the Enlightenment objectified western culture. By Brooks's standards for a heroine or hero (Langston Hughes, Big Bessie, Pepita, Malcolm X, Medgar Evers, and the narrators in the sermons), Satin-Legs fails, not because of an unwillingness to confront a naturalistic world but in the ignorance that keeps him from defining the world.[12] Understanding must precede confrontation.

When Smith "squires" his "lady" to Joe's Eats, his action is just another prelude to sexual intercourse on Sunday. "Squires" evokes the chivalric code of knights, damsels, and jousts, but in the modern world the code lacks meaning. Satin-Legs chooses a different prostitute, an ironic "lady." Each wears Queen Lace stockings and "vivid shoes" without fronts and backs. Thick lipstick characterizes them all, as do Chinese fingernails and earrings. The woman on this particular Sunday has large breasts that comfort Smith in a way that

standard morality cannot serve: "He had no education/In quiet arts
of compromise. He would/Not understand your counsels on control,
nor/Thank you for your late trouble." Here the narrator's consciousness combines with Smith's more closely than anywhere else since
the poem's beginning. Why is "education" ambiguous? Does it imply the listener's hidden carnality, which equals, possibly even surpasses, Smith's? Does it suggest, as well, the inability of this "you" to
distinguish manners, the standardization of values, from the values
themselves? As if to suspend her answers, the speaker describes the
serving methods at Joe's. Fish and chicken come on meat platters; the
coleslaw, macaroni, and candied yams come on the side. Coffee and
pie are also available. The yams ("candied sweets") and the possibly
sugared coffee foreshadow the sexual act that ends the poem. The
scene appears through Satin-Legs's submerging consciousness as the
narrator creates a syntactic paradox. Although parentheses usually
indicate understatement, dashes generally indicate stress. The speaker comments ironically, "(The end is—isn't it?—all that really matters.)" She has shown, rather, that values characterize human life.

"Still do I keep my look, my identity . . . " (*WGB*, p. 49), a Petrarchan sonnet, clarifies a humanistic aesthetic by alliteration and
plosive, by tension between movement and inertia, and by juxtaposition of heredity with environment. In general, the poem associates a
soldier's personal or individual style in lovemaking, here ambiguously showing both violence and grace, with the invariant self that
appears regardless of social class or life's experiences. Although this
self is untranslatable in terms of landscape and finally in terms of this
dead soldier's casket, the self does become visible in forms and
situations as different as baseball and school. In the poem, depicting a
soldier who died during World War II, the surviving narrator interprets the man's life, as empathy and love bind the living with the
dead. In thinking highly of her own life-style, the narrator values his.
The particular therefore leads to the general, and the poem is less
about this soldier than about everyone. Two quatrains and the sestet
create the narrator's introspection, as the first lines emphasize
beauty.

With the "p" in "push of pain," the plosives in "precious prescribed
pose" suggest harshness and abruptness as well as death. The timeless narrator portrays a man once alive and transitory. Can form
bridge their two worlds? She recalls his grief, his ambiguous "hatred
hacked." The latter is narrowness, the racial prejudice that he with-
stood and overcame. Although the poem states neither race nor color,
the man is black. Like Brooks's persona in "The Mother" (also in

Street), he lives in Bronzeville, a black section of Chicago; he is at the same time universal because here too the particular represents the general. The soldier waltzed—showed grace—when confronting pain, inertia, and prejudice. As with Brooks's Satin-Legs Smith, his environment determined his style. So war and dress vary in artistic mode but not in human desire.

The second quatrain reinforces the dead soldier's "pose," his earlier blending of heredity with environment: "No other stock/That is irrevocable, perpetual/And its to keep." The off-rhymes imply human indomitability—"irrevocable, perpetual." The archetypal need to create, to give form, differs as to social class, for the soldier became his style "In castle or in shack./With rags or robes. Through good, nothing, or ill." This last line stands out. Whereas ill is lethargy and apathy, good is dynamism. As in Brooks's "Sadie and Maud," living and posing surpasses not living at all. By symbolizing life, style is the measure of vertical and horizontal space: "And even in death a body, like no other/On any *hill* or *plain* or crawling cot" (my emphasis). Height and breadth end in alliteration and perplexity. Does a cot crawl, or do people? And do people advance, regress? Brooks ended *A Street in Bronzeville* with "The Progress," a poem that portrays well civilization's vulnerability. In "still do I keep my look, my identity," however, the imaginative mind is invulnerable. Having twisted, gagged, and died, the soldier "Shows the old personal art, the look. Shows what/It showed at baseball. What it showed in school."

In sonnet 2 of "Children of the Poor" (*WGB*, p. 100), the narrator more impersonally desires a humanistic aesthetic. For Brooks, the verse reunited the formal with the emotional and determined her future techniques. *Annie Allen* showed her decision to create engaged narrators of the present rather than detached ones of the past. When appearing impersonal ("Bronzeville Mother . . . ," "The Chicago *Defender* Sends a Man to Little Rock"), her later speakers mask their actual involvement and sincerity. Here the narrating mother relates directly her children's distressed inquiries. The children request not an easy life but a life with meaning, because they see themselves as dehumanized objects, the heirs of the nineteenth-century slaves who escaped safely to the northern lines. Social reality undermines the children's religious belief, for what God could possibly create such a world? The narrator herself, of course, reflects this powerlessness rooted in social injustice, because she ends by being neither alchemist, magician, nor God. She is only a woman, signifying the writer who creates her, whose planning and love (although

great) cannot redeem her children from autumn's cold. Here objec-
tivity, irony, and polish deceive.[13]

The poem opens with the parallelism and balance of a rhetorical
question: "What shall I give my children? who are poor,/Who . . .
/Who. . . . "[14] Plosives emphasize again the children's plight: "adjudged," "leastwise," "land," "demand," "velvety velour," "begged."
Because the narrator's listeners and readers live outside the sonnet, it
nearly becomes a monologue written to them. Her children, however, live in the poem's world of suffering, although outside its
dramatic action. They speak not through dialogue but through the
narrator's memory. Looking for fulfillment rather than for wealth,
they are less the individual than the type, and so is she. The second
quatrain blends the two viewpoints when her words indirectly recreate theirs. With alliteration and metaphor she questions the fate of
those "graven by a hand/Less than angelic, admirable or sure." Does
she evoke the myth of Hephaestus-Vulcan, craftsman, symbol of the
artist as well as the writer? What were his limitations? What are hers?
Must she now rehumanize the metaphor and myth as well as restore
it? From "mode, design, device" the narrator advances to grief and
love, but her world lacks magic, the alchemical stone. Her poem ends
in "autumn freezing" because she has come as far as woman and man
can. Having illuminated poverty, she sees her poem end at that magic
and divinity that transcend craft. Even the writer and artist finally
must speak from a fallen world.

> My hand is stuffed with mode, design, device.
> But I lack access to my proper stone.
> And plenitude of plan shall not suffice
> Nor grief nor love shall be enough alone
> To ratify my little halves who bear
> Across an autumn freezing everywhere.
>   (*WGB*, p. 100)

Brooks explores this idea further in "Langston Hughes,"[15] a short
poem that combines cheer and praise with images of speech and
muscle. Here the writer's "infirm profession" suggests human life,
but Hughes's bond with nature is ambivalent. While opposing its
apparent determinism, he demonstrates its aliveness. His name signifies historical black man, black/creative writer, and humanistic
man-woman. The poem blends synchrony with diachrony when the
narrator's final command "See" compels the reader to share the
writer's eternality. Although they are not exclusive, these roles help

the student to outline the poem into four parts. The first (lines 1–3) fuses writer, humanist, and historical figure; the second (lines 4–7) emphasizes a quest for meaning; the third (lines 8–15) develops the theme of art; and the fourth (lines 16–18) extends the narrator's invitation to the reader. As the present tense indicates continuity, Hughes synthesizes joy and freedom. He combines integrity with quest (the "long reach"), and his "strong speech" anthropomorphizes language.[16] His "remedial fears" and "Muscular tears" relate him first to a cultural perception of black suffering and second to a powerful compassion. His world is an oxymoron, and his patterns of struggle, memory, dramatic action, and celebration suggest Brooks's other writings.

Since 1963 Brooks has portrayed the heroic self as confronting nature's undeniable power. By choice her Langston Hughes timelessly "Holds horticulture/In the eye of the vulture." Having identified with his humanness in sections one and two, the narrator apocalyptically fuses her vision with his in section three. As the storyteller and artist, she represents Gwendolyn Brooks, the creator in the externally historical world. But that parallel (yet real) world can never be identical to the poem's. Brooks has given the speaker autonomy, an eternality like the Hughes in the title when readers recreate the poem. She carefully establishes the bond between narrator and persona; between persona, narrator, and reader. All relate to wind imagery that exposes at once man's internal and external worlds. The complementary element of water appears within a framework that implies innovation and illumination. Here alliteration adds fluidity: "In the breath/Of the holocaust he [Hughes]/Is helmsman, hatchet, headlight." The light imagery in the third section blends with the one-word line "See" that begins the last section. The narrator, en route, commands the reader to assume the poet's role, the highest level of possibility. When she calls writing poetry an "infirm profession," her sadness occurs because the limitation (compression) appears within the framing context of style, quest, being, sordidness, and passion. The poem ends by celebrating more than the Harlem Renaissance of the 1920s; it represents more than a writer and a man. It signifies the eternal type that defines itself as freedom, courage, and health: "See/One restless in the exotic time! and ever,/Till the air is cured of its fever."

In "Boy Breaking Glass" (WGB, pp. 408–9), the humanistic aesthetic is social and subjective. The poem presents art, the paradox of beauty, ugliness, destruction, and creation; it fuses desecration with reverence. Complexity grows from allusions to the nineteenth century, as the poem shows that loneliness and neglect reap hardship and revenge. Brooks ironically contrasts the narrator who speaks artificially with the boy who speaks somewhat neurotically. Congress, the Statue of Liberty, the Hawaiian feast, and the Regency Room ironically foreshadow the cliff, the snare, and the "exceeding sun." Mental instability, animal imagery, and social upheaval, in other words, form an unbreakable chain, and Brooks illuminates this continuity against the background of the riots in America during the late 1960s.

The poem has eight stanzas, two having six lines and the remaining six having two. The narrator recognizes both traditional and non-traditional worlds—what W. E. B. Du Bois calls double consciousness.[17] In both instances beauty concerns myth-making. It approximates Coleridge's primary imagination, the first symbolism and vision of the Western world. But counter-myth-making renews the primary myth so as to satisfy contemporary need. When myth-making declines to science (formalism), the true artist rehumanizes craft; his or her new form changes traditional aesthetics.

The sensitive narrator loves the black boy because his art suits his socialization. Temporal and mental space separate him from "us," the listener. His aesthetic, a paradox, is both revolutionary and reactionary, because it resurrects for the future that humanism lost in the past: "I shall create! If not a note, a hole./If not an overture, a desecration." Destruction and creation differ in degree rather than in kind, a degree that represents perspective.[18] Within a structure implying racial and literary history, the narrator's kind tone in the first and third stanzas complements the boy's defiant tone in the second. Recalling the cargoes in stanza three, the ship imagery in stanza four alludes by interior monologue to his slave ancestry:

> "Don't go down the plank
> if you see there's no extension.
> Each to his grief, each to
> his loneliness and fidgety revenge.
> Nobody knew where I was and now I am no longer
>   there."
>
> (WGB, pp. 408–9)

The narrator, however, speaks satirically from the viewpoint of traditional aesthetics: "The only sanity is a cup of tea./The music is in minors." Her artificiality and delicacy muffle the "cry" of the first stanza as well as the overture of the second. The gentility recalls Brooks's juxtaposition in "The Progress" of Jane Austen's politeness with the carnage of World War II, her masterful incongruity suggesting moral sordidness. In "Boy Breaking Glass," however, politeness facilitates detachment: "Each one other/is having different weather." The narrator indicates that the boy's destruction of a window contrasts with her creation of the poem, even though she understands his need for political power, his expensive food, his lodging, and his freedom; she knows that art explodes as well as beautifies. She appreciates him

> Who has not Congress, lobster, love, luau
> the Regency Room, the Statue of Liberty,
> runs. A sloppy amalgamation.
> A mistake.
> A cliff.
> A hymn, a snare, and an exceeding sun.
>   (WGB, p. 409)

because art must reveal the cultural self.

Can understanding the type broaden scholars' readings of Brooks's "The Chicago Picasso"? (WGB, pp. 412–13). When reviewing In the Mecca, Brian Benson praised the poem's "most starkly beautiful description," and later William Hansell discussed Brooks's self-justification of art in the poem.[19] The piece was written for the occasion of Mayor Richard Daley's dedication of a statue, which some called that of a bird-woman, to the city on August 15, 1967. By contrasting the willingness to explore life with cowardice and insensitivity, the poem resolves itself in the possibility of human perception. Yet will is necessary to see. The stanzas, nineteen lines altogether, present the nature of creativity (lines 1–7), the paradox of its appreciation (lines 8–15), and the narrator's resulting insight (lines 16–19). First comes the rhetorical question: "Does man love Art?" By exiling one from comfort, home, and beer, aesthetic experience necessitates pain and quest, as balance and personification show: "Art hurts. Art urges voyages—." Both artist and reader transcend animalism ("belch, sniff, or scratch") imperfectly to seek divinity.

Humanism is paradox: "we must cook ourselves and style ourselves for Art, who/is a requiring courtesan." But a courtesan, a prostitute, sells herself to the upper classes. How is art a prostitute? Does it make one abandon the private self for the public one? Does the creator sacrifice selfhood and humanity? "We do not," the speaker says, "hug the Mona Lisa." "Yes" partially answers the last two questions, although prostitution here implies frailty more than corruption. For the narrator's listeners, artifacts have autonomous meaning. People ("We") admire romantic spectacles ("astounding fountain"), traditional sculpture ("horse and rider"), or standard animal ("lion"). We can bear any burden but our own humanity.

Do the people feel? The poem ends in cold. After the engaged "we," the viewpoint becomes again that of the detached narrator. Her objective poem has been "The Chicago Picasso," because Chicago is American and Picasso is Spanish—even if not parallel—the two representing the impersonalization of art in the Western (modern) world. To the narrator, form should include pain, rawness, and love. Like Brooks's speaker in "Second Sermon on the Warpland," this one shows tension between idealism and realism, black and white, hatred and love, order and chaos. Resembling a woman and a bird, Picasso's cold steel can only imply flight, but the narrator represents the eternal need to soar, at least to sculpt and to write. Her imperative ending contrasts sharply with her interrogative beginning. Why has a statue now become a blossom to her? Here eternality depends less upon form (plants are transitory) than upon human perception and sincerity, the necessary qualities for a world facing sunset:

> Observe the tall cold of a Flower
> which is as innocent and as guilty,
> as meaningful and as meaningless as any
> other flower in the western field.
> (*WGB*, p. 413)

Brooks reaffirms the ontological self. With style and posture her personae withstand the science and barbarism of war or even death. Identity includes vertical and horizontal space as well as time. Living between animalism and divinity, the self seeks resolution; finding grief where magic disappears, it must be content with love. Whether by breaking glass or by creating an overture, separate people diversely experience a common end. To hear Brooks's universal voice, to transcend her form, the reader must ultimately be human.

Notes

1. George E. Kent, "Preface: Gwen's Way," Preface to *Report from Part One*, by Gwendolyn Brooks (Detroit: Broadside Press, 1972), p. 31.

2. Gwendolyn Brooks, *The World of Gwendolyn Brooks* (New York: Harper and Row, 1971). Hereinafter cited in the text as *WGB*.

3. In *Myth and Meaning* (New York: Schocken, 1977), Claude Lévi-Strauss views invariance as being the central unity in structures of human creativity.

4. For convenience, "prostitute" appears here as a sensible term. "Woman" is inadequate, because the poem implies looseness on the woman's part. Yet "looseness" is inexact for the same reason that "whore" would fail. The latter two terms imply the absence of dignity, which Brooks gives to this kind of woman in "a song in the front yard" (*WGB*, p. 12). Prostitute here is a generic rather than a moral category.

5. John Lyons, *Noam Chomsky* (New York: Viking Press 1970); Claude Lévi-Strauss, *The Savage Mind* (Chicago: University of Chicago Press, 1966); idem, *Myth and Meaning* (New York: Schocken, 1979): Jacques Derrida, *Speech and Phenomena: And Other Essays on Husserl's Theory of Signs* (Evanston, Ill.: Northwestern University Press, 1973).

6. "Re-search," as used here, linguistically demonstrates the problem of dehumanization. Etymologically the term implies subjective knowing, yet it has been reduced to meaning the verification of scientific data.

7. To observe the way Brooks's speakers function, see R. Baxter Miller, "'Define . . . the Whirlwind': In the Mecca—Urban Setting, Shifting Narrator, and Redemptive Vision," *Obsidian* 4 (Spring 1978): 19–31; and idem, "'My Hand Is Mode': Gwendolyn Brooks' Speakers and Their Stances," TV videotape for the University of Tennessee Division of Continuing Education, 1978.

8. Miller, "'Define . . . the Whirlwind,'" pp. 19, 30.

9. Andrew Marvell, *Selected Poetry* (New York: Signet, 1967), p. 76.

10. Compare the female typology in "a song in the front yard," *WGB*, p. 12.

11. This reading expands and applies the idea in Arthur P. Davis, "Gwendolyn Brooks: Poet of the Unheroic," *College Language Association Journal* 7 (Dec. 1963): 114–25. The unheroism that Davis observes was probably true until 1963.

12. See Miller, "'Define . . . the Whirlwind,'" where I observe this typology in the second half of *In the Mecca*.

13. Miller, "'Define . . . the Whirlwind,'" p. 26.

14. George E. Kent, "The Poetry of Gwendolyn Brooks, Part II," *Black World* 20 (Oct. 1971): 36–48. Kent considers the "Children of the Poor" sequence the most masterful description in poetry of the black mother's dilemma and one of the most memorable, as well as rhythmical, pieces in English.

15. Gwendolyn Brooks, *Selected Poems* (New York: Harper and Row, 1963), p. 123.

16. Compare the theme of reaching (questing) in "Life for my child is simple, and is good," *WGB*, p. 104.

17. In "The Achievement of Gwendolyn Brooks," *College Language Association Journal* 16 (Sept. 1972): 23–31, Houston A. Baker, Jr., says that Brooks's poetry demonstrates white form and black content. Are these terms difficult to define? Are they mutually exclusive?

18. In "'Define . . . the Whirlwind,'" my explication of *In the Mecca*, I describe it as a volume that "seeks to balance the sordid realities of urban life with an imaginative process of reconciliation and redemption" (p. 20).

19. Respectively, "Review of *In the Mecca*," *College Language Association Journal* 13 (Dec. 1969): 203; "Aestheticism versus Political Militancy in Gwendolyn Brooks' 'The Chicago Picasso' and 'The Wall,'" *College Language Association Journal* 17 (Sept. 1973): 11–15. See also R. Baxter Miller, *Langston Hughes and Gwendolyn Brooks: A Reference Guide* (Boston: G. K. Hall, 1978), p. xxiv.

II

"A Brisk Contour": Analysis of the Poetry

ERLENE STETSON

8

Songs After Sunset *(1935–36):*

The Unpublished Poetry

of Gwendolyn Elizabeth Brooks

All of my works will die—
You know, I know it too.[1]

A nineteen-year-old poet of lyrics and songs, Gwendolyn Brooks can be forgiven for the less-than-visionary complaint cited above. The reader and critic is singularly rewarded that her question: "Why should I try and try/For *no sake?*" (*Songs*, p. 10)[2] has the retrospective tinge of an impatient poet. Indeed, the mature Brooks writes "words [that] hold, oh so much of wonderful import" (*Songs*, p. 9), and thrice over proves herself wrong when she laments that "all of my works will die—/You know, I know it too." (*Songs*, p. 10).

Not only does Brooks's poetry live, but she is also a prolific poet whose resurgence in the sixties resulted in her long-awaited auto-biography, *Report from Part One,*[3] in 1972. Interest in Brooks continues largely unabated, because *Report* only whets the appetite for more about her as artist and person. For now, Brooks defies neat encapsulation. She remains a tantalizing kaleidoscope, a virtual construct of transformations. She is at once the young voice of Maud Martha, a "nice" lady in the "nice" sense of the word, and Annie Allen ("The Anniad"), an ambitious woman of epic proportions; she is Brooks the cultist and universalist; she is also seriously engaged in the development of a methodology that can consider the philosophical and artistic meaning of being a black poet fully aware of the psychosocial and political relevances, of historical realities, as both determinants and results of the poetry she now writes; she is an artist of a kind of psychic split that allows her to write lyrics and sonnets as well as narratives and ballads while still remaining too subtle and sophisticated a poet to make uncritical equations anywhere.[4] Brooks doesn't fall into partisan pitfalls. As one reads *Report*, one is privileged to see her move, rather effortlessly from Negro to black. As an unwitting historiographer, she chronicles her own canon that transcends the covert and suppressed violence of the social order of the fifties to the recognized and overt violence of the social order of the sixties that resulted in upheaval in Bronzevilles all over urban America.

In view of the enormous interest in Brooks as person and poet, fueled in part by the unanswered questions in *Report*, this essay will explore both theme and content in her little-known and unpublished "homemade" volume titled *Songs After Sunset*. I believe that for now, the best way to understand Brooks is by reading her poems. For a brief although compact treatment of the poetics of Gwendolyn Brooks, the reader is referred to Gloria T. Hull's "A Note on the Poetic Technique of Gwendolyn Brooks."[5]

Songs After Sunset is handwritten in indelible ink with typical schoolgirl flourish; the inside cover page bears an inscription:

> Hope you like them,
> Ima Twin,
> Despite their slightness!—

It is signed, "Gwendolyn" and dated July 23, 1936. However, it is not the inscription that captures one's attention as much as does the appearance of the slim 5 by 7 inch volume itself. Its appearance suggests faded significance, a passing grandeur, a sign of some previous vital, majestical presence. The cover is faded blue construction paper bound with a brilliant red corded string. The title page, also signed, reveals an ink drawing of a female singer, opened songbook in hand, with shoulder-length, luxuriant hair covered by a broad-brimmed hat. She is wearing a long-sleeved, full-length bouffant dress that reveals a pair of shoes peeping prettily from beneath. Heavily inked marks above the girl poised in song suggest the illusion of sunset. On the reverse title page, signed "Gwendolyn Elizabeth Brooks" and dated July 23, 1936, is a dedication to Lemuel H. Randolph:

> Whose letters
> Contain the very quintessence
> of friendliness

It carries a notation to "see page 12," which has an eight-line, two-stanza poem, "For Lemuel H. Randolph." This poem is dated the same day as the inscription and dedication.

Both the dedication and the inscription link Brooks with poets of an earlier age. Both are reminiscent of the spirit of platonic love, itself invoking a platonic dedication—an extravagant Petrarchan compliment. The slim volume reminds one of those "slight" manuscripts that it was the habit to circulate among the sophisticated, witty, and cultured members of Elizabethan and Jacobean circles. In fact, the theme of this collection of poems and the effect of the title-page drawing suggest that Brooks is thematically and stylistically located somewhere between Edmund Spenser's *Foure Hymnes* (1596) and John Donne's *Songs and Sonnets* and *Divine Poems* (1633).[6] The overall effect is that of an old Elizabethan songbook with such titles as: "Continuity," "Familiar," "Hidden Memories," "Myself," "Eternal," "Province," "Lesson," "Now Every Hour," "Alteration," and "Change." The dominant mood of these poems is love, both worldly (friendship, marriage, nature) and divine (animism, God, Nature). The reader is easily struck by the young poet's awareness of history and historicity, because all of these poems (except one, for which the day is missing) are dated to the day, month, and year. Only one poem, "Do Not Pull Her Hands Away," dated April 1, 1936, bears a notation: "Made up on street car, on my way back from having my college picture taken." The volume attests to the fact that April (of both years), the love month, was Brooks's most prolific. She wrote three poems on April 2, 1936; three on April 3, 1936; and numerous others during the period from April 1 to April 23, 1936. Most of her longest poems were written in December 1935. Her shortest poem, the two-line, "We," is dated Friday, May 1, 1936. Augmenting this sense of conscious history and continuity is the closing inscription of the last page, written appropriately in the past tense:

> Hope you liked them,
> "Ima Twin,"
> Despite their slightness![7]

Bearing her first-name signature and the date, this inscription bears the notation "Thursday night," the volume ostensibly having moved from day to evening, the "song after sunset."

One approaches the task of explication with a mix of temerity and trepidation in view of Brooks's statement that "Not until I was twenty-one or twenty-two did I write any poems that I want seen today" (*Report*, p. 140). Yet she proceeds to mention three of the poems that appear in *Songs*, thereby inextricably linking them to the poetry and person of Gwendolyn Brooks.

Unlike the mature Brooks, whose poetry is often linked to Shelley and is lauded for its economy of language, polished diction, and technically well-written structure, the young Brooks had not developed a poetic voice that can be articulated to the reader. First, she occasionally forgot to indent consistently a first or second line as the case may be. Second, she used far too many articles (yet, ironically, not enough when it is an article that she needed) and prepositions, thus betraying a lack of rhythm and metric sense. She had not developed her flair for unconventional words and phrasings, but one can already see such a predilection. Chances are that Brooks's debt to an older tradition was still strong; it appears that her indebtedness to John Donne, Ben Jonson, and John Milton is considerable. For example, her poem, "Not in the Face of Failure," makes use of words in the Jonsonian and Miltonic style:

> Not in the face of failure,
> After the furious tuggle
> With iron-armored fate, to
> Resign the struggle.
>   (*Songs*, p. 12)

The use of the word "tuggle," an obsolete word meaning struggle, is not unlike the Jonsonian and Miltonic style of using archaic (usually Latin) words.

A similar effect is created in "Darling," a twenty-line poem in free verse consisting of three stanzas and two unrhymed lines of uneven length. The last two lines: "But—darling, darling, darling,/Is all I need to say," (*Songs*, p. 14) repeat (with the addition of "but") the first two lines of the poem. Brooks uses an ingenious construction—antithesis—utilizing an even more ingenious turn of thought much like the style of a Petrarchan conceit. First, she establishes a series of praise possibilities:

> Oh, I could exclaim
> On the tender light
> That moves gently in your eyes;

Or:

> I could say the bright
> Glimmer of the sun
> Pallid is, compared
> With the radiance of your smile.

Then comes the tantalizing twist (appropriately written in parentheses) to undercut the preceding stanza, the lover notwithstanding:

> (Though smiles have never glowed
> At me with the bold
> Impudence and scorn
> That hot, powerful orb has
> Many a breathless morn!)

The poet is exacting and is not yet finished:

> I could cry—"Your voice is
> Sweet as airs of May!"

To abruptly return the welcome Parthian shot:

> But—darling, darling, darling,
> Is all I need to say.
>   (*Songs*, p. 14)[8]

The reader might note that the word "pallid" is a word appearing frequently in Spenser's *Faerie Queene* (1590) and Dryden's *Fables* (1700), among others. It is an old word whose usage is chiefly in poetry before the 1800s.[9] Similarly, "orb" is more commonly an English usage to be found in works by William Shakespeare and John Milton.

The work of the early, unpublished, and unself-conscious Brooks seems to alternate between the dignified, weighty tone of Milton (for example, her poem "Eternal"), the cloying sweetness of the Elizabethans (as in her poems "People," "Relief"), and the colloquial style implied in John Donne and perfected in modern poetry (as in her poems "Let Them Laugh At Me," "Always," "Continuity"). Ironically, the early Brooks shares yet another characteristic with Donne: an imaginative and intellectual struggle that takes place in her poems. On one hand, their surface import can be one of distortions and oversimplifications: "Pour the blood of your heart—/It has bled so long"; "It twists my soul in burning knots/To look at people long"; "The dawn's red will continue red,/Noon blue, and Sunset gold" (*Songs*, pp. 2–4). On the other hand, one finds verses of compact and dense erudition, as in "Keep The Faith": "Nine little letters/That are singing birds/Sent from heaven/To cheer me on/Crying—After darkness/Dawn." Or, as in "Province": "My province is my poetry/My castle is my soul." With audacious cleverness Brooks creates a unitary effect so that province carries a dual meaning: Province is to the body as the castle is to the soul, with God as "the shining sovereign"—all combined to equal a person:

'A small world, a cramped world,'
I hear you, mocking, cry.
But, oh, sufficient for a thing
As self-complete as I!
(*Songs*, p. 5)

Although this slim volume of thirty-three poems reveals no standard versification pattern, Brooks's poetic strategies are primarily versions of the conventional English poetic tradition. She seems most comfortable with iambic pentameter, although she is equally at home with free verse and adhering to no fixed metrical pattern. Although I have suggested at some length that Brooks's volume is on the surface like an Elizabethan songbook, it is equally true that her poems are universal in appeal in deference to the personal and confessional mode. She herself has articulated these concerns in defining the themes of her earlier poetry as being about: "Nature, love, death, the sky. I was very much infatuated with the sky. I would sit out on the back porch and look up there and see the clouds and pretend things, particularly about my future. I think my dreams were based on the fairy tales I was reading. The future was very vague, but it was very beautiful; it had a fascinating sort of glamour. So that's what those poems were made of" (*Report*, pp. 169–70).

Such articulation defies any period label. The allusions in these poems are more personal than general and cultural. Brooks's concern is to present her feelings on things that she has felt, seen, heard, or imagined. In these poems her attitude, her vision, and her world are plausible, simple, and attractive, so much so that in a two-line poem, "We," the young poet can exult:

An old man said this thing to me:
"The loveliest word of all is 'we.' "
(*Songs*, p. 7)

Or she might enhance the mundane realism of a mouse made important by its inclusion:

I killed a mouse today,
A little, new-hatched bit
With scarce enough of legs
To carry it.
(*Songs*, p. 16)

The reader will note that the word "of" is clearly superfluous, and recall James Weldon Johnson's comments to Brooks on another poem: "The transfer [deletion] would change your metric scheme but would improve both sense and rhythm" (*Report*, p. 202).

The final purpose of this essay is to identify the similarities and differences between the "then" Gwendolyn Elizabeth Brooks and the "now" Gwendolyn Brooks. Has she changed a great deal? The answer is both yes and no.

Clearly, Brooks sustains a lifelong animist concern: "Be pleased with the things of life that are called little. The talk of birds. The first light of morning. The look of the sky to the west at sunset." (*Report*, pp. 63–64). This sentiment compares to her poem "Cat and Poplar," wherein she recognizes her kinship with both as an "enchantment of God." Her poplar has "hair" of "green," and of the cat and poplar Brooks notes: "I mention them together/They like each other so" (*Songs*, p. 18). She sees herself as "sister of them," and thus succeeds in bringing together two separate images, including herself as well, into a unified whole—that of God's creation. Clearly revealed in this poem and others is her habit of personifying inanimate objects with human characteristics. The older Brooks, for instance, writes: "The ground springs up;/hits you with gnarls and rust,"[10] and a younger Brooks writes: "And old dark poplar with her/Green hair so near the sky" (*Songs*, p. 18). Like the older Brooks, she shows a distinct fascination for the verb "is" and a pattern of repetition. Her poem "Past" is a good illustration: "It's past, it's done, it's finished,/It is all over now." This becomes fashioned and perfected in the later Brooks, whose poem "Boy Breaking Glass" is more sophisticated in its repetitious use of "is": "Whose broken window is a cry of art/ . . . is raw: is sonic: is old-eyed première" (*Mecca*, p. 26). Similarly, the irony and the quiet desperation of "Let Them Laugh At Me!" is reminiscent of Brooks's prose lyric narrative, "The Life of Lincoln West,"[11] where the curtain of romanticism hides the pain of being gaped at:

> I should be proud, I guess,
> That I inspire
> This present surge
> Of merriment's ecstatic fire.
> (*Songs*, p. 13)

The difference of the one is in Lincoln West's acceptance and "comfort" in being "the real thing," and in the other, the poet's acceptance without grace, but with a retort: "Well, let them laugh."

Songs After Sunset, then, consists of major revelatory fragments concerning the art of Gwendolyn Brooks. Whatever her present richness, resonance, and complication, her unpublished poems—*Songs After Sunset*—establish a provocative literary framework that begs to be explored, understood, and analyzed. Rather than deal singly with each poem in the volume, I have suggested a context for evaluating Brooks's person and poetry. The critic, in trying to approach a fusion of style and structure in order to produce a total coherence, must consider Brooks's entire canon. As yet, Brooks is multifaceted and ever-evolving. She promises yet another "report," ostensibly a "part two,"[12] implying either deliberately or inadvertently that several personae are evolving within one body. This brings to mind that most pregnant of all possibilities hinted at in the cryptic "Ima Twin" appearing on the front and back cover of *Songs*. Does Brooks suggest that this is "a twin" to another volume? Whatever its meaning, it is a tantalizing construct that invites speculation on the two faces (indeed many faces) of Brooks that readers have been privileged to note. At any rate, one is forced to agree with Brooks, then as now, that

> The written word holds, oh so much
> Of wonderful import—
> Here in these little books of mine
> Shines gold of every sort.
>
> (*Songs*, p. 9)

Notes

1. *Songs After Sunset*, July 23, 1936. An unpublished original, Brooks's handwritten manuscript consists of twenty pages and thirty-three poems, of varying lengths, dated from Friday, October 18, 1935, to Thursday, July 23, 1936. It is the exclusive property of the Lilly Library, a specialized collection of holdings at Indiana University, Bloomington. Hereinafter cited in the text as *Songs*.

2. Emphasis on the last two lines of the first verse is the poet's.

3. Gwendolyn Brooks, *Report from Part One* (Detroit: Broadside Press, 1972). Hereinafter cited in the text as *Report*.

4. See Brooks's "Of Flowers and Fire and Flowers," *Black Books Bulletin* 3 (Fall 1975): 16–18.

5. Gloria T. Hull, "A Note on the Poetic Technique of Gwendolyn Brooks," *College Language Association Journal* 19 (Dec. 1975): 280–85.

6. This date refers to the first collected edition of Donne's poems, published posthumously.

7. Unlike the first inscription, the cryptic "Ima Twin" on the back page is in quotation marks.

8. This poem, "Darling," like many of the others, contains erratic and inconsistent indentations, first of the second line, then not in another stanza. Like others in this volume, this poem adheres to no standard pattern of versification.

9. This is not meant to exclude its use by others, such as Edgar Allan Poe, Robert Southey, and Sir Walter Scott. The word has a scientific orientation (as in *pallor*), but is favored by poets.

10. Gwendolyn Brooks, *In the Mecca* (New York: Harper and Row, 1968), p. 12. Hereinafter cited in the text as *Mecca*.

11. Gwendolyn Brooks, "The Life of Lincoln West," in *New Writings by American Negroes, 1940–1962*, ed. Herbert Hill (New York: Alfred A. Knopf, 1968), pp. 316–17.

12. See Gloria T. Hull and Posey Gallagher, "Update on Part One: An Interview with Gwendolyn Brooks," *College Language Association Journal* 21 (Sept. 1977): 19–40.

GARY SMITH

— *9* —

Paradise Regained: The Children of Gwendolyn Brooks's Bronzeville

What shall I give my children? who are poor,
Who are adjudged the leastwise of the land,
Who are my sweetest lepers, who demand
No velvet and no velvety velour;
But who have begged me for a brisk contour,
Crying that they are quasi, contraband
Because unfinished, graven by a hand
Less than angelic, admirable or sure.
My hand is stuffed with mode, design, device.
But I lack access to my proper stone.
And plenitude of plan shall not suffice
Nor grief nor love shall be enough alone
To ratify my little halves who bear
Across an autumn freezing everywhere.[1]

One of the enduring paradoxes of Gwendolyn's Brooks's long and prolific writing career is that she is one of America's most honored and popular poets, yet she is also one of its most difficult and demanding. Like the modernist poets T. S. Eliot and Ezra Pound, with whom she is often favorably compared, her poetry is intellectual, urbane, and carefully crafted. However, to the American reading public—especially the rather modest segment that routinely reads poetry—she is chiefly known for a handful of widely anthologized poems, "kitchenette building," "the mother," "The Lovers of the Poor," and "We Real Cool." These select poems, however representative they are of her larger body of work, do not challenge the reader with the subtle, complex patterns of her more demanding poetry; at worst, the poems actually create the impression that Brooks is primarily a populist poet in the mold of Langston Hughes or Carl Sandburg. But unlike Hughes's and Sandburg's verse, Brooks's best poetry is not written at a casual level. Although she shares the populist tradition in her thematic concern for the unheralded masses, her poetic techniques—the ways in which she expresses her populism—are not common to the more prosaic approach of populist poetry. As many critics have noted, her poetic techniques are more in line with the elliptical, allusive, and imagistic verse of modernist poetry. Her poetic voice offers a distinct balance between the thematically populist yet technically *belle lettrist*. And, in spite of her often-quoted desire to mediate these extremes in her poetic voice and techniques, to write poetry that would appeal to a tavern as well as classroom audience, Brooks's craftsmanship belongs to a literary tradition that extends itself to seventeenth-century metaphysical poetry.

Another oddity of Brooks's popularity is the bleakness of her poetic vision. To be sure, her bleakness is tempered by an optimism that she inherited, in part, from the New Negro poets of the Harlem Renaissance: Hughes, Countee Cullen, and, to a lesser degree, Claude McKay.[2] But even a casual survey of the subject matter in Brooks's poetry reveals a world fraught with violence and human failure: abortion in "the mother," fratricide in "the murder," prostitution in "My Little 'Bout-town Gal," homicide in "A Bronzeville Mother Loiters," and child abuse in "In the Mecca." Long before existentialism became fashionable in American literary circles, Brooks's poetry described a world in which alienated human beings flirt daily with personal and social disasters that edge them close to the abyss of madness.[3]

The paradox here, of course, is not that Brooks's bleakness is without precedent or unexpected of a black woman poet, but rather that it is not consistent with her official title as Poet Laureate of Illinois and her public demeanor as a popular, optimistic poet. For the most part, though, Brooks's bleakness has not received much critical attention. When her readers have taken notice, they often ignore its darker depths. In the labyrinth corridors of Brooks's poetic vision, most of her characters grope in futile search for some meaning or purpose in their lives.[4] At best, the few who find an escape either through religious intoxication ("hunchback girl: she thinks of heaven") or militant self-belief ("Negro Hero") find themselves alienated from those who do not share their beliefs. Moreover, their confidence is often undercut by the radical strategy of Brooks's poetry: her use of ellipses, metaphysical images, and parodic use of rhyme and meter actually expose her character's confusion and mistaken identity rather than reinforce his or her self-belief ("The Sundays of Satin-Legs Smith").

The bleakness of Brooks's poetic vision is not, as some critics maintain, entirely characteristic of her pre-1967 poetry, before she became a celebrated spokesperson for the Black Arts Movement.[5] While bleak to an admittedly lesser degree, her poetry after 1967 reveals the same uncertainties and frustrated longings. To be sure, her poems portray characters who are more often militantly self-assertive and positive about their black identities, yet their lives are no less haunted, ever defeated by complex socioeconomic and psychological problems that defy immediate solution. Although, for example, intraracial discrimination is no longer a persistent theme after 1967, racial discrimination, poverty, and violence are still a part of her poetic world. And, in spite of the measures her characters take to improve their lives, they continually fail. Brooks's poetry, therefore, realistically describes the personal pain, frustration, and futility of Afro-American history; in her poetic vision, heroism, self-sacrifice, and brotherhood are articulate ideals, but they remain, for the most part, at the level of idealization, and very infrequently are they realized in concrete terms.

However, if Brooks's poetry about adults is bleak, her poetry about children is even more so. As the most vulnerable members of society, children are the most likely victims in a world plagued by personal and social violence. In Brooks's world view, the suffering of children is irrefutable evidence that the rituals that give meaning and substance to human lives are subordinate to the daily struggle to survive. Hence, two predominant themes in Brooks's poetry, entrapment and the desire to escape, are graphically displayed in the lives of her children. They are born into a labyrinth world of corridors and makeshift apartments, where they soon become trapped by poverty. Quite expectedly, then, the overwhelming desire for many of her children is the need to escape, to flee, the various forms of socioeconomic and psychological oppression that thwart self-fulfillment and threaten to destroy their lives. Because it is to a world free of adults where most of her children wish to escape, their unique ability to imagine this world—albeit on the wings of fantasy—distinguishes them from adults and creates some sense of hope.

Brooks has written poems *about* children and poems *for* children. Of the two groups, the first is the larger and the more meaningful because, in each of Brooks's published works, children are central to its thematic design. *A Street in Bronzeville* (1945) contains no less than ten poems written about children, while several others, "obituary for a living lady," "a song in the front yard," and "of De Witt Williams on his way to Lincoln Cemetery," establish a definite link between a character's traumatic childhood and his or her tragic adult life. The first section of *Annie Allen* (1949) is titled "Notes from the Childhood and the Girlhood" and, in the third section, "The Womanhood," Brooks includes one of her most distinguished sonnet sequences, "The Children of the Poor." *In the Mecca* (1968), the volume that is often cited as the turning point in her career, contains her epic poem, "In the Mecca," that focuses on the senseless murder of an adolescent girl. Finally, in her most recent volume, *To Disembark* (1981), Brooks again dramatizes her concern for the plight of children with two of her longer poems, "The Life of Lincoln West" and "The Boy Died in My Alley."

Brooks has also published three works for children. The first, *Bronzeville Boys and Girls* (1956), is her most sustained effort at portraying children in society from the perspective of the child. Written in vignettes of three or four stanzas, each poem discloses a particular moment in a child's life; each is further individualized by a name or title: "Beulah at Church," "Mirthine at the Party," and "Eunice in the Evening." Although few of these children reappear in her other poems, they are of pivotal importance in Brooks's poetry because the crisis that engages their lives is, in a simplified manner, the same crisis that her characters also confront as adults: how to find meaning and purpose in a world that ostensibly denies their very existence. Brooks's two other books for children, *Aloneness* (1971) and *The Tiger Who Wore White Gloves* (1974), are interesting for their prescriptive value. They contain explicit moral themes: aloneness is not loneliness and, in the case of a tiger who mistakenly identifies with something other than his black stripes, be what you are.

In general, though, Brooks's poetry for and about children avoids moral prescription. In theme and design, the poems portray a naturalistic world in which environment dictates the terms by which one lives one's life. And, almost without exception, the environment in Brooks's poetry about children is an enclosed space: alleyways, front and back yards, vacant lots, and back rooms. On a symbolic level, these marginal spaces represent the social restrictions that prevent the mental and physical growth of children; they indicate the margins in which children are expected to live their lives. Although trees, flowers, and grass poke through the concrete blocks of the urban environment, they are only reminders of a forbidden Eden, one that is beyond the reach of Brooks's children. Ironically, elm trees and dandelions become strange exotic life forms, objective correlatives for the children's imaginary flights.

The children in Brooks's poems are unable to escape the perils of their environment. The personae in "a song in the front yard," "the ballad of chocolate Mabbie," and "The Life of Lincoln West" are characterized by a willingness to accept the limitations imposed upon their lives and, accordingly, to live perilously close to self-destruction. In "a song in the front yard" (WGB, p. 12), the adolescent girl exists in an enclosed space. She longs for the naturalistic world of the back yard and alley where other children play:

> I've stayed in the front yard all my life.
> I want a peek at the back
> Where it's rough and untended and hungry weed grows.
> A girl gets sick of a rose.
>
> I want to go in the back yard now
> And maybe down the alley,
> To where the charity children play.
> I want a good time today.

The girl desires the untended, hungry weed that symbolizes her need for freedom and growth. Yet her mother stifles her imaginative longings:

> They do some wonderful things.
> They have some wonderful fun.
> My mother sneers, but I say it's fine
> How they don't have to go in at quarter to nine.
> My mother, she tells me that Johnnie Mae
> Will grow up to be a bad woman.
> That George'll be taken to Jail soon or late
> (On account of last winter he sold our back gate.)

The mother's "sneers," although they are intended to protect her child from a *bad* life, do not provide meaningful alternatives to the front and back yard. Nonetheless, it is the girl's lack of imaginative fulfillment that prefigures her ominous fate as a woman. Unable to repudiate or negotiate the perilous limitations of her world, she defies them with naive bravado that will inevitably entrap her:

> But I say it's fine. Honest, I do.
> And I'd like to be a bad woman, too,
> And wear the brave stockings of night-black lace
> And strut down the streets with paint on my face.
> (WGB, p. 12)

In "the ballad of chocolate Mabbie," the immediate barrier to
Mabbie's self-fulfillment is intraracial discrimination: black judgment of physical beauty by white standards. For Mabbie, a seven-
year-old girl who looks as if she "was cut from a chocolate bar," the
divided worlds of the previous poem—front or back yard—are defined by the grammar school gates:

> It was Mabbie without the grammar school gates.
> And Mabbie was all of seven.
> And Mabbie was cut from a chocolate bar.
> And Mabbie thought life was heaven.
>
> The grammar school gates were the pearly gates,
> For Willie Boone went to school.
> When she sat by him in history class
> Was only her eyes were cool.
>
> (*WGB*, p. 14)

On one side of the gates is a romantic world with her secret lover,
Willie Boone; on the other side is a naturalistic world where the
degree of one's blackness determines questions of love and devotion.
Mabbie, of course, innocently waits "without the grammar school
gates." Like the youthful song of the previous poem, Mabbie's ballad
is set apart from the rituals of innocence that give meaning and
substance to human life. She is literally trapped in a racial paradox
that aggravates the debilitating socioeconomic circumstances of her
life. In the next two stanzas, her naiveté is underscored by the dogged
persistence of her quest:

> It was Mabbie without the grammar school gates
> Waiting for Willie Boone.
> Half hour after the closing bell!
> He would surely be coming soon.
>
> Oh, warm is the waiting for joys, my dears!
> And it cannot be too long.
> Oh, pity the little poor chocolate lips
> That carry the bubble of song!

If Mabbie is a victim, her wounds are prefigured in the racial
limitations that she cannot imaginatively overcome:

> Out came the saucily bold Willie Boone.
> It was woe for our Mabbie now.
> He wore like a jewel a lemon-hued lynx
> With sand-waves loving her brow.

It was Mabbie alone by the grammar school gates.
Yet chocolate companions had she:
Mabbie on Mabbie with hush in the heart.
Mabbie on Mabbie to be.

Like the "bad woman" of the previous poem who wears "brave stockings of night-black lace," Mabbie cannot project her self-identity beyond her "chocolate companions." She accepts "with hush in the heart" the obvious choices of her personal world.

Nonetheless, Mabbie's fate pales by comparison with the adolescent boy of "The Life of Lincoln West."[6] In a poem that is as prosaic in its voice as it is poetic in its craft, the narrator retells the ordeal of Lincoln as he searches for self-identity and acceptance in a world where his very existence is an affront. As the "ugliest boy that everyone ever saw," he is isolated from any meaningful circle of human relations; his life is enclosed by class and racial caste and by his unnatural physical appearance:

. . . The pendulous lip, the
branching ears, the eyes so wide and wild,
the vague unvibrant brown of the skin,
and, most disturbing, the great head.

Lincoln is rejected by his father who "could not bear the sight of him"; by his relatives who felt "indignant about him"; by his school teacher who "tried to be as pleasant with him as with others"; and finally by his playmates who, although they "enjoyed him because he was/resourceful, made up/games, told stories," reject him "when/ their More Acceptable friends came."

However, Lincoln's life is not without meaning and purpose. When he inspects his mirror image, he sees himself as others see him:

He spent much time looking at himself
in mirrors. What could be done?
But there was no
shrinking his head. There was no
binding his ears.

Ironically, this acceptance of his image becomes a triumph of self-identity and racial pride when a white man calls him the "real thing":

One day, while he was yet seven,
a thing happened. In the down-town movies
with his mother a white
man in the seat beside him whispered

loudly to a companion, and pointed at
the little Linc.
"THERE! That's the kind I've been wanting
to show you! One of the best
examples of the specie. Not like
those diluted Negroes you see so much of on
the streets these days, but the
real thing.
Black, ugly, and odd. You
can see the savagery. The blunt
blankness. That is the real
thing."

The "real thing" symbolizes his acceptance of and triumph over his natural conditions:

All the way home he was happy. Of course,
he had not liked the word
"ugly."
But, after all, should he not
be used to that by now? What had
struck him, among words and meanings
he could little understand, was the phrase
"the real thing."
He didn't know quite why,
but he liked that.
He liked that very much.

Lincoln's appearance and his natural inclination to "love Everybody" give Brooks's character a sense of pride in what he is. Lincoln's triumph, therefore, is a victory for racial pride which, when charged with love, transforms harsh realities into hopeful possibilities, a rare achievement in Brooks's poems about children.

Most of the poems Brooks has written for children are similar to those about children. In these poems, poverty and alienation characterize the child's life. The various titles of the poems, "John, Who Is Poor," "Rudolph Is Tired of the City," "Michael Is Afraid of the Storm," and "Robert, Who Is Often a Stranger to Himself," suggest children trapped by socioeconomic circumstances, whose very existence is threatened. However, in other poems for children, there are several important differences. First, the children are more receptive to the imaginative possibilities of their limited lives. Although survival remains the key to their existence, they are able to transcend the socioeconomic limitations of their environment by projecting their identities beyond its harsh realities. For these children, love and friendship are attainable ideals; they exist in spite of the physical and material differences between children. Although adults lurk menacingly on the fringes of the children's world, they do not prevent the children's self-fulfillment. The children readily distinguish between their hopes and the oppressive world of adults. Indeed, in such poems as "Mexie and Bridie," "Luther and Breck," and "Narcissa," the children are able to find self-fulfillment in an imagined world that exists apart from their natural environment; in other poems, such as "Val," "Timmy and Tawanda," and "Ella," the adolescents are able to mediate the differences between their imagined world and actual environment.

The two adolescent girls of "Mexie and Bridie"[7] escape from their urban environment by simply moving their fantasy outdoors:

> A tiny tea-party
> Is happening today.
> Pink cakes, and nuts and bon-bons on
> A tiny, shiny tray.
>
> It's out within the weather,
> Beneath the clouds and sun.
> And pausing ants have peeked upon,
> As birds and God have done.
>
> Mexie's in her white dress,
> And Bridie's in her brown.
> There are no finer Ladies
> Tea-ing in the town.

The important feature of the poem is the imaginative similarities of the two girls. As alter egos, they have a common identity that is based not upon shared social disabilities, but rather upon imaginative possibilities. Although Mexie is dressed in white and Bridie in brown— colors that obviously invoke a racial caste system—there is no apparent intraracial discord between them. In their ritual of innocence, they give meaning and substance to what, we infer, is a rather trivial event in their daily lives. Their tea party takes place "out within the weather/Beneath the clouds and sun." In this, the two girls enjoin nature in their youthful ritual. They are, at once, free in their imagination of the enclosed spaces of their environment, yet they realize a place within a projected natural order. Ants, birds, and God partake of their afternoon happening.

In "Luther and Breck" (*BBG*, p. 16), two adolescent boys also reject the enclosed spaces of their urban environment and escape to an imagined world of historical England:

> In England, there were castles.
> Here, there never are.
> And anciently were knights so brave
> Off to bold deeds afar,
> And coming back to long high halls
> So stony, so austere!
> These little boys care nothing for
> Their wooden walls of HERE.
> Much rather mount a noble steed
> And speed to save the Queen;
> To chop, in dreadful grottoes,
> Dragons never seen.

The antithetical worlds of the two boys, "there" and "here," are symbolized by the high, stony walls of an English castle and the wooden walls of their apartment building. The important difference, though, is not simply material, stone versus wood, but psychological: The children transpose their identities to a timeless moment in human history. Therefore, they enlarge their identities and become less vulnerable, less given to the emotional paralysis that often afflicts Brooks's children. By prefiguring themselves as knights, they assume social identities as men of action, who are in control of their lives and who are able to act against the forces of evil, "To chop, in dreadful grottoes,/Dragons never seen."

The adolescent girl in the poem "Narcissa" (*BBG*, p. 4) uses flowers that grow in her back yard as the vehicle for her imaginative flight:

> Some of the girls are playing jacks.
> Some are playing ball.
> But small Narcissa is not playing
> Anything at all.
>
> Small Narcissa sits upon
> A brick in her back yard
> And looks at tiger-lilies,
> And shakes her pigtails hard.
>
> First she is an ancient queen
> In pomp and purple veil.
> Soon she is a singing wind.
> And, next, a nightingale.

> How fine to be Narcissa,
> A-changing like all that!
> While sitting still, as still, as still
> As anyone ever sat!

For Narcissa, the tiger lilies are totems for a complete self-transformation; she identifies herself as "an ancient queen/In pomp and purple veil." She also imagines herself as a "singing wind" and "nightingale," symbols of a creative world in which she projects her identity.

Finally, the boy and girl in "Timmy and Tawanda" (*BBG*, p. 3) also realize a measure of self-fulfillment by defying adult taboos and invading forbidden "territory":

> It is a marvelous thing and all
> When aunts and uncles come to call.
>
> For when our kin arrive (all dressed,
> On Sunday, in their Sunday-best)
> We two are almost quite forgot!
> We two are free to plan and plot.
>
> Free to raid Mom's powder jar;
> Free to tackle Dad's cigar
> And scatter ashes near and far;
>
> Free to plunder apple juice;
> Let our leaping Rover loose.
>
> Lots of lovely things we two
> Plot and plan and quickly do
>
> When aunts and uncles come to call,
> And rest their wraps in the outer hall.

Here, unlike the children in the previous poem, Timmy and Tawanda do not escape to a fanciful world of imagination. Instead, they move between antithetical worlds; one is characterized by self-inhibiting social manners; "our kin arrived (all dressed/On Sunday, in their Sunday-best)," and the other is defined by personal freedom, "We two are almost quite forgot!/We two are free to plan and plot." The freedoms in which the children engage are rituals of innocence; but unlike the other children, Narcissa, Luther, and Breck, who imaginatively project their social identities into the timeless world of history, Timmy and Tawanda raid the identities of their parents: "Free to raid Mom's powder jar;/Free to tackle Dad's cigar." The cigar and powder jar are, ironically, totems of the world from which the children seek to escape.

As Brooks's poetry for and about children clearly indicates, she is one of the few modern poets who has made children an organic part of her poetic vision. Her children do not exist in a pastoral world apart from the socioeconomic and psychological problems that beset her adult characters. As the most vulnerable members of society, her children are at the center of her poetic vision; they are the barometers by which we are compelled to judge a world where to be human is achieved only by the fullest exercise of the imagination. Moreover, while the complexity of Brooks's poetic vision prevents her from offering simple solutions to complex moral and socioeconomic problems, her children remain reminders of the value of the imagination. Indeed, in those instances where her children are able to overcome the poverty and racism that ensnare their lives and thwart their self-fulfillment, it is because they are able to imagine a world that is different in detail, if not in substance, from the one they are forced to live in. Finally, Brooks's children are testimony to her belief as a poet: If the harsh realities of an existential world are to be transformed into hopeful possibilities, then imagination or a radical innocence must be an integral part of the effort.

Notes

1. Gwendolyn Brooks, *The World of Gwendolyn Brooks* (New York: Harper and Row, 1971), p. 100. Hereinafter cited in the text as *WGB*.

2. See Nathan I. Huggins, *Harlem Renaissance* (London: Oxford University Press, 1971), pp. 3–12.

3. See George E. Kent, "The Poetry of Gwendolyn Brooks," *Blackness and the Adventure of Western Culture* (Chicago: Third World Press, 1972), pp. 134–36.

4. See Harry B. Shaw, *Gwendolyn Brooks* (Boston: Twayne Publishers, 1980), pp. 94–95.

5. See William H. Hansell, "The Poet-Militant and Foreshadowings of a Black Mystique: Poems in the Second Period of Gwendolyn Brooks," *Concerning Poetry* 10 (Fall 1977): 37.

6. Gwendolyn Brooks, *Family Pictures* (Detroit: Broadside Press, 1970), pp. 9–13.

7. Gwendolyn Brooks, *Bronzeville Boys and Girls* (New York: Harper and Row, 1956), p. 1. Hereinafter cited in the text as *BBG*.

CLAUDIA TATE

—— 10 ——

Anger So Flat:
Gwendolyn Brooks's Annie Allen

In 1950 Gwendolyn Brooks became the first black American to receive a Pulitzer Prize for literature for *Annie Allen* (1949), a collection of rigorously technical poems, replete with lofty diction, intricate word play, and complicated concatenations of phrases. One particular poem, "The Anniad," which constitutes the second of three sections in the collection, is especially characteristic of Brooks's fascination with "the mysteries and magic of technique."[1] In fact, "The Anniad" seems to possess an inordinate amount of word mystery and magic. Brooks readily admits that "The Anniad" is a "labored" poem, although she also says that she derived a great deal of satisfaction from writing it: "What a pleasure it was to write that poem! . . . I was just very conscious of every word; I wanted every phrase to be beautiful, and yet to contribute to the whole . . . effect" (*Report*, p. 159).

Perhaps the delight she took in creating "The Anniad" was responsible for her indulgence in the complicated techniques that densely pattern the poem's texture, as well as those in the other two sections of the book, "Notes from the Childhood and the Girlhood" and "The Womanhood."

The complicated techniques in *Annie Allen* produce virtual curiosity pieces of intellectual verse, which her critics consistently mention as prize-worthy. But by the same token, these critics seldom focus full critical attention on this book; instead, they discuss those collections that employ subtle social commentary and realistic depictions of urban settings. As a result, *A Street in Bronzeville* (1945), *The Bean Eaters* (1960), *Selected Poems* (1963), and *In the Mecca* (1968) receive the lion's share of critical coverage. By contrast, *Annie Allen* seems peculiarly abstract and extremely esoteric. These characteristics are responsible for that collection being labeled "intellectual" and "academic," and they are also responsible for its smaller allotment of critical attention.

When we examine the surface texture of the poems that map out the events in the poetic life of Annie Allen, the imaginary focal character who is the namesake for this collection, we find no explicit social statement regarding race, caste, or gender. These poems are found in the first two sections of the book, "Notes from the Childhood and the Girlhood" and "The Anniad," and specifically include "the birth in a narrow room," "Maxie Allen," "the parents: people like our marriage Maxie and Andrew," "Sunday Chicken," "the relative," "downtown vaudeville," "the ballad of late Annie," "do not be afraid of no," "my own sweet good," "The Anniad," and "Appendix to the Anniad." Moreover, the verbal complexity of these poems seems to work at cross-purposes with the simplicity and habitual passivity of Annie's life, in that her life reflects a virtual absence of acts of conscious volition and emotional complexity. In fact, her life seems to be comprised of her deliberate refusal both to act decisively and to reveal her emotional responses. Events in her life seem only to happen to her; seldom does she appear to be an active agent, precipitating them. Moreover, the methods used to communicate the series of incidents themselves are extremely commonplace. Hence, there is a marked disparity between the elaborate structural techniques that create the poem and the content of Annie's life that the poem depicts. This discordance constitutes curious features in the text of the poem, which compels me to ask whether the poem is simply veneered in artifice or whether the elaborate techniques that texture the poem contain interpretative significance in their own right.

I suggest that "The Anniad," as well as the poems in "Notes from the Childhood and the Girlhood," are not merely cloaked in elaborate surface design, but rather, that the structural formats for the poems, in and of themselves, communicate discursive content about Annie's life, specifically her emotional response to the series of events that constitute her life. Moreover, formal devices such as diction, imagery, and meter, create the mood and atmosphere for the poems. These techniques express the author's attitude toward her subject in place of her explicit comment. Brooks combines these devices with conventional forms of satirical verse. These verse forms inherently dictate how the subject is to be regarded, that is, whether the subject is to be viewed sympathetically or critically. She further blends this technique with another source of tension found between what is said and how it is said. In literary terms, she combines satirical format with the tension created between content and its communicative image. This duality between content and its corresponding imagery converges, does not fully synthesize, into a unified interpretation. The content seems to be consistently at odds with its expression, and the resulting tension contours and concatenates each poem.

For example, we frequently find that Brooks seems to be ridiculing aspects of Annie's life, but Brooks does not do so by employing explicitly critical, descriptive language. To the contrary, she employs conventional, formal, satirical techniques for expressing her attitude toward her subject. Instead of outwardly criticizing Annie's mother, we find the mother-daughter relationship depicted in "Maxie Allen" rendered in doggerel. Doggerel is a satirical form that inherently suggests ridicule independent of content. Thus, the loose meter itself informs us that Brooks is censuring the poem's narrative content. This technique of using form to communicate content is repeatedly employed in both "Notes from the Childhood and the Girlhood" and "The Anniad." In fact, this tension climaxes in "The Anniad," where Brooks relies on mock-heroic conventions in order to underscore the gravity of her criticism of Annie's adult life.

On first meeting Annie Allen, we find her described as an ordinary black girl, born in an urban ghetto in the early 1900s. Her parents, Maxie and Andrew Allen, are hardworking, decent, very moralistic people, who believe that their kindness, simplicity, and humility will merit them their just rewards. All they need to do is wait patiently for their receipt. Annie is the necessary product of such a union. She is a docile, well-behaved child, whose total dependence on her mother's dispensation of approval and subsequent affection shapes her life. Maxie has suppressed the possibility of disobedience in her daughter. Maxie has also eliminated the outward expression of Annie's longings in the process by insisting that she be thankful for what she has instead of yearning for what she does not possess. In most social circles Maxie would be credited with having successfully raised a daughter; however, on close observation, we notice that her maternal wisdom has stifled Annie's willfulness and driven her imagination underground.

Brooks expresses her criticism for Maxie's ultimate failure as a mother by rendering the poem in doggerel. Here, technique, rather than merely explicit comment, is the vehicle for censuring, even ridiculing the mother's inability to nurture Annie's emerging imaginative spirit:

> Maxie Allen always taught her
> Stipendiary little daughter
> To thank her Lord and lucky star
> For eye that let her see so far,
> For throat enabling her to eat
> Her Quaker Oats and Cream-of-Wheat,
> For tongue to tantrum for the penny,
> For ear to hear the haven't-any,
> For arm to toss, for leg to chance,
> For heart to hanker for romance.[2]

Brooks reduces all the lessons that this mother must teach her daughter in order to promote her survival and happiness to lessons in gratitude for possessions that are not adequate to nurture Annie's emotional development—Quaker Oats, Cream-of-Wheat, and a penny. In this manner the subject is trivialized and combined with the monotonous doggerel meter. These techniques communicate Brooks's criticism of Annie's mother. Moreover, whenever desire surfaces in Annie's consciousness, her response is to suppress this desire. As a result, her anger, resentment, and guilt arise, but these emotions cannot be revealed as well. Consequently, Annie represses all of her emotional responses and denies them expression by flattening them out until only her gratitude is perceptible. These repressed emotions only resurface in her daydreams. But in this imaginary realm, her desire for adventure is transformed into the wish for someone else to enact her plans. Someone else must engage her wish, and this person, we are told, is a husband.

Brooks also describes Annie as an "unembroidered," "chocolate" brown-skin girl, who is plain in appearance and excessively compliant. Yet in the place where surface pattern would be if she were pretty or spirited is her wondrous and "stupendous" imagination that fancies a private life for which she has no outward expression:

> Sweet Annie tried to teach her mother
> There was somewhat of something other. . . .
>   . . .
> She did not know; but tried to tell.
>   (*WGB*, p. 68)

Rather than try unsuccessfully to explain the life of her imagination and her longings to her mother, she conceals them within herself, again by flattening them out and, thereby, denying them visible surface expression. But no matter how hard she tries to suppress her imaginary world, it inevitably confronts the real circumstances of her life, and this confrontation creates a sense of vague dissatisfaction.

When we recall the first poem in *Annie Allen*, "the birth in a narrow room," not only do we note Annie's humility, reflected in the lower case letters of the title, but we also see that this poem fore-shadows the inevitable conflict between the real circumstances of her submissive life and her imaginary projections of adventure:

> "I am not anything and I have got
> Not anything, or anything to do!"—
> But prances nevertheless with gods and fairies
> Blithely about the pump and then beneath
> The elms and grapevines, then in darling endeavor
> By privy foyer, where the screenings stand
> And where the bugs buzz by in private cars
> Across old peach cans and old jelly jars.
>
> (*WGB*, p. 67)

Annie's admission of her feelings of personal inadequacies do not incite physical activity, but they do cause her to frolic with imaginary sprites. In this way she finds adventure among embellished com-monplace objects, in the recesses of her mind. Hence, the first poem in the collection foreshadows the emerging duality in Annie's charac-ter, which is composite of her outward expression of inactivity, acquiescence, and resignation (a role prescribed for her by her mother as well as by society at large) and her inner life of fantastic, willful adventure. This type of duality develops throughout the collection to poem XV in "The Motherhood," where imaginative and suppressed longings verge upon conscious assertion, ultimately to become new directives for living.

But until that time, the only occasion when Annie demonstrates filial rebellion occurs at the funeral of a relative. Here, she displays her contrary feelings, but only when no one can witness her trans-gression:

> She went in there to muse on being rid
> Of relative beneath the coffin lid.
> No one was by. She stuck her tongue out; slid.
>
> Since for a week she must not play "Charmaine"
> Or "Honey Bunch," or "Singing in the Rain."
>
> (*WGB*, p. 72)

Her resentment is hidden beyond the sight of disapproval. Rather than face parental rejection for impudence, she squeezes herself into that "pinchy" space, where "[her] own sweet good[ness]" dominates her personality, and where her rebelliousness cannot be observed. Annie's behavior demonstrates that she is acutely aware of the struggle between the dual sides of her character—her external, exaggerated "sweet good[ness]" and her internal desire to create a "stupendous," autonomous self. But in order to make her dreams real, she knows she must exercise a "darling endeavor" and cast off others' expectations with the adamantly audible "no."

Brooks records Annie's attempt to say no in "do not be afraid of no." In this poem Annie admits that

> To say yes is to die
> A lot or a little. . . .
>
> . . .
>
> It is brave to be involved,
> To be not fearful to be unresolved.
>   (*WGB*, pp. 76–77)

But instead of enacting her decision to say "no" and live, she elects another way to say what she thinks is "no," although she does not realize the implications of her choice. Hence, not only does she not say "no," but she does not elect to be either involved or resolved in any course of action. She merely continues essentially as she had before. But instead of enacting her decision to say no and live, that is, to utter the word and externalize her internal life, she elects a new wish that is merely another way of saying yes: "Her new wish was to smile/When answers took no airships, walked a while." Rather than reply with the audible no, she smiles sweetly and sighs with the hope that her reluctance to speak would be perceived as the unuttered "no." But her choice of action is not effective. She forfeits the possibility of independence and continues to spin bits of an imaginary life in her daydreams, described as "spilling pretty cherries."

For Annie, there is only one acceptable way to escape from saying yes to her mother and to grasp a life of her own. That course is outlined in "the ballad of late Annie":

> Late Annie in her bower lay,
> Though sun was up and spinning.
> The blush-brown shoulder was so bare,
> Blush-brown lip was winning.
>
> Out then shrieked the mother-dear,
> "Be I to fetch and carry?
> Get a broom to whish the doors
> Or get a man to marry."
>   (*WGB*, p. 74)

Annie's mother literally tells her to obey her orders or to get married (which is the only proper course to freedom beyond a mother's reign for a young woman in Annie's day). Because Annie cannot say "no" in an audible voice, her choice is to use her "own sweet good[ness]" in order to secure a man worthy of her fancying spirit. In this manner, she plans to flee her mother's dominion and establish her own kingdom with the help of a suitable mate. Moreover, the text of the poem itself is veiled in coded meaning, which can be explained by examining the act of sleeping, which is both the dominant event and the unifying, figurative motif in the poem. Here, the act of sleeping underscores Annie's languid, dormant, and unresisting character. The events described in this poem—her oversleeping and the resulting chastisement—both serve as a paradigm for Annie's thwarted emotional development and foreshadow the events described in the poetic discourse of "The Anniad."

We recall that Annie has not learned to say "no," but instead says nothing with a smile and a sigh. We surmise that this behavior is repeatedly misunderstood as an expression for "yes," which she has already equated with death. Then when we recall the multiple meanings of the word "late" in "the ballad of late Annie," we note that not only has Annie overslept, but also that the entire poem addresses her as if she were deceased, that is as if the poem were an elegy for the unresisting Annie. Although Annie is not, in fact, dead, her defeat is clearly predicted, and this ominous shadow of defeat falls across Annie's effort to establish her domestic kingdom in "The Anniad."

"The Anniad" is a long poem which Brooks says deliberately alludes to Homer's *Iliad* (*Report*, p. 158). Although "The Anniad" is not of book-length proportions, like its analogue, it is an episodic, narrative poem that is long by contemporary standards. Although "The Anniad" does not employ a setting that is remote in time and place, and the major character does not possess heroic stature, "The Anniad" does conform to other epic conventions. The poem focuses on a universal problem, the deteriorating relationship between men and women. Furthermore, the poem reveals the consequences of the intervention of fate, in the form of world war, on these relationships. In addition, when we refer to *The Iliad*, we are mindful that both poems concentrate on the activity of brooding. *The Iliad* depicts Achilles' physical inactivity while he externalizes his anger and refuses to fight. "The Anniad," on the other hand, depicts Annie's deliberate refusal to act with conscious volition, while she simultaneously suppresses the outward show of both her emotions and desires by relegating them to the internal region of her daydreams.

The very complicated "Anniad" also recalls the somewhat legendary events surrounding the marriage ritual. The poem records Annie's anticipated courtship, its actuality, her marriage, separation because of war, her husband's return, his temporary infidelity, their reconciliation, followed by his permanent desertion. In other words, the poem recounts a series of girl wins boy episodes, and her ultimate loss.

Throughout these domestic crises, Annie remains sweet, good, and polite, believing that these virtues alone will ultimately merit her happiness. Therefore, in the face of turbulent domestic activity, Annie remains virtually inert and exhibits no perceivable emotional response. In fact, the absence of her emotions seems to work at cross-purposes with the complex expression that gives the details of her life their expression. Her life, although particularly eventful, seems peculiarly emotionally static. Moreover, her inability to say "no" seems to exaggerate the passivity of her inactive life. Events seem to happen to her, and her only response is to wait for these events to have occurred.

At the beginning of "The Anniad," Annie is described as a brown-skin girl, reclining on her bed, daydreaming about her virgin knight. He represents freedom from her parental abode:

> Think of sweet and chocolate,
> Left to folly or to fate,
> Whom the higher gods forgot,
> Whom the lower gods berate;
> Physical and underfed
> Fancying on the featherbed
> What was never and is not.
> . . .
> Watching for the paladin
> Which no woman ever had, . . .
> (*WGB*, p. 83)

Annie endows her knight with fullness of character and the will to act, aspects that she is aware of but does not possess or seem to desire herself. Her imagined suitor is "paradisaical and sad"; thus, he has broad expanses of emotions and intellect. In addition, he has height, breadth, and depth of moral as well as physical vigor. He is "Ruralist and rather bad/Cosmopolitan and kind." Hence, her potential mate possesses a full 360 degrees of character. He can say both "yes" and "no," whereas she is a flat 180 degrees of "yes," or silence with a sighing smile. She is described as a "thaumaturgic lass"; her brilliance has been dulled, her height has been leveled, and her will has been rendered inactive by conventional codes of decorum. The only way she can hold onto some bit of her former thaumaturgy, brilliance, "stupendous" self, is by "Printing bastard roses [her ill-conceived daydreams] there" on her image in the looking glass. The anger and resentment she feels, because she cannot reveal the vitality of her internal life, is patted down, suppressed, and flattened like her unruly hair:

> Then emotionally aware
> Of the black and boisterous hair,
> Taming all that anger down.
> (*WGB*, p. 84)

Again, flattening and silencing her displeasure are the ways in which she responds to the circumstances of her life. Such responses function to inhibit the possibility of her resolving to act decisively with full conscious volition.

Annie's emotional and intellectual lives, therefore, neither synthesize nor achieve autonomy. As a result these aspects of her character retain their duality. One side surfaces as contortions of virtual physical inertia, while the other side is dynamic but remains submerged in her internal life. She counteracts the possibility of the latter surfacing by tensing her face in a hard, tight smile and by flattening the unruly volume of her "boisterous" hair. In other words, she flattens the angry contours of her face into a sighing smile, and smooths the expanding height of her rebellious, voluminous hair into a composed, compressed, and compliant style.

Our expectations for the conventional, heroic character conflict with the submissiveness of Annie's life. "The Anniad's" impelling form and erudite diction seem peculiarly inappropriate for describing her inert life. Moreover, the missing expression or exalted emotions, typically found in the epic, are startling in their absence. These aspects, in juxtaposition, function to accentuate one another, disturbing us as we try to make form and content synthesize into a unified structure. As a result, first, we are forced to look beyond the description of Annie's submissive life, as seen in the narrative content of the poem, in order to determine if her emotional life is given expression in other ways. And second, we are compelled to look beyond the surface texture of the poem in order to reevaluate the suitability of epic format for the poem.

During this reevaluation process, we recall that there has consistently been a clear separation between Annie's two selves in all of the poems in the first two sections. On one hand, Annie's internal emotional complexity appears in the textual activity in the poems that depict her life; on the other hand, her external, inert life is depicted in the narrative content of "The Anniad." Thus, a system of reversals operates throughout the poem relating to the conflict between the content and the manner of its expression. In this context, Annie is much like a landscape of fertile hills and valleys that has been leveled to ordinary starkness. Whereas she once possessed contours of character, she has now been flattened out into a smooth plane. Whereas she was once a "stupendous" being, she has now been squeezed into a too-small, restricted space. As a result her splendor has literally been choked out of her:

> Now, weeks and years will go before she thinks
> "How pinchy is my room! how can I breathe!
> I am not anything and I have got
> Not anything, or anything to do!"—
> (*WGB*, p. 67)

When the reader understands the results of Annie's careful maternal and social nurturing, which are described above, the anger that Annie suppresses is located. It originates in Brooks and is transferred to the reader. Brooks incites our response not only by revealing Annie's fate of unhappiness and loneliness, but Brooks also compounds our disturbance by inciting our impatience with the poem's extreme artifice and with the seeming inappropriateness of the epic format. Thus, the erudite descriptions are, in themselves, indirect expressions of Brooks's anger, which has been suppressed and flattened out into complex, static language. In this manner, Brooks supplies Annie and her readers with the missing anger. The anger, therefore, is simply not in the narrative of the poem but in the work at large, which is the product of "the convergence of the text and the reader's response."[3]

When we read "The Anniad" in this manner, the poem cannot be regarded as an epic poem, as the allusion to *The Iliad* might suggest. "The Anniad" is not a poem that depicts heroic character or events. To the contrary, I contend that "The Anniad" is a mock-heroic satire, in that commonplace characters and events have been elevated in a ceremonious manner by using lofty diction and complicated techniques. It bears repeating that this literary form is, in itself, also the embodiment of Brooks's indirect expression for anger. Hence, Brooks deliberately cloaks her own anger, arising from the events she represents in the poem, in satire as the vehicle for expressing Annie's suppressed anger. By using satire, Brooks does not have to engage in a severely direct and explicit form of censorship. The form inherently ridicules; it ridicules the destructive domestic forces in the life of a young black woman as well as those in the lives of most women. By relying on this literary form, Brooks uses it to communicate not only emotional content, but also social and moral criticism.

Although marriage, in and of itself, is not described as a destructive force in the poem, it can become the site on which the fullness of a woman's evolving character and ambitions are sacrificed. In this manner, maturity and ambitions are often exchanged for "domestic bliss." And domestic bliss is often nothing more than one spouse electing either to say "yes" or to smile in silence with a sigh. This tragic scenario is both recorded and severely ridiculed by relying on the literary form of mock-heroic satire.

The text of "The Anniad," when seen as a literary work, becomes a powerful statement about the cost of extreme forms of role-playing. Consequently, the work becomes an emotionally charged satirical comment about the tragedy of a woman's inactive life, a tragedy compounded by racial prejudice. In fact, the high epic allusion is nothing more than an inversion of the epic form, and although mock-heroic satire is normally associated with a burlesque or comic presentation of its subject, here the mockery is bitter, that is, Juvenalian, in nature. This satire operates by not only relying on the narrative content of the poem, but also and more importantly by using a literary form as a vehicle for communicating both emotional and factual content.

When "The Anniad" is seen as a literary work that must be responded to in order to attain its interpretative significance, the work becomes a powerful statement about the cost of subscribing to extreme forms of role-definition. In this way, the poem ceases merely to be a complex, intellectual exercise, but becomes a serious statement about the destructive social and domestic rituals that are unquestioningly followed. Moreover, when we heed the color codes interwoven throughout the poem, we discern that Brooks is also criticizing the color caste system that further circumscribes Annie's life within barriers of racial prejudice. The reader's response to this woman—and to the social contingencies that design her life—is anger; this anger converges with Brooks's own, and both forms occupy the place where Annie's absent emotional response should be.

When we regard "The Anniad" as a satire, not only do we see the poem as an expression of cloaked anger, but we also understand how the other poems in the collection are to be read. We see that Brooks has crowded Annie's anger back into "pinchy" obscurity of form in poem after poem, where she contends it takes a little bit of patience to see the rage.[4]

Once we have located the rage, encoded on Annie's tightly smiling face and patted-down hair, Brooks does not abandon us. She suggests a route for her sisters in spirit to take in order to escape Annie's fate and cross the "screaming weed" of desperation, referred to in the last poem of the collection, XV in "Womanhood." Here, the unidentified speaker declares that it is all right to acknowledge openly her pain:

> Men of careful turns, haters of forks in the road,
> . . .
> Grant me that I am human, that I hurt,
> That I can cry.
>
> (WGB, p. 123)

She contends that after the pain has been acknowledged, she must celebrate by affirming her life in the presence of other women, despite the fact that she has arrived late both to this level of self-awareness (an internal region) and to this party of women (an external event):

> Open my rooms, let in the light and air.
> . . .
> And let the joy continue. Do not hoard silence
> For the moment when I enter, tardily,
> To enjoy my height among you. And to love you.
> . . .
>
> (WGB, p. 123)

When she is asked to sit down and be quiet, she is compelled to demand "a chair, but the one with broken straw," so that she might sit, but sit uncomfortably in order to be compelled to stand. When she is told "intelligence/Can sugar up our prejudice with politeness . . . ," she remembers to "extend [her] hand and teeth" in a tight, sighing smile, which is an indirect expression of anger. And finally, Brooks has her speaker demand that her sisters stand and join hands to map out new expectations:

> . . . Rise.
> Let us combine. There are no magics or elves
> Or timely godmothers to guide us. We are lost, must
> Wizard a track through our own screaming weed.
>
> (WGB, p. 124)

The word "wizard" of Gwendolyn Brooks's *Annie Allen* maps out the route for Annie's sisters not to take and points, instead, to another. In "wizard[ing] a track through [their] own screaming weed," they locate the untrodden course, which leads to discovering and learning how to nurture themselves.

Notes

1. Gwendolyn Brooks, *Report from Part One* (Detroit: Broadside Press, 1972), p. 158. Hereinafter cited in the text as *Report.*

2. Gwendolyn Brooks, "Maxie Allen," in *Annie Allen* in *The World of Gwendolyn Brooks* (New York: Harper and Row, 1971), p. 68. Hereinafter cited in the text as *WGB.*

3. Wolfgang Iser, "The Reading Process: A Phenomenological Approach," in *Reader Response Criticism*, ed. Jane P. Tompkins (Baltimore: Johns Hopkins University Press, 1981), p. 50.

4. Claudia Tate, ed., *Black Woman Writers at Work* (New York: Continuum, 1983), pp. 42–43.

—— 11 ——

The Women of Bronzeville

An obvious difference between Gwendolyn Brooks and male writers such as Richard Wright and Ralph Ellison who have used the urban environment as the setting for their works is the greater amount of attention she devotes to the experiences of females. While women are not absent from Wright's or Ellison's ghetto worlds, they remain background figures who are of secondary importance, at best, to the central actions of their novels. Like Ann Petry, Brooks focuses on the impact of the urban experience on females as well as males. Her sexual identity as well as her racial identity has molded her vision of the city. Although this aspect of her work has been generally ignored by critics, occasionally one can find comments about the value of the insights she has gained as a result of her sex.

> The life of women, particularly Negro women, and the life of Negroes, particularly those who have grown up since World War I in the North, where America's big towns are, figure prominently in Miss Brooks' poetry. Moreover, it does seem true that she is a woman writing, although not in the manner of the damned mob of scribbling women who so distressed Hawthorne—nor because of any mysterious and occult woman's intuition which seems to guide her inner labors . . . Miss Brooks is a woman, and yet not one in an ignoble way. . . . There is a general way in which women do tend to know women and also a general way in which they tend to know men, largely because our culture makes it so. Miss Brooks, whether she is talking of women or men . . . constantly speaks as a woman. . . . [1]

Although one might disagree with this assessment of her as a woman writer, it is difficult to ignore her numerous portraits of the women who inhabit Bronzeville,[2] the setting for much of her poetry.

Like Richard Wright, she explores the tragic aspects of black ghetto life, but she also probes beneath the surface in order to illuminate those areas of the slum dweller's life that often go unnoticed and should not be seen as ugly or horrifying. Ironically, then, her poems reveal both the destructive and the nurturing aspects of the black urban environment. Brooks's paradoxical vision is perhaps best revealed in a statement concerning her plans for *In the Mecca* that appears in the appendix of her autobiography.

> I wish to present a large variety of personalities against a mosaic of daily affairs, recognizing that the *grimmest* of these is likely to have a streak or two streaks of sun.
> In the Mecca were murders, loves, lonelinesses, hates, jealousies. Hope occurred, and charity, sainthood, glory, shame, despair, fear, altruism.
>
> (*Report*, pp. 189–90)

A central paradox of her composite portrait of Bronzeville is the ability of its residents to transcend, if only temporarily, the sordid conditions of their lives. They are not dehumanized or paralyzed by the poverty that engulfs them. It is against this backdrop of Brooks's overall vision of Bronzeville that her images of urban women as they appear in selected poems from *The World of Gwendolyn Brooks* will be examined. Although a discussion of the urban woman in *In the Mecca, Riot,* and *Family Pictures* will not be included, it would be interesting in a more comprehensive study of Brooks's women to compare the images projected in her pre–1967 poems with these later ones.

The diverse nature of Brooks's females enables her to reveal the many facets, complexities, and paradoxes of the urban black experience. They range from the death-in-life figure of a woman in "obituary for a living lady"[3] to the life-in-death figure of a woman in "the rites for Cousin Vit." The unnamed woman in the first poem, based on a person Brooks knew well (*Report*, p. 154), is the antithesis of Cousin Vit. Although she was a "decently wild child" and as a girl was "interested in a brooch and pink powder and a curl," as a young woman she would not permit sexual contact between herself and the man with whom she had fallen in love. She continued to wait by the windows in a "gay (though white) dress," and finally decided to say "yes," although by this time it was too late because he had found a woman "who dressed in red." Although red traditionally has negative connotations where women's dress is concerned, here it is being used positively to contrast the latter woman's *joie de vivre* with the lack of it in the main character; her purity and paleness of spirit (which the white dress symbolizes) cause her to be rejected. Here Brooks has taken the conventional "scarlet woman" figure usually associated with the corrupt, sinful city and transformed her into a positive, vital

force. After mourning for a long time and "wishing she were dead,"
the woman in white turns to religion and away from the world of the
flesh.

> . . . Now she will not dance
> And she thinks not the thinnest thought of any type of
>   romance
> And I can't get her to take a touch of the best cream
>   cologne.
>
> (*WGB*, pp. 18–19)

Cousin Vit, on the other hand, has lived an exciting, full life and
even in death refuses to be confined.

> . . . it can't hold her,
> That stuff and satin aiming to enfold her . . .
>   . . . Even now, surmise,
> She rises in the sunshine. There she goes,
> Back to the bars she knew and the repose
> In love-rooms and the things in people's eyes.
> Too vital and too squeaking. . . .
>
> (*WGB*, p. 109)

She has tasted much of life's pleasures and sorrows. Disappointments
have not caused her to withdraw from life and miss out on its more
pleasant aspects.

> Even now she does the snake-hips with a hiss,
> Slops the bad wine across her shantung, talks
> Of pregnancy, guitars and bridgework, walks
> In parks or alleys, comes haply on the verge
> Of happiness, . . .
>
> (*WGB*, p. 109)

She has taken chances in order to find joy. Ironically, she seems more
alive in death than the living woman in the previous poem. One critic
has commented on her and other women in Brooks's poems who are
to be admired for attempting to get the most out of their basically
narrow and drab lives.

> Whatever her shortcomings, Cousin Vit has asserted her pagan self
> without asking questions or whining. It may be that she, Sadie, and
> others like them, girls who "scraped life/With a fine-tooth comb," girls
> who seize their love in hallways and alleys and other unconventional
> places—it may be that these carefree souls have a deeper understanding
> of the modern scene than any of their sedate sisters and friends. Perhaps
> they are the only ones who do understand.[4]

"Sadie and Maud" (alluded to in the previous quote) deals with two sisters whose contrasting approaches to life are somewhat analogous to the women discussed in the two previous poems. Sadie, like Cousin Vit, has gotten out of life all it has to offer, despite her limited resources.

> Sadie scraped life
> With a fine-tooth comb.
>
> She didn't leave a tangle in.
> Her comb found every strand.
> Sadie was one of the livingest chits
> In all the land.
>
> (*WGB*, p. 16)

Although she bore two illegitimate daughters and shamed her family, she has left her offspring a rich heritage—her fine-tooth comb—so that they will presumably also squeeze as much joy out of life as possible. She does not have wealth to leave them, but she leaves them something perhaps equally valuable. Maud, on the other hand, who followed the more conventional path and went to college, is, at the end of the poem, alone and like a "thin brown mouse." Like the unnamed woman in "obituary for a living lady," she has followed society's rules, but her life has lacked the vitality and fullness that makes one's existence meaningful.

Brooks also explores the impact of poverty on the lives of her women characters; "the mother" deals with a poor woman who has had a number of abortions, and who experiences anxiety and anguish as a result of these decisions. In the appendix of her autobiography, Brooks refers to her as "hardly your crowned and praised and 'customary' Mother; but a Mother not unfamiliar, who decides that *she* rather than her World, will kill her children" (*Report*, p. 184). Accepting full responsibility for her "crime," she nevertheless remains ambivalent about her actions and exactly what she has done. Although she realizes that she has shielded her unborn babies from the harsh realities of the life they were sure to lead, she also admits having stolen from them whatever joys they might have been able to experience. She wonders if she had that right.

> . . . if I sinned, if I seized
> Your luck
> And your lives from your unfinished reach,
> If I stole your births and your names,
> Your straight baby tears and your games,

> Your stilted or lovely loves, your tumults, your marriages, aches,
>   and your deaths,
> If I poisoned the beginnings of your breaths,
> Believe that even in my deliberateness I was not deliberate.
>
> (WGB, p. 5)

Throughout the poem, one has the feeling that if circumstances had been different, if she had been able to provide adequately for them, they would have been allowed to live. Ironically, it was her deep concern for them as well as her own situation, which caused her to have the abortions.

> Believe me, I loved you all.
> Believe me, I knew you, though faintly, and I loved, I
>   loved you
> All.
>
> (WGB, p. 6)

She knew perfectly well what their fate would have been.

> You will never neglect or beat
> Them, or silence or buy with a sweet.
> You will never wind up the sucking-thumb
> Or scuttle off ghosts that come.
> You will never leave them, controlling your luscious
>   sigh,
> Return for a snack of them, with gobbling mother-eye.
>
> (WGB, p. 5)

Although George Kent criticizes the poem for failing "to convey the attitude of the author toward her subject—the several abortions of the mother,"[5] there is no question in my mind nor probably in the minds of women who have had abortions for similar or even other reasons where Brooks's sympathies lie.

"When Mrs. Martin's Booker T." contains a contrasting portrait of a mother and provides another view of the black urban resident. The code of behavior to which she adheres is more conventional. Mrs. Martin is disgraced by her son Booker T., who "ruins" Rosa Brown when he impregnates her before marriage. She is embarrassed to the point that she cannot face her community, so she moves to the other side of town and renounces her son. The intensity of her feelings is revealed in the simile "He wrung my heart like a chicken neck." The only cure for her damaged pride would be for her son to marry Rosa— "But tell me if'n he take that gal/And get her decent wed." Her strong sense of honor and decency will not permit her to condone behavior that reflects badly on the family. "Good" people marry when babies are on the way. It may also be that Mrs. Martin insists on marriage because she does not want Rosa and her illegitimate child to experience the hardships that usually befall those in their situation.

We also get glimpses into the lives of female ghetto dwellers in other poems from *A Street in Bronzeville* and *The Bean Eaters.* Although their world is drab and ordinary, and sometimes even fraught with danger, they go about their daily lives accepting their plight and somehow managing to survive. In "the battle," the persona (probably Hattie Scott because this poem belongs to that series) would like to believe that she would have behaved differently from Moe Belle Jackson who, after being beaten by her husband the night before because of a domestic quarrel, probably arose the next morning and continued with business as usual.

> I like to think
> Of how I'd of took a knife
> And slashed all of the quickenin'
> Out of his lowly life.
>
> But if I know Moe Belle,
> Most like, she shed a tear,
> And this mornin' it was probably,
> "More grits, dear?"
> (*WGB*, p. 39)

In "when I die" (from the same series) there is a similar acceptance of the realities of life, no matter how unpleasant. An unnamed female, again presumably Hattie, imagines that when she dies, there will be no fanfare but simply "one lone little short man/Dressed all shabbily." Her husband or boyfriend will bring his cheap flowers— "He'll have his buck-a-dozen"—but immediately after the funeral he'll shed his mourning clothes and wipe away his tears. She also has no illusions about what will happen next—"And the girls, they will be waitin'/there's nothin' more to say." She does not romanticize him or their relationship. In "the murder"[6] a mother must face the tragic death of her barely one-year-old son, which was caused by his brother, who "with a grin,/Burned him up for fun." She may also have to live with a guilty conscience for the rest of her life because it might not have happened had she been there.

> No doubt, poor Percy looked around
> And wondered at the heat,
> Was worried, wanted Mother,
> Who gossiped down the street.
> (*WGB*, p. 22)

There is no explanation for Brucie's behavior, which is even more terrifying.

> No doubt, poor shrieking Percy died
> Loving Brucie still,
> Who could, with clean and open eye,
> Thoughtfully kill.
>
> (WGB, p. 22)

Despite their frustrations and limitations, however, happiness does penetrate the lives of the Bronzeville women, although it has to be found in small things. The woman in "patent leather" is thrilled at having a man whose hair is so slick, black, and straight that it looks like patent leather. Although the other men "don't think he's such/A much" because of his shrill voice and "pitiful" muscles (unmasculine traits as far as they are concerned), she "strokes the patent-leather hair/That makes him man enough for her." Similarly, the woman in "when you have forgotten Sunday: the love story" experiences extreme pleasure on Sundays when she is able to stay in bed late with her mate and forget about the cares of the week. She remembers ordinary matters such as how he reacted to interruptions during their lovemaking sessions, how long they stayed in bed, and what they finally had for dinner. Although their apartment is tiny and unappealing and they don't eat exotic meals, they are still able to enjoy each other on this one day of the week when their usual problems don't intrude.

> . . . we finally went in to Sunday dinner,
> That is to say, went across the front room floor to the
>   ink-spotted table in the southwest corner
> To Sunday dinner, which was always chicken and
>   noodles
> Or chicken and rice
> And salad and rye bread and tea
> And chocolate chip cookies—
>
> (WBG, p. 20)

Although this seems to be all she has to look forward to, she's happy.

> Or me sitting on the front-room radiator in the limping
>   afternoon
> Looking off down the long street
> To nowhere,
> Hugged by my plain old wrapper of no-expectation
> And nothing-I-have-to-do and I'm-happy-why?
> And if-Monday-never-had-to-come—
>
> (WGB, p. 20)

Although life in Bronzeville is seldom without frustrations, its inhabitants do experience moments, however temporary, when they are glad to be alive.

Other urban poems reveal the plight of the dark-skinned or kinky-haired girl because of the color prejudice within the black community. Because this problem is shared by black women no matter where they live, it will not be dealt with in detail here, although a discussion of Brooks's images of women generally would include a thorough analysis of such poems as "the ballad of chocolate Mabbie," "Ballad of Pearl May Lee," "Jesse Mitchell's Mother," and selected poems from *Annie Allen.* Beauty parlors are a crucial part of the Bronzeville world as they are in other black environments, and a critic explains their significance. "The worship of 'good' hair naturally suggests the importance of beauty parlors in Bronzeville. They tend to become miracle-working shrines to which the dark girl goes in search of beauty. . . . They know that it is tough to be 'cut from chocolate' and to have 'boisterous hair' in a land where 'white is right.' To be black is to be rejected. . . . "[7]

"At the hairdresser's" contains a portrait of a black girl who is almost ecstatic over the passing from the vogue of long hair. Her short hair, which Madam Walker's and Poro Grower could not help, is no longer a problem now that the "upsweep" is in style. She no longer has to feel inferior to the girls with long hair.

> Gimme an upsweep, Minnie,
> With humpteen baby curls.
> 'Bout time I got some glamour.
> I'll show them girls.
>
> (*WGB*, p. 37)

Brooks's urban world is also inhabited by older women who have a different kind of struggle. The persona in "A Sunset of the City" can be seen as a victim of a modern, urbanized environment, not necessarily Bronzeville, where close family ties have broken. She is resentful as she approaches middle age because of the way she is now treated by her children, husband, and lovers.

> Already I'm no longer looked at with lechery or love.
> My daughters and sons have put me away with marbles
>   and dolls,
> Are gone from the house.
> My husband and lovers are pleasant or somewhat polite
> And night is night.
>
> (*WGB*, p. 337)

"Night is night" rather than a time for fun and adventure as it was when she was younger. Not only is it "summer-gone" where the seasons are concerned, but she is also approaching the winter of her own life. She is like the flowers and grass, which are personified.

> The sweet flowers indrying and dying down,
> The grasses forgetting their blaze and consenting to
> brown.
>
> (*WGB*, p. 337)

She sees herself as a hopeless woman whose needs are no longer satisfied in her cold, empty house.

> There is no warm house
> That is fitted with my need.
>
> I am cold in this cold house this house
> Whose washed echoes are tremulous down lost halls.
>
> (*WGB*, p. 338)

Like old furniture, she is "dusty," and now "hurries through her prayers," because they seem useless. She contemplates suicide as an alternative to a numb existence where she would do nothing, feel nothing, and desire nothing. This death-in-life quality has been seen before in one of Brooks's women. The poem ends on a pessimistic note with her concluding that Fate has played a cruel joke on her. One critic sees this poem as "another indication of the spiritual bankruptcy of our times," of "the meaninglessness of modern living," and "our loss of faith."[8] While the poem can be seen as having a universal theme, its central purpose should not be overlooked—the revelation of the inner turmoil of a woman as she faces a critical point in her life. The nature of the frustration she feels is in many ways different from what a man growing old would experience, yet similar.

Often Brooks's older women are seen in their relationships with their husbands, although these portraits tend to be less sharply focused than the ones that include a female figure only. In "the old marrieds" she explores, among other things, the negative impact of cramped ghetto quarters on a couple's relationship. Although the possibilities for romantic love have been perfect on this day, they are unable to communicate with each other because of circumstances beyond their control.

> And he had seen the lovers in the little side-streets.
> And she had heard the morning stories clogged with
> sweets.

It was quite a time for loving. It was midnight. It was
   May.
But in the crowding darkness not a word did they say.
                           (*WGB*, p. 3)

One would surmise that although it is dark, they still do not have the privacy desired for intimate contact. So, they remain silent. One might also conclude that the passage of time has caused their relationship to deteriorate to the point where it is impossible to express love.

In "The Bean Eaters," which also deals with an older married couple, Brooks explores the effect of poverty on their lives. They, like others in Bronzeville, attempt to make the most of their economic deprivation.

They eat beans mostly, this old yellow pair.
Dinner is a casual affair.
Plain chipware on a plain and creaking wood,
Tin flatware.
                    (*WGB*, p. 314)

Although they go about their daily lives in an almost mechanical manner, they refuse to give up.

Two who are Mostly Good.
Two who have lived their day,
But keep on putting on their clothes
And putting things away.
                    (*WGB*, p. 314)

Their memories, some of which are unpleasant, keep their lives from being totally meaningless.

Remembering, with twinklings and twinges,
As they lean over the beans in their rented back room that
   is full of beads and receipts and dolls and cloths,
   tobacco crumbs, vases and fringes.
                    (*WGB*, p. 314)

Although the couples in these two poems do have companionship, life seems to be just something to be endured. However the latter poem gives a more positive portrayal of the mates having endured together.

Without the perspective of the black woman writer, certain aspects of life in the urban black ghetto would possibly remain hidden. Brooks explores not only what it is like to be poor and black and male, but also what it is like to be poor and black and female. She treats the relationships between males and females and the joys and frustrations that women experience in a way that is different from her male counterparts. The female images she creates reflect her personal experiences with black women, her observations of them in the community, and her general knowledge of their history in this country. These images are as varied as the human types present in any community.

Brooks's poems present a more realistic view of the diversity and complexity of black women than the stereotypes (matriarch, whore, bitch, for example) that have persisted in other literary works by black and white artists alike. The lack of uniformity in her portraits of black women would contradict the notion that there is a monolithic black woman. There are females in her poems who commit adultery ("the vacant lot") and are sexually inhibited ("obituary for a living lady"); they are aggressive ("when Mrs. Martin's Booker T.") and passive (Maud of "Sadie and Maud"); they are extraordinary (Madam Walker of "southeast corner") and ordinary ("Mrs. Small"); they are exploited (unnamed women in "The Sundays of Satin-Legs Smith") and protected (young girl in "a song in the front yard"). They dream in the midst of adversity ("Callie Ford" and "hunchback girl: she thinks of heaven"), and they wallow in despair ("A Sunset of the City"). Although they share a common environment and heritage, they are still presented as individuals with different priorities and values, different levels of tolerance for misery, and different ways of dealing with problems. The major portion of Gwendolyn Brooks's work does indeed reflect, among other things, an intense awareness of black women's identities and an unusual insight into the problems that they face.

Notes

1. Blyden Jackson and Louis D. Rubin, *Black Poetry in America: Two Essays in Historical Interpretation* (Baton Rouge: Louisiana State University Press, 1974), p. 82.

2. In a 1967 interview with Illinois historian Paul Angle, Brooks says that Bronzeville was not her own title but was "invented" many years ago by the Chicago *Defender*, a black newspaper, to refer to the black community. Gwendolyn Brooks, *Report from Part One* (Detroit: Broadside Press, 1972), p. 154. Hereinafter cited in the text as *Report*.

3. Gwendolyn Brooks, *The World of Gwendolyn Brooks* (New York: Harper and Row, 1971), p. 8. Hereinafter cited in the text as *WGB*.

4. Arthur P. Davis, "Gwendolyn Brooks: Poet of the Unheroic," *College Language Association Journal* 7 (Dec. 1963): 118.

5. George E. Kent, "The Poetry of Gwendolyn Brooks, Part II," *Black World* 20 (Oct. 1971): 38.

6. Brooks says that this poem was also based on a real-life situation, except that the mother was really working instead of gossiping down the street. She adds, "I guess I did her an injustice there" (*Report,* p. 154).

7. Arthur Davis, "The Black-and-Tan Motif in the Poetry of Gwendolyn Brooks," *College Language Association Journal* 6 (Dec. 1962): 95–97.

8. Davis, "Gwendolyn Brooks: Poet of the Unheroic," p. 117.

GARY SMITH

——— **12** ———

Gwendolyn Brooks's "Children of the Poor," Metaphysical Poetry and the Inconditions of Love

> It is not a permanent necessity that poets should be interested in philosophy, or in any other subject. We can only say that it appears likely that poets in our civilization, as it exists at present, must be *difficult*. Our civilization comprehends great variety and complexity, and this variety and complexity, playing upon a refined sensibility, must produce various and complex results. The poet must become more and more comprehensive, more allusive, more indirect, in order to force, to dislocate if necessary, language into his meaning.
>
> —*T. S. Eliot*, The Metaphysical Poets[1]

Despite Gwendolyn Brooks's recent protest that the sonnet is irrelevant to her artistic goal of blackening English,[2] she is arguably one of America's finest sonneteers. Throughout the early phases of her writing career, before her association with the Black Arts Movement of the 1960s, she repeatedly turned to the sonnet to express her dual commitment to socially relevant and well-crafted poetry. Moreover, she was able to sustain these two often contradictory purposes without creating polemical verse or writing in an art for art's sake mode. Her success in achieving both commitment and craftsmanship is underscored by the many awards she has received for her poetry— especially her sonnets. Her initial public recognition as a sonneteer came in the form of the Eunice Tietjens Award (1944) for "Gay Chaps at the Bar"; this poem along with nine others form the antiwar sonnet cycle that concludes her first published volume, *A Street in Bronzeville* (1945). Her second volume, *Annie Allen* (1949), for which she won a Pulitzer Prize (1950), contains no less than eight sonnets. And in her third volume, *The Bean Eaters* (1960), Brooks includes two of her most critically acclaimed sonnets, "A Lovely Love" and "The Egg Boiler."

In part, Brooks's attraction to the sonnet might be traced to the influence of the New Negro poets, her immediate literary predecessors during the Harlem Renaissance, had upon her work. From these poets, Brooks learned that the four-hundred-year-old and largely genteel sonnet form could be used as a devastating instrument of social protest and that the inherent tensions in the sonnet's syllogistic structure could be used to argue against racism and social injustice. She also knew that the sonnet form had been mastered by most of the major poets writing in the English language.

For example, Claude McKay and Countee Cullen, two of the leading sonneteers among the New Negro poets, primarily used the English romantic poets as models for their sonnets. In two of their most famous sonnets, "If We Must Die" and "From the Dark Tower," the poets freely adapted the Romantic themes and literary styles of Keats, Wordsworth, and Shelley.[3] Their poems, written in iambic pentameter with exact rhymes, are models of traditional Shakespearean and Petrarchan sonnets. However, both poets were obviously immune to the modernist rebellion against romantic lyricism, pastoral imagery, and traditional versification that was underway when their poems were written. Nonetheless, their sonnets indirectly address the paradoxical questions of racism and socioeconomic injustice in America. The metaphorical language of McKay's sonnets—"hogs," "dogs," "monsters," and "kinsmen,"—has inspired any number of outcries against oppression and injustice; whereas the "Dark Tower" of Cullen's sonnet describes any place of forced labor and captivity. The two sonnets are not only timeless in their social protest but also noticeably colorless.

While the New Negro poets demonstrated to Brooks that race was incidental to the tradition of well-crafted and universal poetry, two other individuals had decisive influences upon her distinctly modern poetic voice. The first was the distinguished poet and statesman, James Weldon Johnson; the second was Inez Stark, the Chicago socialite and reader for *Poetry* magazine. In his brief but incisive commentary on several poems Brooks sent him, Johnson wrote: "You have an unquestionable talent and feeling for poetry. Continue to write—at the same time, study carefully the work of the best modern poets—not to imitate them, but to help cultivate the highest possible standard of self-criticism."[4] The immediate effect of John-son's advice was to provide a "standard" for Brooks's poetry other than the one she found in the New Negro poetry. To her substantial reading list that already included Milton, Spenser, Donne, and Shake-speare, Brooks added Frost, Eliot, Cummings, and Pound.[5]

Stark complemented Johnson's theoretical advice with practical criticism of Brooks's poetry. In the poetry workshop she organized for a group of aspiring poets on Chicago's Southside, Stark gave Brooks lessons in traditional versification as well as modernist poetics. Her classroom texts included Robert Hillyer's *First Principles of Verse* as well as *Poetry*, the magazine that featured many of the modernist poets. As the following quotation indicates, Stark translated into plain, outspoken English the very essence of modernist poetics:

> All you need in this poem are the last four lines. . . . You must be careful not to list the obvious things. They, in these days (wartime) are more than ever a weakening influence on the strengths we need. Use them only to illustrate boredom and inanity.
>
> I don't understand too well what it's all about but it has three FINE lines.
>
> Dig at this until you have us see all the skeleton and no fat.
>
> (*Report*, pp. 66–67, emphasis in the original)

The criticism Stark offered Brooks emphasizes imagistic compres-sion, ironic understatement, and temporal and spatial dislocations. These characteristics, of course, were radical departures from the romantic and generally discursive styles of McKay and Cullen.

Johnson and Stark's stylistic advice provides a partial explanation for Brooks's difficulty as a modern poet. Her best work comprehends not only the protest tradition of the New Negro poetry, but also the traditional and contemporary styles of European and American po-etry. To be sure, it is the precise juggling of these various and complex traditions that contributes to the metaphysical quality of her verse. Like John Donne, the seventeenth-century metaphysical poet, Brooks creates a depth and range of feeling in her poetry that often overshadows her commonplace subject matter; she also displays a metaphysical wit that features startling and incongruent figures of speech; and she uses poetic diction that is a mixture of formal and colloquial speech.[6]

Donne's *Holy Sonnet XIV*[7] offers a striking example of the diffi-culties associated with metaphysical poetry. Its octave summarizes the persona's paradoxical religious feelings:

> Batter my heart, three-personed God; for you
> As yet but knock, breathe, shine, and seek to mend;
> That I may rise and stand, o'erthrow me, and bend
> Your force, to break, blow, burn, and make me new.
> I, like an usurped town, to another due,
> Labor to admit You, but Oh, to no end!
> Reason, Your viceroy in me, me should defend,
> But is captivated, and proves weak or untrue.

The speaker literally implores God to save him from the inner forces that threaten to destroy his religious faith. His heart-felt desperation is dramatized by the plosives that accompany his penitential outburst: "break," "blow," and "burn." However, the ninth line, with its volta, begins the turn toward a partial resolution of the persona's ordeal:

> Yet dearly I love You and would be loved fain,
> But am betrothed unto Your enemy:
> Divorce me, untie or break that knot again
> Take me to You, imprison me, for I,
> Except You enthrall me, never shall be free,
> Nor ever chaste, except You ravish me.

In a voice less strident than the one that controls the poem, the persona finally resolves his predicament with a simple declaration of love: "Yet dearly I love You."

The initial difficulty one experiences while reading the sonnet is structural. Donne has altered the conventional Petrarchan rhyme pattern by adding a Shakespearean couplet to the final quatrain. Within the sonnet, this structural change creates two voltas: at the end of the second and third quatrains; whereas, in the conventional Petrarchan sonnet, the volta usually occurs at the first point, and in the Shakespearean sonnet, it is withheld until the penultimate line. On one level, one doubling of the volta thwarts the reader's expectation for an early resolution of the persona's paradoxical dilemma; on another level, it lessens the dramatic distance between the opening conceit, "Batter my heart, three-personed God," and the final one, "Except you enthrall me, never shall be free."

This structural complexity is compounded by the sonnet's metaphorical language. In the initial quatrain, God is prefigured as an artisan capable of transforming the persona, who imagines himself a misshapen vessel. But rather than draw this metaphorical analogy to a point of conclusion, the second quatrain introduces another conceit: The speaker is a beleaguered town and God a liberating force.

And in the final quatrain, the speaker equates God to a lover. Of course, this triunal metaphor, vessel-town-woman, lends itself to a multitude of interpretations, none of which totally answers the sonnet's paradoxical question: How can the persona's fractured religious faith be restored by a three-personed God? One possible answer— that the speaker's love negotiates the logical gaps between the three different conceits—is plausible on an emotional or metaphysical level but not a rational one.

The final complexity within the sonnet is Donne's poetic diction. In the opening lines, he takes his words from the metal arts: "batter," "knock," "shine," and "mend"; whereas in the second quatrain, he turns to the military: "usurped town," "viceroy," "defend," and "captived." Finally, he utilizes the diction of love and courtship: "betrothed," "enthrall," "chaste," and "ravish." These disparate choices are intended, in part, to startle the reader into an awareness of the subliminal relationships between words and ideas. They reinforce the complex and paradoxical nature of Donne's religious faith. But more important, the words, like the sonnet's structure and metaphorical conceits, characterize Donne's metaphysical sensibility.

Brooks's sonnet sequence, *The Children of the Poor*,[8] contains many of the same stylistic difficulties one finds in Donne's *Holy Sonnets*, but it also presents a distinct departure from many of his themes. While Brooks consistently experiments with the sonnet's syllogistic structure, she does not always adhere to the theme of resolution. Her sonnets do not attempt to resolve their paradoxical dilemmas as much as they graphically display a mind that alternately associates and disassociates itself from the dilemmas. Like Donne, Brooks also entertains questions of religious faith in her sonnets, yet she rejects religion as a viable means of resolving complex social problems. Finally, as in Donne's *Holy Sonnets*, love plays a decisive role in Brooks's sonnets, but she is most adept at describing its absence. Indeed, her overriding theme, "the inconditions of love," examines the sociopsychological forces in modern society that deny love.

The Children of the Poor consists of five sonnets. As protest sonnets, they address the question of socioeconomic injustice. Brooks's thematic focus is upon the most vulnerable members of society—black children. Throughout *The Children of the Poor*, Brooks manipulates form to underscore her theme. In each sonnet, she uses a mixture of both Petrarchan and Shakespearean forms. While the octave conforms to the Petrarchan rhyme pattern, *abba* and *abba*, the sestet offers a series of complex variations on the Shakespearean rhyme pattern: *efef* and *gg*. This diversity reinforces the complexity of the emotional responses to the paradoxical questions within each sonnet. Furthermore, the multiple couplets that Brooks employs in the sestet—especially in the first three sonnets—thwart the expected resolution of the sonnets' dilemmas; instead they heighten the sense of the mother's frustration and her inability to provide meaningful answers to her children.

In the first sonnet, for example, the Petrarchan rhyme pattern of the octave underscores the ordered yet constrained lives of childless people:

> People who have no children can be hard:
> Attain a mail of ice and insolence:
> Need not pause in the fire, and in no sense
> Hesitate in the hurricane to guard.
> And when wide world is bitten and bewarred
> They perish purely, waving their spirits hence
> Without a trace of grace or of offense
> To laugh or fail, diffident, wonder-starred.

Here, the world of childless people is characterized as essentially callous and ingrown. Without children, they are indifferent to human and natural disasters, "pause in the fire" and "hesitate in the hurricane," as well as to their own lives, "they perish purely." The world of people with children, however, is marked ironically by self-containing contradictions:

> While through a throttling dark we others hear
> The little lifting helplessness, the queer
> Whimper-whine; whose unridiculous
> Lost softness softly makes a trap for us.
> And makes a curse. And makes a sugar of
> The malocclusions, the inconditions of love.
>   (*WGB*, p. 99)

In this sestet, Brooks uses multiple couplets to reinforce the mother's feeling of enclosure. As opposed to a "mail of ice," parents are entrapped by the emotional needs of their children. The multiple couplets also thwart an expected resolution to the sonnet's implied, paradoxical question: Is human life more fulfilling with or without children? Rather than offering a possible answer, the couplets present a series of oxymorons: soft trap, soft curse, and sugary malocclusions. These oxymorons become the metaphorical equivalents for the inconditions of love.

In the second sonnet, ingenious and incongruent figures of speech also reinforce the anti-love theme. The mother begins by comparing her children with lepers; this conceit is raised to a level of abstraction when she further compares them with "contraband"; and, finally, in the last quatrain, the speaker employs the mythological conceit of the alchemist's stone:[9]

> What shall I give my children? who are poor,
> Who are adjudged the leastwise of the land,
> Who are my sweetest lepers, who demand
> No velvet and no velvety velour;
> But who have begged me for a brisk contour,
> Crying that they are quasi, contraband
> Because unfinished, graven by a hand
> Less than angelic, admirable or sure,
> My hand is stuffed with mode, design, device.
> But I lack access to my proper stone.
> And plenitude of plan shall not suffice
> Nor grief nor love shall be enough alone
> To ratify my little halves who bear
> Across an autumn freezing everywhere.
>
> (*WGB*, p. 100)

At first reading, these heterogeneous metaphors startle the reader into a more acute awareness of the complex social problems of poverty; the disjunction, however, creates certain historical parallels that add to the richness of the mother's emotional stress in response to her paradoxical question: "What shall I give my children? who are poor?" Indeed, the movement of metaphors is from simple abstractions, "leastwise" and "poor," to Biblical and historical referents, "lepers" and "contraband,"[10] and finally to mythology, "proper stone." These figures of speech obviously avoid a concrete description of poverty and help distance the persona from her painful dilemma. Psychologically, her children are not simply shoeless and malnourished; they are freely associated with other outcasts in the Bible and in Afro-American history. The mother's awareness is further underscored by the descriptive terms she uses for her children, "sweetest lepers" and "little halves." These euphemisms connote a tacit acceptance of the judgment of her children as social undesirables. More important, they suggest the mother's "sweet" refusal to counter the social images of her children or, perhaps, to accept them as mirror images of herself. Thus, the sonnet's paradoxical question precipitates not an unequivocal defense of human love apart from poverty, but rather a dramatization of the mother's inner conflicts: how poverty has weakened the emotional underpinnings of her love.

Brooks's use of both colloquial and literary poetic diction plays a part in dramatizing the psychological problems of love and poverty. The octave of the third sonnet is particularly suggestive of this mixture of two poetic dictions:

> And shall I prime my children, pray, to pray?
> Mites, come invade most frugal vestibules
> Spectered with crusts of penitents' renewals
> And all hysterics arrogant for a day.
> Instruct yourselves here is no devil to pay.
> Children, confine your lights in jellied rules;
> Resemble graves; be metaphysical mules;
> Learn Lord will not distort nor leave the fray.
>
> (*WGB*, p. 101)

In the first line, the sonnet's paradoxical question contains an implied answer. The word "prime" is an elliptical expression that implies teaching at a primary level; when combined with the other two accented words in the line, "pray, to pray," it becomes an alliterative but sarcastic answer to the question. In the second line, "mites" is both a reference to insect pests and a diminutive qualifier for "children" as well as an ingenious reference to the small boxes used for special, Sunday school offerings. These connotations coalesce in the phrase, "invade most frugal vestibules," the nearly empty anteroom of the church where the children have come to pray.

In the third line, "spectered" connotes the mysterious, ghostly nature of Christian mythology, while "crusts of penitents' renewals" suggests bits of the sacramental wafer as well as the more domestic image of a nearly empty food closet. Moreover, in keeping with the mother's pessimism about religious belief, "all hysterics" infers an emotional catharsis that, "for a day," accompanies the children's intense religious worship.

While the word choices in the initial quatrain are allusively literary, those in the second are colloquial. The mother sarcastically admonishes her children, "instruct yourselves here is no devil to pay" and "confine your lights in jellied rules." The word "lights" signifies both religious enlightenment and self-knowledge, but ironically the mother instructs her children to confine their self-knowledge in the "jellied rules" of their religious training. This spiritual food, like the earlier "crust," does not, however, respond to the basic need of the poor children for nourishment. Without food, the children will "resemble graves." Finally, in a striking example of Brooks's use of colloquial and literary diction, the mother commands her children, "be metaphysical mules." She encourages her children to accept religion's meager offerings, and as the final two lines of the sonnet suggest, the mother will apply a "bandage" on their eyes to conceal their spiritual impoverishment.

While the first three sonnets dramatize the emotional paralysis and pessimism of a mother whose love has been undermined by poverty, the fourth sonnet presents a radical shift in tone and viewpoint. The poetic diction is more forceful and less encumbered by allusive figures of speech. Its perspective omits the dichotomies that characterize the mother's ambivalence in the earlier sonnets; its point of view is the collective, second person plural, "you." Its deliberate, self-assertive tone suggests someone who is actively engaged in the life struggles of her children:

> First fight. Then fiddle. Ply the slipping string
> With feathery sorcery; muzzle the note
> With hurting love; the music that they wrote
> Bewitch, bewilder. Qualify to sing
> Threadwise. Devise no salt, no hempen thing
> For the dear instrument to bear. Devote
> The bow to silks and honey. Be remote
> A while from malice and from murdering.
> But first to arms, to armor. Carry hate
> In front of you and harmony behind.
> Be deaf to music and to beauty blind.
> Win war. Rise bloody, maybe not too late
> For having first to civilize a space
> Wherein to play your violin with grace.
>   (WGB, p. 102)

The spondee, "First fight. Then fiddle," interrupts the regular iambic pentameter of the initial line. As plosives and imperatives, they underscore an emotional commitment to militant action as a response to the sonnet's implied, paradoxical question: How can the ideals of art—beauty and truth—be reconciled with the demands for socioeconomic justice?

This commitment is also conveyed in the sonnet's form and imagery. The octave, for example, argues that music-making and the discipline it involves have certain sociopsychological virtues: "Ply the slipping string," "muzzle the note," "Qualify to sing," and "Devote the bow to silks and honey." However, the sestet, with its volta in the ninth line, defiantly argues that militant action is necessary "to civilize a space / Wherein to play your violin with grace." Unlike the incongruent and heterogeneous figures of speech in the earlier sonnets, the images are neatly divided between militancy and music: "Carry hate in front of you and harmony behind."

The introspective and elegaic tone of the initial three sonnets returns in the final poem. As a protest sonnet, its paradoxical question, how can the poor—who have lived marginal lives—accept death, is perhaps a response to the previous sonnet's exhortation to militant social action.[11] The mother's commitment to socioeconomic justice for her children is still firm:

> When my dears die, the festival-colored brightness
> That is their motion and mild repartee
> Enchanted, a macabre mockery
> Charming the rainbow radiance into tightness
> And into a remarkable politeness
> That is not kind and does not want to be,
> May not they in the crisp encounter see
> Something to recognize and read as rightness?
> I say they may, so granitely discreet,
> The little crooked questionings inbound,
> Concede themselves on most familiar ground,
> Cold an old predicament of the breath:
> Adroit, the shapely prefaces complete,
> Accept the university of death.
>
> (*WGB*, p. 103)

In the octave, the euphemism, "dears die," replaces the earlier oxymoron, "sweetest lepers," as a descriptive term for the mother's children. The alliterative and playful word choices, "motion and mild" and "rainbow radiance," also help create an optimistic and enchanting tone in the poem. Furthermore, death becomes another euphemism, "crisp encounter."

The sestet, then, with its volta, "I say they may," answers the paradoxical question in the affirmative. The poverty and "crooked questionings" that characterize the children's lives have prepared them to accept death as a natural consequence of living. But by placing a couplet after the volta, Brooks thwarts our expectation for a stoic resolution of the sonnet. The last three lines further imply that death will actually begin life, because its "university" will provide answers that have eluded the mother. Death is a universal that ignores matters of race and class.

In retrospect, *The Children of the Poor* demonstrates Brooks's success in writing poetry that is both socially conscious and intricately crafted. Her sonnets belong to the modernist tradition in that they contain the variety, complexity, indirection, and dislocation T. S. Eliot suggests are the hallmarks of poets in our civilization. Nonetheless, she subscribes to the New Negro's faith in art as an instrument for social change. Like Cullen and McKay, her protest sonnets avoid specific mention of race as a social issue inextricably tied to poverty; moreover, as illustrated by the abrupt tonal shifts between the third and fourth sonnets, she often vacillates between overt militancy and painful introspection. Finally, if Brooks has abandoned the sonnet form as a means of addressing the socioeconomic concerns of blacks in her latest poetry, she remains committed to art as a means of negotiating racial differences. And in this sense, her commitment to art remains, by implication, a commitment to human life.

Notes

1. T. S. Eliot, "The Metaphysical Poets," in *Selected Essays* (New York: Harcourt, Brace, 1950), p. 248.

2. See Martha H. Brown, "Interview with Gwendolyn Brooks," *The Great Lakes Review* 6 (Summer 1979): 55.

3. See Blyden Jackson and Louis D. Rubin, Jr., *Black Poetry in America: Two Essays in Historical Interpretation* (Baton Rouge: Louisiana State University Press, 1974), pp. 46–47.

4. Gwendolyn Brooks, *Report from Part One* (Detroit: Broadside Press, 1972), p. 202. Hereinafter cited in the text as *Report*.

5. See George Stavros, "An Interview with Gwendolyn Brooks," *Contemporary Literature* 11 (Winter 1970): 10.

6. See Herbert J. C. Grierson, *Metaphysical Lyrics and Poems of the Seventeenth Century* (New York: Oxford University Press, 1959), pp. xiii–xxviii.

7. For an interesting discussion of John Donne's *Holy Sonnets*, especially "Sonnet XIV," see *John Donne's Poetry*, ed. A. L. Clements (New York: W. W. Norton, 1966), pp. 246–59.

8. Gwendolyn Brooks, *The World of Gwendolyn Brooks* (New York: Harper and Row, 1971), pp. 99–103. Hereinafter cited in the text as *WGB*.

9. See R. Baxter Miller, " 'Does Man Love Art?': The Humanistic Aesthetic

of Gwendolyn Brooks," in *Black American Literature and Humanism*, ed. R. Baxter Miller (Lexington: University Press of Kentucky, 1981), pp. 104–6.

10. Besides the usual meaning of goods forbidden by law, "contraband" was also used during the Civil War to identify slaves who fled to, or were smuggled behind, the Union lines or remained in territory captured by the Union Army.

11. See Harry B. Shaw, *Gwendolyn Brooks* (Boston: Twayne Publishers, 1980), pp. 114–15.

—— 13 ——

"Tell It Slant": Disguise
and Discovery as Revisionist Poetic
Discourse in The Bean Eaters

When *The Bean Eaters,* Brooks's third collection of poetry, was published in 1960, America was beset by the upheaval of the civil rights movement. On the black American literary front, fiery spokesperson James Baldwin dissected and rebuked white Americans in his essays, while dramatist Lorraine Hansberry protested racial housing discrimination in the first Broadway play by a black woman, *A Raisin in the Sun* (1959). Brooks's audience, like that of Baldwin and Hansberry, was presumably white liberals, because many of the poems in *The Bean Eaters* originally appeared in major American magazines such as *Harper's, Poetry,* and *Voices.* Brooks's topical race themes, including the lynching of Emmett Till, Jr. in 1955 and the 1957 court-ordered integration of Arkansas schools, seemed to indicate that in the genre of poetry she assumed a poetic role parallel to that of Hansberry and Baldwin as witness and conscience for white America. But reactions to *The Bean Eaters* by that audience were oddly mixed.

Some reviewers found *The Bean Eaters* sufficient in content and form, while others found it too tame in its protest mission; still others were upset and put off by what they deemed an unseemly social emphasis. Thus, one reviewer pointed up the book's "deep compassion" and "concern for human misery,"[1] and another praised Brooks for touching on a "universal pattern of human suffering."[2] But others denied the book's accessibility, accusing Brooks of a "complacent handling of . . . racial themes."[3] Another group attacked Brooks's style as "an impressionistic method . . . too elliptical, private . . . and obscure," with the effect of making "social judgments

difficult."[4] Finally, some found *The Bean Eaters* a book of "disturbing overtones," presumably with reference to its social criticism.[5]

In fact, according to Brooks herself, it was the "too Social" quality
of *The Bean Eaters* that frightened reviewers into an initial silence.[6]
Not "folksy" like her first volume, *A Street in Bronzeville* (1945), not
"mandarin" like her second Pulitzer Prize-winning volume, *Annie
Allen* (1949), *The Bean Eaters*, from its inception, presented a problem of interpretation for its critics.

One reason *The Bean Eaters* aroused such a range of disparate
critical assessment was the way Brooks yoked her "social" message
to a variety of classic high modernist techniques. By 1960, it should
be remembered, the high modernism of Eliot, Pound, and Stevens
was already paralleled by a burgeoning countermovement of post-
modernism, sometimes labeled "personalism."[7] Brooks, despite her
social concerns, was temperamentally committed to the high-modernist concept of poetry impressed upon her as an apprentice writer
(*Report*, pp. 66–67). From this perspective, the duty of the modernist
poet was to produce poetry that, in Richard Wilbur's words, "accom-
modates mixed feelings, clashing ideas, and incongruous images . . .
the full discordancy of modern life and consciousness . . ." (Poulin, p.
460). Added to this was the tradition of distance between poet and
poem, a tradition that downplayed the poet's own personality and
assorted private demons, and demanded instead the type of "verbal
scrupulosity"[8] promoted by the New Criticism. In contrast, post-
modernist poets of the late 1950s such as the black poet LeRoi Jones
(now Imamu Baraka) and the female poet Sylvia Plath, spilled their
"psychic guts" with unabashed forays into personal emotional suffering, while their contemporaries, the Beat poets, practiced other more
social forms of personalism, with Ferlinghetti, Ginsberg, and others
howling private/public jeremiads at America's sins.

Brooks avoided either extreme. If late modernists such as Plath and
Baraka seemed obscure because of their poetry's inward biographical
resonance, Brooks's obscurity rested on her meticulous craft. And if
the visionary Beat poets were embarrassingly loud in their denuncia-
tions of America's social ills, Brooks was content with "disturbing
undertones." Thus, Brooks located her rhetoric of social critique, her
poetic discourse, in a range of studied poetic techniques, a *slanted*
intentionality. This strategy allowed Brooks to "insinuate" her
truths rather than to resort to the old-fashioned didacticism that, for
many new critics, marred the work of her older contemporaries, such
as then-poet-laureate Robert Frost. It equally allowed her to move
beyond an entropic exclusive high-modernist "art for art's sake"

aesthetic, and to do what her predecessor Emily Dickinson once advised: "Tell all the Truth, but tell it slant."[9]

Therefore, even in the most potent "social" poems of *The Bean Eaters*, Brooks practices a modernist eclecticism, manipulating modes and infusing mixed techniques from different genres into her poetic architecture. In particular, as many critics have noted, Brooks uses characters and personae as her modernist predecessor T. S. Eliot used them, with attendant settings, situations, and voices to express her ideas. The result is that many of her poems achieve a dual purpose: They present a "drama of human consciousness"[10] at the same time that they present disguised arguments or systems of discourse. From semicomic poems like "Mrs. Small" to the tragic "Ballad of Rudolph Reed," *The Bean Eaters*[11] poems frequently show characters struggling to piece together fragments of perceptions of a variety of social forces. These people try to make sense of what is happening in the world around them and in the process provide a unifying revisionist project for *The Bean Eaters.* By presenting this collage-like series of vignettes, this gallery of persons immobilized or driven by frayed hopes and frustrated wants, Brooks, in *The Bean Eaters*, makes "hit-and-run" attacks on a number of beliefs, values, or ideals that were destructive to mid-twentieth-century America.[12]

As characters in *The Bean Eaters* struggle with "the full discordancy of modern life and consciousness," despite their Eliotian aura, their ultimate function is not to provide a mimetic rendering of spiritual *angst* in a Wasteland tradition, but to uncover negative social relations. Thus naming, gestures, and dramatic portrayals of character function extradiegetically, or outside the text's plot and depiction of character. This function is often revealed in narrative tone, particularly where the tone is satirical or caricatural, as in two poems about encounters between blacks and whites, "Mrs. Small" and "Lovers of the Poor." The result of this added layer of text is an intensification of disguise and duplicity. To further enrich her poetic texture, the disguise and duplicity inherent in Brooks's rendering of character is then extended to ancillary aspects of the text—its setting, situation (dramatic encounter), metaphors, images, and figures. For the initiated reader, the unfolding disguise leads to discovery as Brooks shatters conventional expectations. Let us look at setting as an example. In many *Bean Eaters* poems, Brooks uses typical women's space—domestic scenes in bedrooms, living rooms, and kitchens—with a revisionist thrust. Usually settings for dalliance or harmonious domestic activities such as cooking or caring for family members, Brooks makes them the loci of conflict, disruption, or tragedy. In this way she plays on the 1950s American popular ideal of home life and housewifery, promoted in large part to get World War II working mothers back into the kitchen. Instead of bolstering this myth, Brooks reveals the underlying racial or gender conflicts it obscures. Thus setting is often discordant with situation, as when sexual encounters occur in urban hallways instead of romantic pastoral locations ("A Lovely Love"), or when murder takes place among "neighbors" on the neighborhood block ("The Ballad of Rudolph Reed"), or when home becomes a hell rather than a haven ("A Sunset of the City," "Mississippi Mother"). Love in alleys, death in boudoirs, and violence in the community establish an antithetical, oxymoronic use of setting consonant with modernist irony.

Excellent examples of Brooks's exposure of gender and racially biased myths, particularly regarding women, are found in four of the best poems in *The Bean Eaters*. These are three narrative portraits: "Mrs. Small," "A Bronzeville Mother Loiters in Mississippi. Meanwhile a Mississippi Mother Burns Bacon," "Jessie Mitchell's Mother," and the vocative sonnet, "A Lovely Love."[13] Each of these poems presents a drama of female consciousness but with a modernist narrative distance between reader, character, and author that allows for a wide-angled, ironic, slanted vision. The effect is that without heavy-handedly forcing her views upon her readers, Brooks exposes the "relation of women to discourse and of discourse to women"[14] as reified in American society. While none of her characters achieves true empowerment, the fact that each experiences varying degrees of awakening constitutes Brooks's own disguised indirect discourse. Thus, to examine these poems closely is to understand how Brooks enriches the dominant American poetic discourse, not simply by subverting it, but by making it subtle, by expanding it and giving it alterity.

Simultaneously a narrative and portrait, "Mrs. Small," on the surface, simply describes an amusing encounter between a housewife and a salesman. In the process of making coffee and apple pie, a busy, absentminded mother of ten is interrupted by a visit from the insurance man who has come to collect. Thus, the poem's central dramatic encounter consists of an intrusion into typical women's space and the disruption of womanly rituals such as preparing food and nurturance. Startled by her visitor, Mrs. Small distractedly offers him her coffee pot instead of money and accidentally spurts two brown spots of coffee onto his immaculate white shirt. This "accident" is the central, rather comic "event" in the poem, yet a careful reading reveals its larger significance, the poem's subverting, revisionist complexity.

For instance, on the level of onomastics, or the naming process, Brooks gives her heroine a diminutive patronym with several implications. As Mrs. *Small*, the woman's name conforms to the gender-based stereotype that women's lives are narrow and that women are preoccupied with unimportant matters. Yet this appropriative last name is offset by Mrs. Small's first name, Delphine, which suggests her hidden complexity and power by associating her with the ancient oracle of Apollo at Delphi.[15] Thus, respect for Mrs. Small functions outside the poem in the implied disguised discourse between narrator and reader. The informed reader would know the associative aspects of her name. While to the insurance man Mrs. Small is virtually nameless and to her husband she is simply "Delphine, the best coffee maker in town," the reader would see her quite differently and appreciate the irony of the way in which the men perceive her. Here the relationship of women to discourse and of discourse to women is exemplified onomastically in the fact that, from a male perspective, Mrs. Small is either reduced to nothing or subsumed by patriarchy. Her situation illustrates the principle that "in a system where discourse goes hand in hand with power, to be named is to undergo reification, but not to be named signifies exclusion from the system and effective disappearance" (Cohen, p. 793). The result is that women are either misnamed or occulted or totally appropriated.

Not only is naming a function of the poem's discourse, but Mrs. Small's mock-heroic confrontation with the intruding insurance man is presented by a subversive narrative voice that underscores the complexity of this ostensibly commonplace, unheroic encounter. For instance, when Mrs. Small returns from the kitchen with the coffee pot instead of her pocketbook, we are told:

> The insurance man was waiting there
> With superb and cared-for hair.
> His face did not have much time.
> (*WGB*, p. 325)

On one level, the two characters are metaphors, their confrontation a syntagmatic enactment of a clash of cultures, gender, and ethos. The mechanistic "white" world of business, immersed in discrete time, dominated by the clock and the pursuit of capital gain, is evoked in a single image: "His face did not have much time." With

neometaphysical use of analogue, Brooks communicates male impersonality, impatience, and dominance. Looking at the flustered
woman, the insurance man sees Mrs. Small as less than real; he sees
"the half-open mouth and the half-mad eyes and the smile half-
human" (*WGB*, p. 325). To him, the world of women is domestic,
suspended in pre-history, unreal and unrelated to the temporal *reality* of the business world. To the informed reader, however, Mrs.
Small's distractedness suggests other mythic associations, not with a
demimonde but with a higher spiritual sphere. Delphi, where Apollo's oracle lay, was not an out-of-the-way place, but a sacred center of
the world, visited by many pilgrims. These anxious truth-seekers
sought answers to questions delivered by a priestess who went into a
trance before she spoke. Thus, Mrs. Small's "weird" state could be
the mark of a priestess unrecognized by her intruder, who is looking
for money, not truth.

On a narrative level, Mrs. Small's disguised wisdom—her informed consciousness—is clearly indicated by the narrator's tone.
The insurance man's perfect appearance is undercut by the slyly
ironic tone with which its "defilement" is described:

> For there can be no whiter whiteness than this one:
> An insurance man's shirt on its morning run.
> This Mrs. Small now soiled
> With a pair of brown
> Spurts . . .
>
> (*WGB*, p. 326)

On an imagistic level, the insurance man is disembodied like a
figure in a Magritte portrait when referred to by his surrogate, the
shirt. But more important, the "defilement"—the climax of the encounter—is imaged by tragicomic symbolism with devastating racial
undertones—white is "soiled" by brown. This single image signifies
the underlying theme of failed racial and gender communications and
rituals. Mrs. Small, associated with female rituals of nurturance,
kitchen, coffee, and apple pie, is "rejected" when the insurance man
scorns her absentminded offer of the coffee pot. The man wants
money, not food. Thus, a whole history of economic relations with its
attendant myths of social hierarchy between whites and blacks is
suggested in this encounter.

Finally, and most importantly, the narrator interiorizes Mrs. Small
and ascribes a vocative to her that indicates her own correct perception of what is taking place. Playing her role by seeming to conform to
the stereotype of the "dizzy dame," Mrs. Small tells the insurance

man, "I don't know where my mind is this morning." Here a dual
revision takes place: To the extent that Mrs. Small seems to fit many
stereotypes of the American housewife, her characterization also
revises cinematic stereotypes of the American black woman who,
during the thirties and forties, were either domineering mammies
(Beulah in *Gone with the Wind*), shrill dialect-speaking naggers
("Amos 'n Andy"'s Sapphire), or "red-hot street mamas" (Dorothy
Dandridge in *Carmen*). Brooks debunks these stereotypes by making
her focal character a black woman who is a shrewd housewife.

From this undercutting, revisionist, "commonplace" perspective,
Mrs. Small is a person of subtle wisdom who knows only too well
what is happening, as this passage reveals:

> "I don't know where my mind is this morning,"
> Said Mrs. Small, scorning
> Apologies! For there was so much
> For which to apologize! Oh such
> Mountains of things, she'd never get anything done
> If she begged forgiveness for each one.
>
> (*WGB*, p. 326)

Apologize for being black, apologize for being female, apologize for
having so many children, . . . Now Mrs. Small is in a hurry. She, too,
has a schedule, and "apologies" and her hurry will not mix. With a
final sly pun, the narrator describes Mrs. Small as continuing her
"part of the world's business," even if it is not recognized as such.

Just as in "Mrs. Small," the central encounter in "A Bronzeville
Mother Loiters in Mississippi. Meanwhile, a Mississippi Mother
Burns Bacon" involves the intrusion and disruption of domestic
rituals. This time, on an onomastic level, the two characters are
identified by region, making them function with even greater symbolic significance. Representing different races, ethos, and points of
view, the texture of the relationship between the white Mississippi
mother and the black Bronzeville mother is enriched by the com-
monality underlying the ostensible opposition of characters—both
are women and mothers. In situating her characters, Brooks places
the white Mississippi mother where she "belongs"—in her kitchen,
preparing breakfast for her husband and children. Earlier her "community" space had been invaded by the northern black "Bronzeville"
mother, who has returned "down home" to retrieve her lynched
child's body. This earlier intrusion is followed by a second intrusion
in the Mississippi mother's memory. The remembered encounter has
become a "problematic" for the Mississippi mother and will even-

tually become a vehicle for her awakening conscience. Brooks's decision to establish this alterego relationship has a revisionist thrust. The poem's dramatic structure suggests not only that female relationships are important, but also that the relation of the "female to suppressed dimensions of her own identity" is a valuable inquiry (Ostriker, p. 319).

On one level, "A Bronzeville Mother . . ." is a protest poem, because it deals with the notorious lynching of a fourteen-year-old Chicago boy, Emmett Till, who was killed when visiting his grandmother in Mississippi. However, rather than focusing on the act of the lynching itself, as many black poets have done, Brooks decided to offer a "drama of consciousness" centered on the conflicting reactions of the white woman on whose behalf the child was murdered. The poem's modernity lies in this "slanted" approach to its theme.

To further complicate her art, Brooks chose to make running attacks on certain literary conventions throughout the poem. Thus, "A Bronzeville Mother . . ." opens with the narrator's references to a western ballad tradition in an attempt to explain the feelings of the poem's everyday "heroine," an ordinary southern housewife. As the Mississippi mother prepares food, her disturbed consciousness grapples with the fact of the murder and the ensuing courtroom trial, which had ended in acquittal. From the beginning, the narrator notes, everything had seemed to her like a ballad, with a "beat inevitable," "blood" and "wildness cut up, and tied in little bunches." References to the ballad tradition suggest the dual southern mythology of a medieval world of lords and ladies and an alter-world of violence and gory battles between good and evil. In the sprawling lines and complex syntax of this long free-verse narrative, it becomes clear to the Mississippi mother that the neat formal and theoretic structures of traditional ballads form an inadequate frame of reference for the massive, tangled patriarchal social forces surrounding her.

A black boy has been murdered on her behalf, but when the Mississippi mother tries to understand what happened by setting up the balladic appellative system referring to a "Dark Villain" (Emmett Till), "A Fine Prince" (her husband), and a "Milk-White Maid" (herself), the naming process merely exposes the artificiality of the dominant social discourse. The relation of the black race and of women to discourse and of discourse to them is simply to legitimate violence and dominance, to legitimate the social order incarnated by her white husband, and to obscure alienation and truth. The exposing narrator discloses this social truth in complicity with the reader by cleverly juxtaposing balladic epithets, themes, and plots with references to a

series of metonymic domestic objects that reify the banality of everyday domestic life: step-on cans, eggs, sour-milk biscuits. The "Fine
Prince" (husband) uses crude gestures, scratches himself at the table,
mutters hate-filled words over his newspaper, and, at the poem's
climactic encounter, slaps his infant in variation on the violence he
has wreaked on another woman's child. What starts out as a commonplace, impressionistic rendering of a domestic ritual becomes an
expressionistic, surreal evocation of the "disturbing undertones" of
reality. Domestic violence is too often the counterpart to myths of
domestic bliss. Metonymic references to the husband's hands
("When the Hand / came down") creates an aura of hysteria. References to the stark triad of colors—red, white, and black—become
symbolic of southern racial conflict. In her revisionist mission,
Brooks makes these colors lose their traditional connotations. In
"Bronzeville Mother . . . ," black (when it is a black child) is not evil
after all, white is not so pure, and red suggests passion turning into
brutality. In one of the poem's final metonymic encounters, Brooks
deconstructs the myth of conjugal love and discovers the truth of
male hegemony. Near the poem's end, the husband's mouth, "wet
and red," closes over his wife's in an act of smothering entrapment,
rendering her immobilized and silent in the entanglement of eros and
violence.

In the thrall of this forced, appropriating kiss, the Mississippi
mother dives into suppressed dimensions of her own identity, hear-
ing "no hoof-beat of the horse and . . . no flash of the shining steel"
(WGB, p. 322): She remembers instead the "decapitated exclamation
points in that Other Woman's / eyes" (WGB, p. 323). Trapped by the
reality of her husband's violence against her own children, the Mississippi mother enters into sisterhood with the grieving black
mother, imagining blood as a lengthening "red ooze . . . seeping,
spreading darkly . . . over her white shoulders" (WGB, p. 322). The
interiorizing narrator can now eliminate the distance between the
Bronzeville mother and the Mississippi mother. The former intruder
is now her "sister," an agent of awakening. A final reference to
flowers changes the romantic southern myth embodied by the magnolia into a new flower rooted in female resistance. The Mississippi
mother now fully comprehends that "the last bleak news of the
ballad" is that the myth of the benign, patriarchal magnolia'd South
must end, for the sake of women, of blacks, and of society itself.

Another *Bean Eaters* poem based on the dramatic situation of
female-to-female encounter is "Jessie Mitchell's Mother." Again, the
characters function antithetically: In this case one represents youth,

health, and futurity, the other represents middle age, illness, and decline. As in "A Bronzeville Mother . . . ," commonalities unite the characters. Both are women, but with an even stronger tie; they are mother and daughter, and they are both female and black, with the attendant joys and dangers of that relationship. One curious twist in this poem is the theme of intraracial color competition. The declining mother is of the highly valued light-skinned ("yellow") complexion, while the daughter, although young and healthy, is black, a distinct stigma and "handicap" in black America before the "Black Is Beautiful" movement of the sixties. In a tightly woven architecture of situation, space, dialogue, and acts, Brooks uses this poem as a paradigm to critique what a recent black feminist critic has called "the narrow space of race, the dark enclosure of sex."[16] The difficulty of decoding this vignette is seen in the reaction of the eminent critic, Arthur P. Davis, who once described "Jessie Mitchell's Mother" as a poem about the "unnatural hatred between a dark-skinned daughter and her light-skinned mother."[17] Davis, a black American who has written perceptively of what he called the "black-and-tan motif" in Brooks's work, did not fully understand the "suppressed dimensions" of black female relations. Yet, it is these very relations that constitute the complex "social truth" of Brooks's not-so-natural psychodrama.

The poem opens with Jessie Mitchell's entrance into her mother's bedroom. Jessie has come to wash her mother who is lying in. The bedroom itself has a metonymic of the paradoxically nurturing and destructive forces in women's lives, because bedrooms are "women's spaces," places of amour and dalliance, but also loci of illness, childbirth, and death. Thus, alternating visions of sex, procreation, and death surround this mother/daughter encounter. The opening line, "Into her mother's bedroom to wash the ballooning body," sets up both the sisterhood and alienation between the women. They are locked together in a healing ritual: The daughter will bathe her mother's body, big with yet another child, now reduced to a "stretched yellow rag." This once-valued, vibrant woman who can remember an "exquisite yellow youth" is a mere object. The washing of a body also suggests a death ritual rather than a prelude to birth. Birth or death, the mother has been brought to her state precisely by her attractiveness, the valued yellowness that made her the object of male attention. Significantly, in her reductive condition, the mother remains unnamed and defined appellatively by her role; she is "Jessie Mitchell's mother," a woman immobile, passive, and seemingly totally dependent.

To the metonymic space entrapping these women, and the symbolic encounter between them, Brooks adds a vocative element that imposes yet another ironic layer of meaning to the text. Jessie Mitchell, interiorized, thinks:

> "My mother is jelly-hearted and she has a brain of jelly:
> Only a habit would cry if she should die."
> (*WGB*, p. 328)

With the bravado of youth, she accepts dominant values and therefore devalues her mother, precluding feminine solidarity. By devaluing her mother's state, she sabotages her chance to understand fully the sociosexual forces shaping her mother's fate, and, by extrapolation, the suppressed dimensions of her own identity. Jessie Mitchell refuses to consider her own future vulnerability to the same male hegemonic forces that have crushed her mother. She is ingenuous. To underscore Jessie's slanted vision, the narrator establishes complicity with the reader by interiorizing the mother and revealing her own strategies for undercutting what appears to be her total powerlessness. Jessie Mitchell's mother, like Mrs. Small, understands more than she vocalizes. She sees clearly her daughter's scorn, but knows that because Jessie is dark-skinned, her "way" will be harder; that sex and black poverty will be proud Jessie's downfall, and that:

> . . . poor men would bend her, and doing
> things with poor men,
> Being much in bed, and babies
> would bend her over . . .
> (*WGB*, p. 328)

By placing these ideas not in a vocative, but in the unspoken conscious of Jessie's mother, Brooks masterfully builds a text shot through with irony. In an act of anamnesis, or remembrance, Jessie Mitchell's mother can protect herself from her daughter's contempt and restore her self-esteem by reminiscences. She deliberately recalls her "exquisite yellow youth" metaphorized as a drooping flower into which she forces perfume. Therefore, in an effort quite different from the Mississippi mother's, she purposefully sustains the very myths that have reduced her.

Alienation between the two women in "Jessie" remains unarticulated. Articulating that rage could have brought about a higher consciousness between mother and daughter, even if painful. Instead, their relationship remains insincere; the daughter speaks in falsely solicitous tones when she asks: "Are you better, mother, do you think it will come today?" The mother refuses to warn her daughter of the dangers ahead. Yet, behind the poem is Brooks's critical vision not only of female-female relations, but also of a male and racial hegemony in which black men adhere to mainstream American myths about what constitutes female beauty. The resulting nefarious beauty standards create a pecking order that generates rivalry even between mother and daughter. Therefore, the poem's thematic closure lies in its context. If "Jessie Mitchell's Mother" is permeated by implied criticism of gender-based ideas, it ends as a revisionist validation of female-to-female relationships. On an imagistic level, it is a tableau of ablution. Like Mary Cassatt's painting of a mother bathing her daughter, "Jessie Mitchell's Mother" is a "woman-identified" poem that confirms the importance of womanly rituals, with the roles reversed and paradoxical. With overtones of purification, baptism, and absolution, it dramatizes the commonalities that bind women to women in joy, pain, and the business of daily living.

One of the most intricate examples of Brooks's fusion of subverted form with revisionist discourse is found in *The Bean Eaters'* sonnet, "A Lovely Love" (*WGB*, p. 347). The central "episode" of this dramatic monologue and apostrophic sonnet spoken by a female to her lover consists of two encounters: the furtive meeting of the two lovers in sordid circumstances and the encounter between the lovers and a disapproving society. As in the three previously discussed poems, the nexus of space, voice, and situation is crucial, brilliantly undercutting the poem's ostensibly sentimental title. The conventions of romantic myth require a pastoral or boudoir setting; here, however, references to alleys, hall, stairway, and a "splintery box" underscore the realistic, non-bucolic ambiance of this liaison. The presence of a janitor as "chorus" reinforces the "dirtiness" of the lovers' intent. If the Mississippi mother found her everyday kitchen with its step-on can inimical to the idea of chivalric myth, the disjunction between reality and myth is even more jarring in "A Lovely Love."

The so-called "lovely love" is really a quick liaison, motivated by lust and acted out with haste and unabashed force. It concludes with the persona warning, in a voice at once vernacular and eloquent:

> . . . Run
> People are coming. They must not catch us here
> Definitionless in this strict atmosphere.
> (*WGB*, p. 347)

The use of the woman as first-person narrative voice is as subversive as the poem's setting. While the speaker is a woman, the voice is overtly "unfeminine" in its imperative tone throughout the poem. The result is a curious reification of an unholy alliance between sex and violence. At the opening of the poem, while a janitor hurls curses at the lovers and "cheapens" their need for refuge, the narrator not only accepts her portion, but also demands it. In a series of parallel phrases she commands:

> Let it be alleys. Let it be a hall
> . . .
> Let it be stairways, and a splintery box
> (*WGB*, p. 347)

In further consent to a degraded situation she describes the coarse encounter with her lover:

> Where you have thrown me, scraped me with your kiss,
> Have honed me, have released me after this
> Cavern kindness . . .
> (*WGB*, p. 347)

With regard to form, "A Lovely Love" shows modernist syncretistic mixtures, particularly the modernist attraction to metaphysical conventions and to new possibilities for the sonnet form. Brooks uniquely combines the three quatrains and concluding couplet of the Shakespearean sonnet with the *abba* rhyme scheme of the Petrarchan sonnet in each quatrain. In a sense, Brooks's bold manipulation of western forms parallels the boldness of her unconventional speaker. With a subversion of the syllogistic argument common to many Shakespearean sonnets (i.e., the "if-then" discourse), for example, Brooks's speaker's argument rests on a "not this, but this" structure:

> That is the birthright of our lovely love [she explains]
> In swaddling clothes. Not like that Other one.
> Not lit by any fondling star above.
> Not found by any wise men, either. . . .
> (*WGB*, p. 347)

In the above passage, the speaker not only alters the structure of her argument, but also her role; instead of mythologizing it, she makes sarcastic references to the Nativity, rejecting its similarity to her outsider status and its later reification in the chivalric Mary of courtly love tradition. Thus in form, theme, and discourse, Brooks alters both her Shakespearean and Petrarchan antecedents.

To further illustrate how the poem thematically as well as formally alters western concepts of courtly love, it should be remembered that the love situations Petrarchan poets presented were characterized by instability and discontinuity, shifts in tone, mode, and stance. The mythic lady, the one addressed, remained chaste and never let the poet satisfy his desire. Feminine unassailability was the very function of the protean and unstable character of Petrarchan love. Yet poets as early as Spenser reversed the Petrarchan tradition by turning the "endless change and transformation"[10] central to Petrarchism into a celebration of conjugal fidelity and love. By such a reversal Spenser repudiated the idea that celibacy was a superior state. Neither did he celebrate adultery, as was common to Elizabethan convention. He centered instead on the conception of love as sacred when it found expression in a stable, reciprocal marriage. Brooks, however, not only rejects the Petrarchan notion of the lady-lover as agent of transcendence, as seen in her negative references to the heavens ("not lit by any fondling star above"), but she also rejects Spenserian tributes to *stabile*. In "A Lovely Love" instability, discontinuity, and tenuousness are embraced *by the female speaker* herself. She transforms the Petrarchan tradition by not only "challenging and dissolving" the conventional topos, or setting, of Petrarchan love but also by altering the very discourse of love itself. Pastoral, religious referents change to urban referents, with seriously antireligious overtones; and the vagaries of black ghetto love are acknowledged, even confirmed. The terrestrial, with all of its vicissitudes, is ruthlessly endorsed.

On an imagistic level, the cluster of hyacinth, darkness, and rot embodies the poem's central themes of eros, duplicity, and disintegration brought about by the transgression of codes. For instance, the concept of transgression and duplicity permeates these early lines in which the speaker describes the custodian's discovery of their situation:

> Whose janitor javelins epithet and thought
> To cheapen hyacinth darkness that we sought
> And played we found, rot, make the petals fall.
> (*WGB*, p. 347)

In Greek mythology, the hyacinth is associated with the theme of death. Thus, on one level, "A Lovely Love" is about the universal awareness of the coupling of love and death; in this case, real death or the death of myth itself, leading to the sexual liberation of the female persona.

In addition to these subverted metaphors and linguistic strategies, a look at the naming process in "A Lovely Love" reveals another subverting thrust in the poem. In the coda, the poem is ascribed to "Lillian." This speaker may be associated with Lilith, Eve's counterpart in Semitic myth, who was a defiant demon succubus, a dweller in deserted places whose barrenness drove her to subvert the very idea of fertility by attacking other people's children. Eve may have seduced Adam, but she was herself the victim of the snake; Lilith, however, is a far more potent, intentional agent in myth than Eve. The abruptness of the speaker's language and her use of imperative semantic structures dramatizes her dominant Lilith-like role. Thus, the speaker's subversive voice achieves power and authority by demonstrating not only consciousness, but also control.

Appropriately, "A Lovely Love" is framed by alternating syntagmatic movements: a secretive entrance and a forced exit by these transgressors of society's codes of "love," its "strict atmosphere." In "A Lovely Love" the persona's Promethean impulse to defy society, directed against strict codes of gender behavior, becomes yet another aspect of Brooks's project in *The Bean Eaters*: to puncture myth, to expose it, to alter it, to move beyond it. Just as "A Lovely Love" transgresses against the "strict atmosphere" of western literary form, so, to use Genette's phrasing, Brooks's work in *The Bean Eaters* shows exactly how "literary discourse [can be] produced and developed in accordance with structures that it can transgress."[19]

Similar techniques of slanted discourse are used throughout *The Bean Eaters* to critique other myths: the myth of the American West and masculinity, the myth of the American dream, the myth of domestic happiness, and the myth of effective Christianity. If some readers found *The Bean Eaters* to be a book with "disturbing undertones," they were not mistaken; but the awakening of a society's conscience is never pleasant, is perforce, disturbing. That Brooks did not shrink from this revisionist "project" is a testament to her refusal to let "objective" craft obscure her role as a social commentator. In her subsequent volumes this discourse would shed its "insinuating" garb, and she would speak more forthrightly.

Notes

1. Review, *Chicago Sun Times*, 19 June 1960.
2. Herbert Burke, review in *Library Journal* 85 (15 April 1960): 1599.

3. Frederick Bock, review, *Chicago Sun Times Sunday Magazine*, 5 June 1960, sec. 4, p. 12.

4. Leonard E. Nathan, "Four Books," *Voices* (Sept.–Dec. 1960).

5. Review, *Bookmark* (April 1960):171.

6. Gwendolyn Brooks, *Report from Part One* (Detroit: Broadside Press, 1971), p. 78. Hereinafter cited in the text as *Report*.

7. A. Poulin, Jr., "Contemporary American Poetry: The Radical Tradition," in *Contemporary American Poetry*, ed. A. Poulin, Jr. (Boston: Houghton Mifflin, 1967), pp. 459–73. Poulin identifies the "personalization of poetry" as a major difference between modernist and contemporary poetry. Hereinafter cited in the text as Poulin.

8. A term used by James E. B. Breslin in his study, *From Modern to Contemporary Poetry, 1945–1965* (Chicago: University of Chicago Press, 1983), p. 30.

9. Poem no. 1129 in the Thomas H. Johnson variorum edition.

10. Ihab Hassan applies this term to Kafka's work in his study, *The Dismemberment of Orpheus: Toward a Postmodern Literature* (Madison: University of Wisconsin Press, 1982), p. 137.

11. I use the text as it appears in the collection, *The World of Gwendolyn Brooks* (New York: Harper and Row, 1971). All citations to *The Bean Eaters* refer to this text and hereinafter will be cited in the text as *WGB*.

12. See Alicia Ostriker, "The Thieves of Language: Women Poets and Revisionist Mythmaking," in *Feminist Criticism: Essays on Women, Literature and Theory*, ed. Elaine Showalter (New York: Pantheon Books, 1985), p. 318. Hereinafter cited in the text as Ostriker.

13. These poems are found on the following pages of *WGB*: "Mrs. Small," pp. 325–27, "A Bronzeville Mother," pp. 317–23, "Jessie Mitchell's Mother," pp. 328–29, and "A Lovely Love," p. 347.

14. Susan D. Cohen, "An Onomastic Bind: Colette's *Gigi* and the Politics of Naming," *PMLA* 100 (Oct. 1985): 793. Hereinafter cited in the text as Cohen.

15. Paul Rabinowitz, "Naming, Magic, and Documentary: The Subversion of the Narrative in *Song of Solomon, Ceremony* and *China Men*," in *Feminist Re-visions: What Has Been and Might Be*, ed. Vivian Patraka and Louise A. Tilly (Ann Arbor: University of Michigan Press, 1983), pp. 26–42.

16. Gloria Wade-Gayles, *No Crystal Stair: Visions of Race and Sex in Black Women's Fiction* (New York: Pilgrim Press, 1984), p. 246.

17. Arthur P. Davis, *From the Dark Tower: Afro-American Writers, 1900 to 1960* (Washington, D.C.: Howard University Press, 1974), p. 188.

18. Reed Way Dasenbrock, "The Petrarchan Content of Spenser's Amoretti," *PMLA* 100 (Jan. 1985): 28–47.

19. Gerard Genette, *Figures of Literary Discourse*, trans. Alan Sheridan (New York: Columbia University Press, 1982), p. 67.

14

Community and Voice:
Gwendolyn Brooks's "In the Mecca"

Voice as speech and dialogue has long been used in poetry (in fact the first impulse of poetry was to tell a story), and speech as dialogue or monologue contributes to theme, architectonic structure, and characterization in poetry's pace and process. "In the Mecca"[1] by Gwendolyn Brooks can be studied in this context—the multi-logues, interior monologues and speeches that contribute to the dynamics of the poem, its range, and revelations of Afro-American character. The characters are made visible through their speech-acts—both interior and exterior "say"—and it is speech that helps to render the kind of poem that Brooks was seeking to create, as she describes in her autobiography, *Report from Part One*: "I wish to present a large variety of personalities against a mosaic of daily affairs, recognizing that the *grimmest* of these is likely to have a streak or two streaks of sun.

In the Mecca were murders, loves, lonelinesses, hates, jealousies. Hope occurred, and charity, sainthood, glory, shame, despair, fear, altruism."[2]

Brooks's "In the Mecca" is precisely such a multidimensional poem, with blacks in the foreground, visible and individuated. Because of the multitude of community voices and personalities manifest in speech and thought, we have what Gertrude Stein might refer to as the multiple "rhythms of personality." Each character in "In the Mecca" could create an individual poem, but the integration of portraits and voices provides the sense of the Mecca as a world. And the multivoiced poem has a long tradition in Afro-American poetry; for example, such poems are found in the works of Sterling Brown, Robert Hayden, and Sherley A. Williams. Williams has also written of the influences and motives of such poetry in her article "The Blues

Roots of Contemporary Afro-American Poetry": "This complex interweaving of general and specific, individual and group, finds no
direct correspondence in Afro-American literature except in the literary blues. But the evocation of certain first person experiences and
the extensive use of multiple voices in Afro-American poetry may be,
at least in part, an outgrowth from this characteristic of the blues."[3]

Its many voices enable Brooks's poem to operate on many levels at
once and to move in many directions (inward, outward, vertically,
and horizontally, or backward, forward, up, and down). Ruth Miller
has described the time spent in Mrs. Sallie's apartment as "horizontal," the rest of the time/space scheme vertical.[4] Interior monologue
functions on all levels, and although interior monologue has been the
great leap in all twentieth-century poetry and prose, for the Afro-
American poet, it has special significance beyond the technical device. In another article, I have discussed the supra-literary purposes of
Jean Toomer's use of the interior monologue, which may also be
applied to Brooks's use of interior speech:

> though Afro-American innovative writers sometimes share or seem
> to mirror some of the forms of these European-American non-tradi-
> tionalists, it is important to make distinctions and to look for distinc-
> tive purposes. For instance, if we were to compare Jean Toomer's use of
> stream-of-consciousness literary technique in *Cane* with that of James
> Joyce in *Ulysses* we would get some inkling of this. With Jean Toomer,
> the exploration of interior landscape and consciousness of Afro-Ameri-
> can character and personality *adds value* beyond the mere technical
> facility or expertise. Because Afro-American character had not been
> explored from *the inside as complex and serious* (in Euro-American
> literature because not thought to possess this; in Afro-American litera-
> ture because the drama of personality was often secondary or back-
> ground to the drama of oppressive interracial confrontation . . .) the
> technical device becomes a morally (ethically, politically, socially) re-
> sponsible act.[5]

While Mrs. Sallie searches for her lost child Pepita, it is only Pepita
who remains the "invisible person" in the poem. Although we never
"see" Pepita, the search for her enables us to see others, and when
finally we hear her voice, too, it acts as a kind of moral vision and
ethic for the poem. The search for Pepita gives the unity to seemingly
disparate voices of a particular community in a particular time and
space.

The first voice is that of the poet or the narrator. Poetry has two
voices: Poets either move away from, or move toward, speech. Contemporary poetic diction generally moves toward speech—generally

ordinary speech in its word choice, cadences, and syntactical choices. Contemporary prose has also tended to move toward the colloquial. Black poetry, especially, has long been concerned with the "orality" of verse, and often achieves its greatest impetus from the language of speech. In fact, Stephen Henderson has referred to speech as one of the "referents" of black poetry, along with its music. In their introduction to *Giant Talk*, Quincy Troupe and Rainier Schulte also discuss this foundation:

> An important element in Third World writing: the power of music in words. This led the writer back to an oral tradition, to sounds that previously were not considered a part of the poetic language, and he therefore frequently looked for inspiration to the language of the "street." He felt that "elevated" language took some of the energy out of the immediate human expression, and he hoped to revitalize poetic language through the reflection of the word from the streets.[6]

Gwendolyn Brooks moves in both directions in her poetry. It is an eclectic poetic tradition that manages to move both away from and toward the language of (heightened) everyday speech. It is an aggregate language that runs the gamut of "elevated" and "street" without devitalizing either.

"In the Mecca" begins in an "exclusive" rhetoric—a language that seems to set itself apart from the community's voice, although it directs us toward that community. However, it is not exactly the hierarchical "framed" narration of an earlier literary generation, which novelist John Wideman recalls here:

> From the point of view of American literature then, the fact of black speech (and the oral roots of a distinct literary tradition—ultimately the tradition itself) existed only when it was properly "framed," within works which had status in the dominant literary system. For black speech the frame was the means of entering the literate culture and the frame also defined the purposes or ends for which black speech could be employed. The frame confers reality on black speech; the literary frame was a mediator, a legitimizer. What was outside the frame chaotic, marginal, not worthy of the reader's attention becomes, once inside, conventionalized into respectability.
>
> . . . The frame implies a linguistic hierarchy, the dominance of one language variety over all others. This linguistic subordination extends naturally to the dominance of one version of reality over others.[7]

In Brooks's poetry there is no such hierarchy because any kind of language may occupy any space; indeed, different languages may almost occupy the same space.

Brooks's narrator points us toward the Mecca and toward the community, but she uses the imagery and language of the community's more decorative, formal traditions and self-conscious poetic forms: the oratory, the sermon, the spiritual, the proverb. The narrator directs us: "Now the way of the Mecca was on this wise." Although the language is elevated, we the readers are still being spoken to; we are addressed and made to not simply observe or read, but to enter and participate in the poem *and* the upcoming search. This is reminiscent of the way audience functions also in African oral tradition and establishes a reciprocal relationship: "A good speaker . . . makes sure of the participation of the audience in a way analogous to story-telling; he expects murmurs of support and agreement, muttered rejoinders of his rhetorical questions, laughter when he purposely brings in something amusing or exaggerated, and thanks and acknowledgement when he has ended."[8]

"Sit where the light corrupts your face," advises the narrator, and we are invited as well into the paradoxes of the Mecca's existence—the paradoxical being a persistent Brooks theme, as Beverly Guy-Sheftall has observed in her article, "The Women of Bronzeville." Brooks builds "facets, complexities and paradoxes," and often characters exist as "antitheses" of each other,[9] like the antitheses Brooks enumerates in her design for the poem. Certain characters inhabit the Mecca, such as Prophet Williams who is rich in Bible talk, yet whose wife dies in self-defense. Such characters become paradoxes, antitheses of themselves, as the Mecca itself is a grand paradox. The building is no "fair fable," but a tale of paradoxes that even the description of *things* must fall into—"the sick and influential stair." And when we meet Pepita—from others' descriptions—she too is in line with paradoxical representation:

> our Woman with her terrible eye,
> with iron and feathers in her feet,
> with all her songs so lemon-sweet,
> with lightning and a candle too
> and junk and jewels too?
> (*WGB*, pp. 385–86)

It is from the extended viewpoint of Mrs. Sallie, a "low brown butterball," that the reader views the others in the poem. I say "extended" viewpoint, because although we proceed with Mrs. Sallie and encounter those whom she meets, we learn things about the other people that Mrs. Sallie cannot know. In her discussion of fiction, Kit Reed has described the viewpoint that occurs in this poem:

1. The writer has the added ability *to see his character from the outside*: he can describe the character's looks, his aspect as opposed to or indicative of his inner state.
2. The writer can draw the scene before the character walks into it: what the place looks like, what the other people are doing, and he can do so with greater art than he would in the character of a person telling a story. Although more limited than he would be in using an omniscient narrator, the writer has mobility of vision.
3. The writer can pick up subtleties his character may not notice *at the time*: attitudes on the part of other characters, innuendo, speeches made when the point-of-view character isn't really listening.
4. There is greater opportunity for flights of style. This is linked with mobility of vision, but there is another factor. Although the writer assumes a character's way of looking at things, *he is not limited by his character's diction or his vocabulary*.[10]

We first meet St. Julia Jones, whose sermonic rhythms, biblical strategies in dialogue "rich with Bible," perhaps, clue us to (and hark back to) the nature of the beginning of the poem, giving the key to the literary influences of the poet/narrator's own voice. St. Julia Jones's speech is "peppered" with such rich and brimming diction:

> "Isn't He wonderfulwonderful!" cries St. Julia.
> "Isn't our Lord the greatest to the brim?
> The light of my life. And I lie late
> past the still pastures. And meadows. He's the comfort
> and wine and piccalilli for my soul.
> He hunts me up the coffee for my cup.
> Oh how I love that Lord."
>
> (*WGB*, p. 378)

Next we meet Prophet Williams, who is younger than St. Julia, but who has more visible contradictions of character:

> and rich with Bible, pimples, pout: who reeks
> with lust for his disciple, is an engine
> of candid steel hugging combustibles.
> His wife she was a skeleton.
> His wife she was a bone.
> Ida died in self-defense.
>
> (*WGB*, p. 378)

Characters not described through dialogue or narrative which, like the above seem to duplicate thoughts in progress, receive axiomatic presentation, a special trait of Brooks. Hyena is "a fancier of firsts"; and Mrs. Sallie, who wants to decorate, thinks of a "sick kitchen" that would annul such beautifying impulses: "First comes correctness, *then* embellishment." Even descriptive imagery seems axiomatic: "Briggs is adult as a stone." And certainly Briggs's thoughts/ internal speech is axiomatic or aphoristic: "Immunity is forfeit, love / is luggage, hope is heresy."

On the Mecca's fourth floor are Mrs. Sallie's children, and this begins what Ruth Miller has referred to as the "horizontal" section of the poem. There is another "address," this time to the children— "Children what she has brought you is hock of ham." The poet's voice becomes more clearly "spoken," more clearly a part of the community's voice. Sherley A. Williams has also spoken of this kind of narrative blending and vitality of persona in a "diction that hovers marvelously"[11] between the poet's and the community's voices.

Mrs. Sallie's apartment is a space where things can jump to life; where stoves can be "cruel," where mustard can be "mesmerized." Thought patterns as well as speech again take over the narrative:

> Now Mrs. Sallie
> confers her bird-hat to her kitchen table,
> and sees her kitchen. It is bad, is bad,
> her eyes say, and My soft antagonist,
> her eyes say, and My headlong tax and mote,
> her eyes say, and My maniac default,
> my least light.
>
> (*WGB*, p. 380)

This kind of incremental repetition is often shared with poem and prose structures in the blues mode. Ernest Gaines, in an interview, has spoken of this kind of music-inspired repetition:

> I love music, all kinds of music. I think my stories are meant to be read out loud and I think that's because of the musical influence in my work.
> In my work you see a lot of repetition: He said, she said. Repetition of certain things and certain lines. Martin Luther King used a lot of this in his great speeches. It's a rhythmic thing that you develop in your speaking, which is a result of music.[12]

We are introduced to Mrs. Sallie's children: the eldest daughter, the "Undaunted" who once "pushed her thumbs in the eyes of a Thief"; Yvonne, preparing for a lover, uses "Doublemint as a protective device" because it is "unembarrassable" and offers another paradox: "It is very bad, but in its badness it is nearly grand." Other children are described by what they hate, which is also an indication of what they lack:

> Melodie Mary hates everything pretty and plump.
> And Melodie, Cap and Casey
> and Thomas Earl, Tennessee, Emmett and Briggs
> hate sewn suburbs;
> hate everything combed and strong; hate people who
> have balls, dolls, mittens and dimity frocks and trains
> and boxing gloves, picture books, bonnets for Easter.
> Lace handkerchief owners are enemies of Smithkind.
> (WGB, pp. 381–82)

What they like, therefore, becomes a defiance: "Melodie Mary likes roaches." These are seeming inversions of "what the importances are" for children who live in cruel, grim spaces:

> To delicate Melodie Mary
> headlines are secondary.
> It is interesting that in China
> the children blanch and scream,
> and that blood runs like a ragged wound
> through the ancient flesh of the land.
> It matters, mildly,
> that the Chinese girls are grim,
> and that hurried are the seizures
> of yellow hand on hand. . . .
> What if they drop like the tumbling tears
> of the old and intelligent sky?
> Where are the frantic bulletins
> when other importances die?
> Trapped in his privacy of pain
> the worried rat expires,
> and smashed in the grind of a rapid heel
> last night's roaches lie.
> (WGB, p. 382)

But really it is the "privacy of pain" that can raise everything ostensibly minute to the level of immediacy and importance, as if changed to symbol.

There is another address to the reader: "Please pity Briggs." But we do not know whether it is the narrator's request, or Briggs's own request for *any* cognizance. Briggs, like all the children in their individual ways, attempts to cope with his "cruel stoves" and to "proceed."

Suddenly, Mrs. Sallie discovers that Pepita is missing, and we are launched to another level of the poem's revelation—a galvanizing section of the poem—as Mrs. Sallie goes on her search for Pepita. The search might also be seen as a metaphor for any search of discovery and for special searches of discovery that each of us takes for "the other person." In descending and ascending stairs and entering rooms—the beehive steel-box type of this architecture—the poem loses any claim to equilibrium and becomes infused with poetic tension. We continue to meet other voices and hear other personalities revealed, but now they are revealed through what they have to say about Pepita—descriptions of her, speculations and musings on what might have occurred, or their evasions of the question, Where Pepita? Sometimes they are also answering the question of where they themselves are in reference to their world past and present (and anticipated). "Where is Pepita?" often becomes "Where am I?" For instance, the first woman to whom Mrs. Sallie says, "One of my children is missing," responds with a journey into history through what is essentially a (mini) slave narrative, which sets up a personal and historical context and aids in the discovery of *her*, her own modes of perception and being. We have her portrait—"moving picture"— through her speech, and she momentarily, like a jazz-blues soloist, becomes the central figure in this orchestration. Her story seems a nonsequitur, but it brings her into view and provides another angle of vision and reality, momentarily inverting space and time:

> "I ain seen no Pepita. But
> I remember our cabin. The floor was dirt.
> And something crawled in it. That is the thought
> stays in my mind. I do not recollect
> what 'twas. But something. Something creebled in that dirt
> for we wee ones to pop. Kept popping at it.
> Something that squishied. *Then* your heel came down!
> I hear them squishies now. . . . *Pop*, Pernie May!
> That's sister Pernie. That's my sister Pernie.
> Squish. . . . Out would jump her little heel.
> And that was the end of Something. Sister Pernie
> was our best popper. Pern and me and all,
> we had no beds. Some slaves had beds of hay
> or straw, with cover-cloth. We six-uns curled
> in corners of the dirt, and closed our eyes,
> and went to sleep—or listened to the rain
> fall inside, felt the drops
> big on our noses, bummies and tum-tums. . . ."
>
> (*WGB*, p. 387)

The question of Pepita's whereabouts leads Loam Norton not only to speculate on other historical "unkindnesses and harms" that move outward from the self, but also to take into account oneself as part of a "not remote, not unconcerned humanity," the black and the Jewish stories juxtaposed as "twin evils."

In her search for Pepita, Mrs. Sallie's mind turns "epithet, foiler, guillotine"; she must constantly remind herself "Pepita's smart"— but in such a search for a lost child, "everyone in the world is Mean," and meanness itself is personified. In such a world even the door becomes a speaker: "What are you doing here? and where is Pepita the puny—the halted, glad-sad child?" Note the paradoxical description again; the door also contributes to the first descriptions of Pepita through the speech and speech-thoughts of others.

All Mrs. Sallie's children take part in the search, until finally the "Law" is called, thus beginning another principal section of the poem, primarily in its telling of what the poem is not. This is no poem about a "Female of the Negro Race" or any other abstract, monolithic description, but rather about individual, particular Afro-American, human beings. Although "the Law" is thus abstracted, these inhabitants of the Mecca will be looked at, and touched, even though the look and touch can be either "terrible" or "nearly grand." "In the Mecca" is not one of the monolithic "Race Poems" that theorize or "treatise" black humanity.

After the law leaves, Aunt Dill "arrives to help them" and tells essentially more about her own nature. She tells a horror story about a "Little girl got raped and choked to death last week." Another paradoxical figure, Aunt Dill calls herself "doing good," yet even her "pianissimos and apples" are sinister.

When the law returns and trots about the Mecca, we have incorporated into Brooks's poem an interpolated example of the kind of monochromatic race poem she is not writing. Again, her poem is not a romanticized abstraction that one might find for instance in some poems of Negritude that sing "in art-lines of Black Woman" or refer superficially to "the black feet of Africa," nor Afro-American analogous traditions where Klansmen are excoriated like "cartoon ghosts." Brooks incorporates such monomial poetry within her broader poem.

In another surface divergence, Brooks merges "the ballad of Edie Barrow" before returning to the story of the search. I am not totally sure of the entrance of the ballad in the poem. However it does not seem out of place because of the mosaic pattern already established, and it offers a view of experience both lyrical and realistic, as the other experiences have been presented. Edie Barrow could well be an inhabitant of the Mecca. The ballad, one of the first poetic forms and one that joins audience with balladeer/storyteller, offers another view (closely following the "Law" scene) of interracial machinations (this time between Jews and Gentiles) and their dislocating effects on human relationships and perceptions. The ballad seems to sit on an angle of the poem and foreshadows the poem's own discovery of violence, although in this poem's case the violence is inner-directed: both intraracial and internal. Janheinz Jahn has contrasted the ballad with the blues tradition that functions in other sections of the poem. The blues territory is "subjective," as shown in the speech and thought monologues of characters, whereas the ballad describes a third-person experience such as in Edie Barrow's story. Both, however, have either direct or indirect references to the racial background of certain experiences.[13]

Hyena, "the striking debutante," describes Pepita as "a puny and putrid little child." This early description becomes important when we finally discover her for ourselves and discover her sense of herself.

There is something circular in even the vertical and horizontal progressions of this poem, as we return to characters we met in the beginning and see them anew in their responses to the loss of Pepita. Prophet (One Visit Can Keep You Out of the Insane Asylum) Williams, for instance, yawns and asks, "Pepita who?" He solidifies the contradictions of a character who "advertises in every colored journal in the world," who is a bringer of cures and lucky hands but does not know this one "colored" child, much less how to find her.

A quick succession of other characters appears during the search for Pepita: Eunie "the intimate tornado," Simpson "the peasant king," "Great-uncle Beer"—"laughter joker gambler killer," Wezlyn "the wandering woman," "Insane Sophie" ("If you scream, you're marked 'insane'"). Staccato narrative seems to reproduce the rhythms of the "mad life." "But silence is a *place* in which to scream! / Hush. / An agitation in the bush. / Occluded trees. . . . / Things slant."

We are constantly taunted with the question: "How many care, Pepita?" And there is another rapid succession of names and multiple identities: Darkara, who looks at *Vogue* (mischievous paradox, signifying); Alfred's "Apologie"; the sixty-ish sisters "with floured faces"; Way-out Morgan, collecting guns ("Death-to-the-Hordes-of-the-White-Men!"); Marian, mixing "Gumbo File or roux"; Pops Pinkham, who like others "forgets Pepita" and talks of other things;

and Dill, "the kind of woman you peek at in passing and thank your God or zodiac you may never have to know." All the characters, despite their paradoxes, are "black and electric," as Alfred would poeticize them.

At the poem's conclusion we discover Pepita; at least we discover her murderer: "Jamaican Edward denies and thrice denies a dealing of any dimension with Mrs. Sallie's daughter." But it is the "dimensions" of Pepita that are really revealed at the end of the poem, not through the musings of others that have seemed to bring her greater invisibility, although the search has granted them their visibility. We learn about Pepita through what she has *thought* and *said* of herself:

> She never learned that black is not beloved.
> Was royalty when poised,
> sly, at the A and P's fly-open door.
> Will be royalty no more.
> "I touch"—she said once—"petals of a rose.
> A silky feeling through me goes!"
> Her mother will try for roses.
>
> (*WGB*, p. 403)

To the mosaic of voices and multiple black personalities is added Pepita's voice. In its simplicity, however, it becomes perhaps a real answer for the poem and a key to the poem's meaning. In another poem, "First Fight. Then Fiddle," Brooks has used the phrase "civilize a space." It is Pepita who civilizes the space of this poem, and who represents the "streak of sun." Although Pepita has either been invisible through most of the poem, or offered in distorted images through the mirrors of others, in the end she speaks for herself and becomes perhaps the most vital voice of the community in speaking her own (to use Ellison's phrase) "sense of possibility" in the world. Pepita, in fact, might be seen as an antithesis of Mrs. Sallie's vision of self. One need not always wait for correction to decorate; correction—of place or character—can come in the *act of doing*—of "trying for roses."

Notes

1. Gwendolyn Brooks, *The World of Gwendolyn Brooks* (New York: Harper and Row, 1971), pp. 377–403. Hereinafter cited in the text as *WGB*.

2. Gwendolyn Brooks, *Report from Part One* (Detroit: Broadside Press, 1972), 189–90. Beverly Guy-Sheftall quotes this precise section of Brooks's autobiography in her article, "The Women of Bronzeville," in *Sturdy Black Bridges: Visions of Black Women in Literature,* ed. Roseann P. Bell, Bettye J. Parker, and Beverly Guy-Sheftall (New York: Anchor Press/Doubleday, 1979), p. 158.

3. Sherley A. Williams, "The Blues Roots of Contemporary Afro-American Poetry," in *Chant of Saints,* ed. Michael S. Harper and Robert B. Stepto (Urbana: University of Illinois Press, 1979), p. 130.

4. Ruth Miller, ed., *Blackamerican Literature* (Beverly Hills, Calif.: Glencoe Press, 1971), p. 414.

5. Gayl Jones, "Oral Tradition in Modern Afro-American Literature" (manuscript).

6. Quincy Troupe and Rainier Shulte, eds., *Giant Talk* (New York: Vintage, 1975), pp. xxxiv–xxxv.

7. John Wideman, "Frame and Dialect: The Evolution of the Black Voice," *The American Poetry Review* 5 (Sept./Oct. 1976): 36.

8. Ruth Finnegan, *Oral Literature in Africa* (London: Oxford University Press, 1970), p. 456.

9. Guy-Sheftall, "The Women of Bronzeville," p. 159.

10. Kit Reed, *Story First* (Englewood Cliffs, N.J.: Prentice-Hall, 1982), p. 50.

11. Williams, "The Blues Roots," p. 134.

12. Ernest J. Gaines, interviewed by Jeanie Blake, *Xavier Review* 3 (1983): 4. This might also be an example of "worrying the line" that Sherley A. Williams also describes in "The Blues Roots": "repetition in blues is seldom word for word and the definition of worrying the line includes changes in stress and pitch, the addition of exclamatory phrases, changes in word order, repetitions of phrases within the line itself, and the wordless blues cries which often punctuate the performance of the songs" (p. 127).

13. Janheinz Jahn, *Neo-African Literature: A History of Black Writing* (New York: Grove Press, 1968), pp. 173–74.

15

The Ballads
of Gwendolyn Brooks

The ballad is a story told in a particular way. Even a casual reader of Afro-American literature is struck by the place of storytelling across genres. Serious students are especially sensitive to the artifice, to the inner form of tale-telling. For example, in *Bloodline,* an integrated collection of five stories, Ernest J. Gaines creates a folk community of resourceful, tough, knowing individuals whose method of telling about their lives is perfectly suited to their characters and to the events of their days. Gaines's stories seem more oral than written, told by very simple narrators both bawdy and metaphoric. Gaines eschews literary language, digging instead into the black soul field that Richard Wright and Stephen Henderson describe for the homeliness of black folk styling. James Baldwin in his marvelous short story "Sonny's Blues" reveals the ethnic struggle of black Americans, the enervating rage they feel in Sonny's mother's rehearsal of the story of the death of Sonny's uncle—the dead father's brother—when he was a very young man, little more than a boy himself. Readers have been well prepared for this tale of specific woe by Baldwin's use of the sensitive narrator's generalized and lyrical recollections of the foreboding tales he and his contemporaries heard as children gathered about the feet of their elders. The emotional experience of the old folks and of Sonny's mother is made significant, carrying the weight that leads to Sonny's own tale, told haltingly near the end of the story in words, told richly in Sonny's performance as a pianist. Again, in Lonne Elder's *Ceremonies in Dark Old Men,* the occasional and happy tales of Mr. Parker contrast with the blues-singing form of the play. Blue Haven's tale, the story of his relationship with his woman and his son, is his blues. Without this story of his past, Blue Haven would be little more than a stereotypic parasite upon the Harlem community. Without his tales, Mr. Parker could not be perceived by theatergoers as a richly complex individual. The point is that black writers transform a community impulse for tale-telling for a variety of artistic purposes.

The ballad is a special kind of tale. It is a narrative that lifts a character and/or events from the chaotic, undefined flow of experience into a special moment. The ballad differs from the tale in that it is very economical. Details are carefully selected for maximum storytelling effect and for performance with musical accompaniment. Historically, ballads are believed to be communally composed narrative lyrics, orally transmitted and preserved when sufficient linguistic stability exists to make it possible for the material to pass from generation to generation without either vocabulary or syntax becoming unintelligible or verse form awkward.

The ballad is participatory. It goes a giant step beyond the other participatory oral folk forms that all satisfy the desire of humans for a good, exciting story. The ballad satisfies another perhaps more basic human need: the psychic-social need of people to sing, dance, to participate in rituals of enactment, be they familiar, awe-filled, or high-spirited. Ballads, if viewed as they were originally conceived— to satisfy aesthetic and emotional needs—are poetry, music, and drama. Ballads are, in small, what myths and epics are.

The Afro-American ballad is like the ballad *qua sua* in many respects. It is generally impersonal and objective. It tells a definite story. It is lyric. The refrain, an organic part of the work, is structurally important in helping the performer-maker achieve the effect of the story upon an audience. The Afro-American ballad is more than this, however. In the introductory section to "Folk Literature" in *The Negro Caravan*, the distinguished scholar-teacher Sterling Brown makes clear the functional and aesthetic domain of the Afro-American ballad. Black balladeers took (and take) great pleasure in preserving and altering American ballads of the English-Scottish tradition. Their chief pursuit, however, is to "create ballads narrating the exploits of their own heroes and lives . . . to celebrate the outlaw . . . or the swift fugitive . . . or the hero of strength, courage, and endurance."[1] In other words, Afro-American balladeers make redemptive mythology, disagreeing with the definitions that slavery and second-class citizenship impose on blacks.

In ballads like "John Henry," "Bad Man Ballad," "Stackalee," "The Escape of Gabriel Prosser," and "Railroad Bill," characters are busy proclaiming, demonstrating, being somebody in a cultural context that would deny them basic humanity. A community can be heroic, too. In his arrangement of "Gallis Pole," the classic blues and ballad singer Ledbetter alters the lyrics, the attitudes, the meaning of "Hangman" in such a way that an entire community, having accepted the absurd condition of the narrator's jailing, pours out things to preserve one of their own. Parents, friends, wife affirm the narrator's worth by frustrating a culture that demands his death, but will let him live if he will accept being a commodity.

In dealing with the absurdity of the black condition in the United States, balladeers sometimes infuse in their work the play of good humor, of wry wit, of side-splitting exaggeration and bombast. Black heroes occasionally overcome their absurd struggle with a jive-styled reaction, a high seriousness that turns upon a sense of the irony of the situation.

Brooks has written nine ballads. The ones I shall write about are "the ballad of chocolate Mabbie," "Sadie and Maud," "of De Witt Williams on his way to Lincoln Cemetery," "Ballad of Pearl May Lee," "A Bronzeville Mother Loiters in Mississippi. Meanwhile a Mississippi Mother Burns Bacon," "The Last Quatrain of the Ballad of Emmett Till," and "The Ballad of Rudolph Reed."

The first two ballads are, on the surface, alike in their having child personae or in being about children. A reader considers the way these ballads project the depth of the black experience. In "the ballad of chocolate Mabbie,"[2] Brooks creates two kinds of surprises. The first is that the puppy love affair of a little girl for a little boy is lifted to high seriousness. The other surprise is that a child of seven, the girl, learns a most painful lesson: Color caste exists, and her most important human relationships for the rest of her life might be determined by the color of her skin.

The first surprise is not sudden. It slowly develops, as feature by feature Brooks projects a child as a passionate woman. This surprise is opened to readers by the second line of the ballad and is developed through four of the six stanzas in a manner that creates charming and delicate humor. The first lines of the first three stanzas echo the melody, the word choice, and the word order of literary ballads like "The Fair Flower of Northumberland" and "William and Margaret" overlaid with a suggestion of paratactic simplicity appropriate to the subject matter of the ballad:

> And Mabbie was all of seven.
> And Mabbie was cut from a chocolate bar.
> And Mabbie thought life was heaven.
> . . .

> He would surely be coming soon.
> . . .
> It was woe for our Mabbie now.

The word "and" that begins lines two, three, and four of the first stanza contributes further to the "little girl" speaker effects of the ballad in two ways. First, an unsophisticated storyteller is hinted at. Second, metrical regularity is achieved, a bouncy, light rhythm.

When in stanza two, Brooks begins to disclose Mabbie's more than little girl passions, she departs from the original syntactic pattern of completed simple sentences. Here, and in stanza three, she elaborates syntax somewhat for emphasis:

> When she sat by him in history class
> Was only her eyes were cool.

In this complex sentence, "eyes" and "cool" are in emphatic positions, "eyes" as the delayed subject of the sentence and "cool" the last word of the sentence and the stanza, rhyming with "school." Next comes:

> It was Mabbie without the grammar school gates
> Waiting for Willie Boone.

where the second line is a participial modifier.

Brooks varies the sentence patterns of stanza two and the beginning of stanza three at line eleven when, for one line, she plays a melodramatic key. Alarm, impatience, eagerness are all suggested, eased by sibilants and the long open sounds.

> Half hour after the closing bell!
> He would surely be coming soon.

These two lines, as well, briefly change the pace of the stanza with their suggestion of somberness.

Stanza four begins in an uproariously funny fashion. The melodramatic note is struck again, heightened by the word "oh" and the lushness of lengthened nasals and liquids. Jammed against the two lines anticipatory of joys are the next two lines of the stanza, somewhat like the earlier two, which foretell Mabbie's unhappiness. Because ballads do not, as a rule, forecast their conclusions, much of their appeal resides in the economically and generally objective, almost disinterested telling of a story that builds to a startling conclusion. Brooks's variation is simply more of her technique of "swelling" the story. The more it swells, the more trivial it is seen to be, and the funnier. Her laughter is gentle, however. Brooks introduces just the right sentimentally personal tone, inviting readers in ("my dears" could be the ballad audience), instructing them in the proper emotions. For Mabbie *is* sweet as chocolate and an innocent lover.

The penultimate stanza sustains the good fun readers have been having. Mabbie's love is characterized as "saucily bold." Willie has got to be energetic and superbly self-confident. Brooks uses the language of *True Confessions* and *Love Story* circa 1940 to describe Mabbie's competition for Willie's affections:

> He wore like a jewel a lemon-hued lynx
> With sand-waves loving her brow.

The speaker's admiration for Mabbie and, in stanza four, her concern for Mabbie's heartbreak determine the tone of the language with which Mabbie's rival is described. Her skin color and the texture of her hair are noted. But more than that is suggested in the carefully elaborated sentence. Mabbie is precious. She is chocolate sweet, loving, constant. The rival is the color of lemon, and it is suggested that lemons are sour. She is cat-like with all the connotations of slyness and danger. At seven or eight, she is seductive, knowing the arts of hair styling and insinuating walk. Mabbie is badly outclassed.

The second surprise of the ballad is carefully related to the development of the first. Mabbie knew instantly why Willie preferred the lemon-hued lynx to her: the color of her skin. The last stanza is stripped of every fun-making device used earlier. The first line of the poem is repeated as the first line of the final stanza with one major substitution. The word "alone" replaces "without," setting the tone of darkness that penetrates the stanza. In the earlier ones, readers looked out with and at Mabbie at the grammar school gates, the classroom, and Willie's promenade with the other girl. Now, readers are inside Mabbie, in that darkness where she attempts to make meaning of her broken romance. Assonance and alliteration, "Mabbie/Mabbie," "hush/heart," the long open vowels, in this place with this meaning, fit the onset of bitter and painful understanding.

"The ballad of chocolate Mabbie" appears at its beginning to be artless. "Sadie and Maud" (*WGB*, p. 16) seems totally artless. It is a song seemingly told by a child who appears to be skipping rope outside an old house where one of two sisters, Maud, still lives. The story is the history of the family told in light rhythms. And because it is a community story, not furtive and fresh gossip, but set in nursery rhyme manner, it is an old story.

But there is much artifice here. The persona is not a child, for the primary image of the poem, the image that characterizes the absent sister, is mature and knowing.

> Sadie scraped life
> With a fine-tooth comb.
>
> She didn't leave a tangle in.
> Her comb found every strand.

Sadie herself could not have better revealed the quality of her life: full, greedy for experience, knowing pain and pleasure. Sadie's death is described with as much worldliness as her life-style has been characterized:

> When Sadie said her last so-long
> Her girls struck out from home.
> (Sadie had left as heritage
> Her fine-tooth comb.)

Sadie's life has been a series of experiences. She has jauntily waved each one off and on the center stage of her momentary concern. Death, then, is not made any more of than any other experience. There's a dash, a bit of jive to her taking leave of life. And her children have inherited this same way of enduring.

Other family members are revealed even more charily, two of them without benefit of imagery. Maud and the sisters' parents were shamed—nearly to death—at Sadie's pregnancies. Maud, surviving her sister and parents and living in the old house, is now a thin brown mouse.

Brooks's method seldom elicits pity for her characters as melodrama might. Her method, instead, compels readers to respect the people she portrays more often than not. So Brooks controls the family history in the simple, artless form of a nursery rhyme. The method permits the poet to project a tone in which the pathetic, the tragic are handled rather like a loose garment. The catchy, bouncy style gives vigor to the material, capturing the flavor of vital living somehow, anyhow. Tragedy might become a shroud, but it is not allowed to be so. Another feature of nursery rhyme form is that it permits many more words to be emphasized. Nothing is lost: Maud's slight story, Sadie's pregnancies, the parent's shame, Sadie's casual departure from life, her girls' lust for living. So much happening creates a rather scatter-gun effect, an unlikely characteristic of the dramatic or the tragic.

The ballad must be rounded. Sadie has been the subject from lines two through eighteen. Maud must be given her due. And she is, in the final section.

> Maud, who went to college
> Is a thin brown mouse.
> She is living all alone
> In this old house.

Again, apparent artlessness is brilliant artifice. The poem has to end in some way. But by seeming to toss off old Mousy Maud, the poet plumbs the well of the family tragedy. The unrealized, silent sister's story is the equal of Sadie's. Sadie seems to have rushed to her grieving end. Maud passively approaches hers.

"Sadie and Maud" is a superior poem, a delightful, disarming con, and a painful/pleasant memory play about the momentness of the lives of Sadie, her children, Maud, and the parents/grandparents. The ballad "of De Witt Williams on his way to Lincoln Cemetery" (*WGB*, p. 23) is as fine: brief, terse, allusive.

> He was born in Alabama.
> He was bred in Illinois.
> He was nothing but a
> Plain black boy.
>
> Swing low swing low sweet sweet chariot.
> Nothing but a plain black boy.
>
> Drive him past the Pool Hall.
> Drive him past the Show.
> Blind within his casket,
> But maybe he will know.
>
> Down through Forty-seventh Street:
> Underneath the L,
> And—Northwest Corner, Prairie,
> That he loved so well.
>
> Don't forget the Dance Halls—
> Warwick and Savoy
> Where he picked his women, where
> He drank his liquid joy.
>
> Born in Alabama.
> Bred in Illinois.
> He was nothing but a
> Plain black boy.
>
> Swing low swing low sweet sweet chariot.
> Nothing but a plain black boy.

The first refrain, "He was born in Alabama. / . . . nothing but a / Plain black boy," is compressed Afro-American history, post-Reconstruction. With the Chicago *Defender* in the 1920s describing the promised land to Alabama, Mississippi, and Georgia Negroes, the migratory stream became a flood. Two particles floating on the rising tide were De Witt and the adult or adults who brought him North. De Witt's history is told plainly however, in two short, simple, unembroidered sentences, lines one and two. The remainder of the first refrain particularizes, apparently by stereotyping. The phrase "black boy" recalls Richard Wright's lyrical autobiography. Wright suggests the emotional turmoil, the struggle for identity, the conflicts between adult realities and man/child dreams that wash over Brooks's use of the term. The adjective "plain" is chosen to restate the first two lines of the poem, lines that catch the history of a people. Because that history—and De Witt's—is anything but plain, the usage prepares for the possibility of masking, of a kind of ironic poetic statement.

"Of De Witt" contains a second refrain. The first one can be thought of as read by a minister, relative, or good Christian friend over the body of the deceased. The second one seems to continue the sentiments of the first. The first line, for instance, is from a Negro spiritual of funereal and redemptive content. It has been changed however, made jazzy like Louis Armstrong's swinging "When the Saints Go Marching In." The speaker here, a real street buddy of De Witt's, introduces a joyous, urban individuality into the sadness of the funeral. The spiritual line has been expanded, and the voice of the speaker gives both De Witt and himself a unique Isness. The *s*'s can be held a long time. The vowels can be sounded at many different registers. The liquids in the line can have almost any coloration and vibrato. This solo line allows nearly unlimited improvisational freedom in the middle of the quiet refrain.

Stanzas one and two are ordinary even to the point of repetitions in lines seven and eight and in their sing-song rhythms. The rhythms are held to throughout stanza three, varying at the last line of the stanza preceding the double refrain:

> . . . where
> He drank his liquid joy.

Other than at the second refrain, no other line in the ballad is imagistic. The speaker of the second refrain, who has just given a private blues-black sound to the line from the spiritual, does it again with the uplifting and lengthy "liquid joy."

In small space, Brooks reveals a life. Four verbs directly characterize De Witt, only three of them actions for which he is solely responsible. He *picked* his women, he *drank* his liquid joy; he *loved* the city,
the congregated blackness of his turf. These three verbs evoke a man
skillful at symbolic transformation, at putting value in the place
where he was, at lifting the moment up, and making it glitter.

> Swing low swing low sweet sweet chariot.
> Nothing but a plain black boy.

If De Witt represents symbolic transformation, Pearl May Lee of
the "Ballad of Pearl May Lee" (*WGB*, pp. 44–47) is a grown-up Mabbie
with a difference. Mabbie contains her feelings; Pearl May exposes
hers, moaning, screaming them.

> Then off they took you, off to the jail,
> A hundred hooting after.
> And you should have heard me at my house.
> I cut my lungs with my laughter,
>> Laughter,
>> Laughter.
> I cut my lungs with my laughter.
>
> They dragged you into a dusty cell.
> And a rat was in the corner.
> And what was I doing? Laughing still.
> Though never was a poor gal lorner,
>> Lorner,
>> Lorner.
> Though never was a poor gal lorner.

Like "Edward" and "The Three Ravens," Pearl's ballad begins in the
middle, the identity of "they," "you," and "I" held back. What the
"you" has done is not immediately disclosed, but it has stirred a
community and has provoked the "I" to excessive laughter. Setting
the refrain formula in place with the word "laughter," a result of
some crime the "you" has committed, Brooks early establishes the
relation between "I" and "you" as sadistic. The effect is chilling.

The ballad, then, becomes the "poor gal's" history of her relationship with Sammy, of Sammy's relationships with other women, of
his preference for bright and white females, of Sammy's lynching by
the aroused white men in the town, all threaded through the
woman's anguish at her loss of Sammy's love and her anger at
Sammy's rejection.

Pearl's anguish is indicated not only by her admitting she is lonely,
while trying desperately and unsuccessfully to lift herself from her

depression. She also experiences vicariously every event related to the story she tells. She imagines the flirtation between Sammy and the white woman, although it is possible he cockily told Pearl about it! Too, it may have been the subject of community gossip. Sammy could not have told her, however, about the rendezvous or about the accusations of rape, the rat in the cell, the lynching. Pearl is able to enter into the white woman's psyche, to be black man, to penetrate the interrelated attitudes of guilt, rage, lust, sexual fascination, and to contain them all. This reveals the young woman's complexity and near emotional breakdown.

After revealing the event, and the four characters—one the community—in the first five stanzas, the speaker makes quite clear the reason for it all in stanzas six through eight: Sammy's fascination, even in boyhood, with the white female and his love-hate for black women. The speaker suggests Sammy used black women, as one uses food or drink, but that he idolized white women. Because they were unattainable, he desired them.

> Yellow was for to look at,
> Black for the famished to eat.
>
> You grew up with bright skins on the brain.
> And me in your black folks bed.

Disbelieving a young white woman's proposition.

> Then a white girl passed you by one day,
> And, the vixen, she gave you the wink.

Sammy thought about the offer, knowing its potential danger, but could not resist.

Stanzas eleven through thirteen characterize the young white woman and her community. She has been fascinated by Sammy but, after the sexual act, shame and another kind of power, differing from that that seduced Sammy to the rendezvous, the power to incite white men to protect her against her own sexuality, govern her behavior. She says "rape," and the community compulsively lynches Sammy, stealing him from the town jail.

"Ballad of Pearl May Lee" has an unwell-made quality that is deliberate. Pearl has got to talk, so she goes on and on and on for sixteen stanzas, fingering her blues, punishing herself as a black woman for having to tell such a story about losing her man to a white woman. There is an earthiness and forthrightness about the ballad that helps characterize Pearl May as a straightforward, uncomplicated, down-home girl. She uses folk speech and imagery that act as attitudinal reference points in her assessment of black/white/man-woman relations.

White women are honey, milk, cream, nourishment of a kind, unsubstantial. After one has tasted them, one wants—needs—more solid food, "dark meat" that can satisfy a famished spirit. The dinner Sammy had was too costly. Sammy drank his fill of his dream, then paid dearly in the real world with his brown body, Pearl's red heart, and their salty tears. Pinks, whites, yellows pale to insignificance in this hierarchy of valuing words.

Another feature in the making of the ballad is the use of pointed repetition. Early in the poem Brooks emphasizes the speaker's laughter and the hooting when the sheriff speaks. The first blues-bitter note with the juxtaposition of Pearl's voice and the imagined sheriff's voice comes in stanza three:

> "You son of a bitch, you're going to hell!"
> 'Cause you wanted white arms to enfold you,
>   Enfold you,
>   Enfold you.
> 'Cause you wanted white arms to enfold you,

Repetition effectively clarifies the ambiguity of the speaker's voice, which is both chummily friendly and pain-filled, then sarcastic.

> But you paid for your white arms, Sammy boy,
> And you didn't pay with money.
> You paid with your hide and my heart, Sammy boy,
> For your taste of pink and white honey,
>   Honey,
>   Honey.
> For your taste of pink and white honey.

The refrain "honey/honey/honey" is both a term of loving endearment used sarcastically and a referent to Sammy's white love.

Stanza five attempts a forthright statement of the consequences of Sammy's behavior, but it begins with the blues maker's styling to survive her pain:

> Get me a garment of red to wear.
> You had it coming surely,
>   Surely,
>   Surely.
> You had it coming surely.

So, what seems a matter-of-fact statement of results is a masking of Pearl May's pain.

In stanzas six and seven, Brooks repeats entire lines. The word "often" is used with great force. The word is repeated six times, revealing the love/hate relationship existing between the black woman and man.

> Often and often you cut me cold,
> And often I wished you dead.
> Often and often you cut me cold.
> Often I wished you dead.

In stanza eight, the thrice-repeated "you thought" about an affair with a white woman renders Sammy's tortures. In stanza nine, lust is heightened by

> The fire within you winding . . .
> Winding,
> Winding. . . .
> The fire within you winding.

and his satiety by the content of the repeated lines in stanza ten.

> Say, she was white like milk, though, wasn't she?
> And her breasts were cups of cream.
> In the back of her Buick you drank your fill.
> Then she roused you out of your dream.
> In the back of her Buick you drank your fill.
> Then she roused you out of your dream.

Already mentioned are the young white woman's shame and one of the forms of her power. The repetitions are effective in conveying these two qualities:

> "You raped me, nigger, and what the hell
> Do you think I'm going to do?
> What the hell,
> What the hell.
> Do you think I'm going to do?
> . . .
> You got my body tonight, nigger boy.
> I'll get your body tomorrow.
> Tomorrow,
> Tomorrow.
> I'll get your body tomorrow."

The townspeople hooted in the first stanza of the poem. At stanza thirteen, in the act of lynching Sammy

And they laughed when they heard you wail.
    Laughed,
    Laughed.
They laughed when they heard you wail.

Two kinds of laughter shape the poem, the speaker's laughter to keep from crying and the community's laughter at committing violence on one of its members. The speaker's laughter and her toughness in stanza fourteen are more of the doublenesses found in the poem. Throughout "Ballad of Pearl May Lee," poetic significance is primarily achieved by the speaker's saying one thing and meaning another, the mask shown the public giving way in private to blues-black anguish.

And I was laughing, down at my house.
Laughing fit to kill.
You got what you wanted for dinner,
But brother you paid the bill.
    Brother,
    Brother.
Brother you paid the bill.

"A Bronzeville Mother Loiters in Mississippi. Meanwhile, a Mississippi Mother Burns Bacon" (*WGB*, pp. 317–23) is a poem in which Gwendolyn Brooks appears to unfold playfully in the form of the classical ballad the developing agony of the white Mississippi mother whose husband killed a young Negro boy. The ballad is the very muscular substructure of the poem, however, not something overlaying the material. The reason ballad form initially seems an overlay is that it is the white woman who conceives of the events of the last weeks as like a ballad: she, the "maid milk," has been insulted by the dark villain and her prince-husband has defended her honor by killing him. She, confusing ballads with fairy tales and romances, has found them appealing because they exalt chastity and coolly express sexuality while stirring the blood. The Mississippi mother, however, has never understood the form or content of the ballad, for the ballad is a story about visceral anguish that builds through surprises to chilling climaxes. Brooks then very cleverly chose the ballad way of disclosing a deeply despairing story that its main actor thinks no more than an adventure at its beginning.

Bearing the Mississippi mother's misunderstanding of the ballad in mind, the first two segments seem insignificant—the mother playing with concepts she does not comprehend—until one rereads them.

Segment three is somewhat wasted too, although here the mother is perplexed and inattentive to her household responsibilities. She burns the bacon and hides it.

Brooks excels in expanding the heart of the ballad, the developing consciousness of the white mother. The poet achieves the expansion by a technique of transforming early images of villainy, violence, and blood into images of innocence and culpability, while images of goodness, high motives, and princely behavior become inverted and malevolent. The mother begins to question her early definitions of villainy in segment four, although the beginning of segment three, already referred to, is portentous. She learned in high school that ballad villains were grossly evil. Yet, the Dark Villain, now disclosed to have been adolescent, is perceived to have not been totally evil.

> The hacking down of a villain was more fun to think about
> When his menace possessed undisputed breadth, undisputed height,
> And a harsh kind of vice.
> . . .
> The fun was disturbed, then all but nullified
> When the Dark Villain was a blackish child
> Of fourteen, with eyes still too young to be dirty,
> And a mouth too young to have lost every reminder
> Of its infant softness.
>
> (*WGB*, p. 318)

The mother still largely accepts her early definition; "perhaps" he should have been older. But, since he wasn't, there still was a lot of fun and excitement when he was hacked down. Furthermore, as the mother imagines the villain may have thought, he responded in surprise rather than in terror to the rushing onslaught of the prince and his lieutenant. The mother is thinking a little.

While she is beginning to reexamine her ideas about villainy, the mother observes the prince's behavior. As her storybook hero, he was fine, the one who bestowed Happiness-Ever-After on her. Now she perceives him as "something ridiculous," his companion "heavy" as they rushed "rich with breadth and height and / Mature solidness . . ." at the slim villain. Two words are used to prefigure the ominous character of the mother's eventual perceptions and to reveal the horror of the action. The words are "blood" and "hack/hacking." Brooks plays with the words "composition," "pattern," and "breaks" as the mother loses her composure and her pleasure at being the storybook princess. Old ballad ideas and the mother's attitudes toward the death of the villain are being radically changed. "Red," "blood," and "lipstick" become symptomatic of the mother's participation in the horror. She feels the horror most keenly as she prepares for the prince's homecoming. Her sense of worthlessness and growing fear of the prince govern her behavior.

The next four segments of the ballad belong to the prince. Shown dining, talking proudly about the culture he has defended when he killed the villain, slapping one of his two little children for dining-table misbehavior, the prince is distanced further and further from the knightly ideal in which the princess early held him. He is shown to be guilty and callous. Half-sneers work across his sweet and pretty face as he reads northern newspaper accounts of his trial. He looks again and again at the hands that have hacked down the villain, proud of himself.

The suddenness with which the prince slaps their child jolts the mother-princess, bringing to a head the inchoate thoughts, attitudes, fears that have worried her. The "Hand," capitalized now, becomes an evil force, evoker of blood, so frightening that her child becomes for an instant the child-villain. That child becomes any child disappearing in a tide of blood. The cries of her children repeat the child-villain's cramped cries when he was being hacked to death. The cries of all the children startle the mother into recognizing that the villain has become the prince, and she is as fearful as the child-villain was just before his death. Fear "[ties] her as with iron."

The prince puts his hands on the princess. The poet transforms that touch-embrace from the love/lust touch the prince intended to a grip so frightening that the princess-mother imagines herself bleeding as the murdered child did and as she imagines her children doing.

Brooks has inlaid the ballad tradition upon the story of an American region: its undescribed characters, its plot line begun at a moment of crisis, its incremental and significant organization of episodes. She makes ironic and despairing commentary upon the definitions and attitudes the majority culture has assigned to whites and to blacks in that region. The irony is self-evident. It is despairing because the prince in destroying definitions has destroyed a familial relationship that he is too innocent to repair, and the princess finally too aware to restore.

> Then a sickness heaved within her. The courtroom Coca-Cola,
> The courtroom beer and hate and sweat and drone,
> Pushed like a wall against her. She wanted to bear it.
> But his mouth would not go away and neither would the
> Decapitated exclamation points in the Other Woman's
> eyes.

> She did not scream.
> She stood there.
> But a hatred for him burst into glorious flower,
> And its perfume enclasped them—big,
> Bigger than all magnolias.
>
> The last bleak news of the ballad.
> The rest of the rugged music.
> The last quatrain.

"A Bronzeville Mother . . ." is the only one of Brooks's ballads in which the poet assumes the persona of a white person. In her other ballads, a black persona, in typical ballad tradition, has written out of a community consciousness from which the social norms and attitudes of personae and actors have come. Brooks has generally kept qualities of black styling at the forefront of those ballads. In the Mississippi ballad, however, the turbulence the persona undergoes, resulting in the triumph of her conscience over the conscience of her community, has been approximated in the modernity of the poet's presentation: its verse paragraphs, its desertion of rhyme and meter, its ironic mode, its tensive manipulation of the meditative and the dramatic.

"The Last Quatrain of the Ballad of Emmett Till" (*WGB*, p. 324), a fragment, completes "A Bronzeville Mother. . . ." In eight loose lines, Brooks defines the numbness of Emmett Till's mother:

> Emmett's mother is a pretty-faced thing;
>   the tint of pulled taffy.
> She sits in a red room,
>   drinking black coffee.
> She kisses her killed boy.
>   And she is sorry.
> Chaos in windy grays
>   through a red prairie.

The poet chooses a persona observing the profoundly sorrowful woman. The persona shows an exterior, leaving one to infer the interior from what is shown. Mrs. Till is on the other side of suffering, at a place where she is detached and her body's wrenching period has been replaced by frozen prettiness. The action of drinking coffee is formal. One senses her emotional arrest.

Not only do these lines render numbness. Carefully selected color words—taffy, red, black, grey, red again—convey different qualities. "Taffy" carries no special weight at the point where it is used. The "redness" of the room conveys much emotion and many facts: Emmett's blood and pain, Mrs. Till's anger, hatred, and anguish. The "black" of the coffee registers one boundary of her mood—its biliousness, its ugliness, its rot.

The final two lines are imagistic in the Pound manner. They play readers inside the mother's mood and outside to the world where events like Till's murder do happen. Mrs. Till is desolate ("gray"). The desolation boils, writhes, rises. All other mental conditions are overcome by the rising and boiling. The woman's appearance shown in the first two lines of the poem is a fragile mask fronting a potentially cataclysmic whirlwind. The last two lines also repeat the image of "A Bronzeville Mother. . . ." and complete it. The lines read

> . . . a red ooze was seeping, spreading darkly, thickly,
>   slowly,
> Over her white shoulders, her own shoulders,
> And over all of Earth and Mars.

The desolation of aborted human community, the barren black and white lives are expressed in the final lines of "The Last Quatrain. . . ."

However, the basic facts of "The Ballad of Rudolph Reed" (*WGB*, pp. 360–62) are these: Reed, his wife, and their three children, having lived in a rundown neighborhood, move to an area of town largely populated by whites. The Reeds are not wanted there. First rocks and then gunshots threaten the Reeds' safety. A shot on the third night grazes one child. Reed kills four white men and is killed.

This story of violent emotions and actions is told in a very plain, contained manner, established in the first stanza.

> Rudolph Reed was oaken.
> His wife was oaken too.
> And his two good girls and his good little man
> Oakened as they grew.

The image of the oaken Reeds embodies the unique reality this black family endured, a reality that exists for the parents and becomes the children's reality as they grow. It is not particularly fresh. It does not reveal new meanings and associations. As the poem develops, however, it becomes clear that the image is fitting. First, stanzas two through five, Mr. Reed's credo and vision, reveal the extent to which he is controlled by a dream so overpowering that he cannot comprehend any event that would deny it. Stanzas six through nine project the tensions between the real world and the world Mr. Reed dreams of. At this point in the poem, therefore, several contrasts—practical, moral, aesthetic—are engaged, creating in the consciousness of readers a balance of competing motives, moods, and impulses. The oakness-dream contrast is central to this balancing. An oaken man would not seem to be one who can be moved by a dream. In an earlier poem, "kitchenette building," Brooks evokes the dream's wisp-like, tenuous nature. Yet, despite its tenuousness, the Reeds have been seduced by the siren song of their dream to the extent that they are disarmed and undefended against the reality that has oakened them. The reality is expressed in the following ways:

> It was in a street of bitter white
> That [the Reeds] made [their] application

and

> The agent's steep and steady stare
> Corroded to a grin.

and

> A neighbor would *look*, with a yawning eye
> That squeezed into a slit.

The dream attained is simply described.

> For were they not firm in a home of their own
> With windows everywhere
> And a beautiful banistered stair
> And a front yard for flowers and a back yard for grass?

Eventually, the intrusions of the world of rock throwing and sniping upon the dreamed-of world force to the forefront of consciousness the tensions and frustrations the parent Reeds have known for a toil-filled lifetime. The dream becomes a nightmare because a man must be oaken *and* must dream too.

Brooks has been an innovative poet. She is also an artist in whom the forces of tradition and continuity have enriched her craft. She has written carefully disciplined and well-wrought sonnets in the tradition of Shakespeare. Metrical craft and poetic form have been as much a consideration for Brooks as they have been in her antecedents Yeats and Frost. The metaphysical wit and irony of Eliot, Pound, Frost, and the younger Robert Lowell have exerted a significant influence on the poet. The basic and central free-verse tradition that comes to Brooks through Walt Whitman, James Weldon Johnson, Sterling Brown, William Carlos Williams, and her beloved Langston Hughes is especially strong. Certain features of her art originate in the black folk art forms—the blues, the ballads, the folk tales, the sermons Brooks grew up with—as well as in the works of Shake-speare, Frost, Dickinson, et al. The poet's penchant for understatement, her wry and ironic humor, her terseness, her skill in giving her poetry the sound of the human voice, and the ethnotrophic metaphor she creates are brilliantly present in her ballads as they are in the folk ballad antecedents. The Brooks ballad reveals one stream of the multiple literary influences that flow through her poetry.

Notes

1. Sterling Brown, Arthur P. Davis, and Ulysses Lee, eds., *The Negro Caravan* (New York: Arno Press, 1969), p. 425.
2. Gwendolyn Brooks, *The World of Gwendolyn Brooks* (New York: Harper and Row, 1971), p. 14. Hereinafter cited in the text as *WGB*.

—— **16** ——

Gwendolyn the Terrible:
Propositions on Eleven Poems

For more than three decades now, Gwendolyn Brooks has been writing poetry that reflects a particular historical order, often close to the heart of the public event, but the dialectic that is engendered between the event and her reception of it is, perhaps, one of the more subtle confrontations of criticism. We cannot always say with grace or ease that there is a direct correspondence between the issues of her poetry and her race and sex, nor does she make the assertion necessary at every step of our reading. Black and female are basic and inherent in her poetry. The critical question is *how* they are said. Here is what the poet has to say about her own work: "My aim, in my next future, is to write poems that will somehow successfully 'call' . . . all black people: black people in taverns, black people in alleys, black people in gutters, schools, offices, factories, prisons, the consulate; I wish to reach black people in pulpits, black people in mines, on farms, on thrones; *not* always to 'teach'—I shall wish often to entertain, to illumine. My newish voice will not be an imitation of the contemporary young black voice, which I so admire, but an extending adaptation of today's G. B. voice."[1]

"Today's G. B. voice" is one of the most complex on the American scene precisely because Brooks refuses to make easy judgments. In fact, her disposition to preserve judgment is directly mirrored in a poetry of cunning, laconic surprise. Any descriptive catalog can be stretched and strained in her case: I have tried "uncluttered," "clean," "robust," "ingenious," "unorthodox," and in each case a handful of poems will fit. This method of grading and cataloging, however, is essentially busywork, and we are still left with the main business. What in this poetry is stunning and evasive?

To begin with, one of Brooks's most faithfully anthologized poems,

"We Real Cool," illustrates the wealth of implication that the poet
can achieve in a very spare poem:

> We real cool. We
> Left school. We
>
> Lurk late. We
> Strike straight. We
>
> Sing sin. We
> Thin gin. We
>
> Jazz June. We
> Die soon.[2]

The simplicity of the poem is stark to the point of elaborateness. Less
than lean, it is virtually coded. Made up entirely of monosyllables and
end-stops, the poem is no non-sense at all. Gathered in eight units of
three-beat lines, it does not necessarily invite inflection, but its
persistent bump on "we" suggests waltz time to my ear. If the reader
chooses to render the poem that way, she runs out of breath, or trips
her tongue, but it seems that such "breathlessness" is exactly required of dudes hastening toward their death. Deliberately subverting the romance of sociological pathos, Brooks presents the pool
players—"seven in the golden shovel"—in their own words and
time. They make no excuse for themselves and apparently invite no
one else to do so. The poem is their situation as *they* see it. In eight
(could be nonstop) lines, here is their total destiny. Perhaps comic
geniuses, they could well drink to this poem, making it a drink-
ing/revelry song.[3]

Brooks's poetry, then, is not weighed down by egoistic debris, nor is
her world one of private symbolisms alone, or even foremost; rather,
she presents a range of temperaments and situations articulated by
three narrative voices: a first-person voice, as in "Gay Chaps at the
Bar,"

> We knew how to order. Just the dash
> Necessary. The length of gaiety in good taste.
> Whether the raillery should be slightly iced
> And given green, or served up hot and lush.
> And we knew beautifully how to give to women
> The summer spread, the tropics, of our love.
> When to persist, or hold a hunger off.
> Knew white speech. How to make a look an omen. . . .
> (*WGB*, p. 48)

an omniscient narrator for the ballads,

> It was Mabbie without the grammar school gates.
> And Mabbie was all of seven.
> And Mabbie was cut from a chocolate bar.
> And Mabbie thought life was heaven. . . .
>
> (*WGB*, p. 14)

and then a concealed narrator, looking at the situation through a double focus. In other words, the narrator ironically translates her subject's ingenuousness. To this last group of poems belongs "The Anniad," perhaps one of the liveliest demonstrations of the uses to which irony can be put.

A pun on *The Aeneid* or *The Iliad*, the title of this piece prepares us for a mock-heroic journey of a particular female soul as she attempts to gain self-knowledge against an unresponsive social backdrop. At the same time, the poem's ironic point of view is a weapon wielded by a concealed narrator who mocks the ritualistic attitudes of love's ceremony. The poem is initially interesting for its wit and ingenuity, but eventually Brooks's dazzling acrobats force a "shock of recognition." Annie, in her lofty naiveté, has been her own undoing, transforming mundane love into mystical love, insisting on knights when there are, truly, only men in the world. Annie obviously misses the point, and what we confront in her tale is a riot of humor—her dreams working against reality as it is. We protest in Annie's behalf. We want the dream to come true, but Brooks does not concede, and that she does not confirms the intent of the poem: a parodic portrayal of sexual pursuit and disaster.

Shaped by various elements of surprise, "The Anniad" is a funny poem, but its comedy proceeds from self-recognition. Brooks gives this explanation: "Well, the girl's name was Annie, and it was my little pompous pleasure to raise her to a height that she probably did not have. I thought of the *Iliad* and said, I'll call this 'The Anniad.' At first, interestingly enough, I called her Hester Allen, and I wanted then to say 'The Hesteriad,' but I forgot why I changed it to Annie . . . I was fascinated by what words might do there in the poem. You can tell that it's labored, a poem that's very interested in the mysteries and magic of technique . . . (*Report*, p. 158).

From the 1949 Pulitzer Prize-winning volume, *Annie Allen*, "The Anniad" may be read as a workshop in Brooks's poetry. Its strategies are echoed in certain shorter poems from *A Street in Bronzeville* and *The Bean Eaters*, particularly the effective use of slurred rhyme and jarring locution in "Patent Leather" and "The Sundays of Satin-Legs

Smith." In narrative scope and dramatic ambition, "The Anniad" anticipates *In the Mecca*, written some twenty years later.

Forty-three stanzas long, "The Anniad" is built on contradictions. Locating their "answer" or meaning constitutes the poem's puzzle and reward. Here are the two opening stanzas:

> Think of sweet and chocolate,
> Left to folly or to fate.
> Whom the higher gods forgot,
> Whom the lower gods berate;
> Physical and underfed
> Fancying on the featherbed
> What was never and is not.
>
> What is ever and is not.
> Pretty tatters blue and red.
> Buxom berries beyond rot.
> Western clouds and quarter-stars,
> Fairy-sweet of old guitars
> Littering the little head
> Light upon the featherbed. . . .
> (*WGB*, p. 83)

After saying all we can about the formal qualities of these stanzas, we are still not certain about the subject of the poem. By means of slurs and puzzles of language, the action is hustled on, and circumlocution—"tell the truth, but tell it slant"—becomes a decisive aspect of the work's style. This Song of Ann is a puzzle to be unraveled, and the catalog of physical and mental traits deployed in the first fifteen stanzas becomes a set of clues. Not unlike games or riddles played by children, the poem gathers its clues in stanzas, and just as the questioner in the child's game withholds the solution, the speaker here does the same thing, often to the reader's dismay. However, once we know the answer, the game becomes a ritual where feigned puzzlement is part of the ceremony. In a discussion of Emily Dickinson's poetry, Northrup Frye points out that the "riddle or oblique description of some object" is one of the oldest and most primitive forms of poetry.[4] In "The Anniad" the form gains a level of sophistication that is altogether stunning.

The dilemma of Annie is also that of "chocolate Mabbie": the black-skinned female's rejection by black males. The lesson begins early for the black woman, as it does for young Mabbie. A too well-known theme of black life, this idea is the subject of several of Brooks's poems, but usually disguised to blunt its edge of madness and pain. With Mabbie's experience in mind, then, we are prepared for the opening lines of "The Anniad" and their peculiar mode of indirection.

The color theme is a crucial aspect of the poem's proposition and procedure, posing light skin and dark skin as antagonists. The question is not merely cosmetic, because hot combs and bleaching creams were once thought to be wonder workers, but it penetrates far and sharp into the psychic and spiritual reaches of the black woman's soul. I know of no modern poet before Brooks to address this subject, and as she does so, she offers the female a way out not only by awakening the phobia, but also by regarding it as yet another style of absurdity. The point is to bury inverted racism in ridicule and obscure reference, but not before contemplating its effects.

In "the ballad of chocolate Mabbie," the situation goes this way:

> Out came the saucily bold Willie Boone,
> It was woe for our Mabbie now.
> He wore like a jewel a lemon-hued lynx
> With sand-waves loving her brow.
>
> It was Mabbie alone by the grammar school gates.
> Yet chocolate companions had she:
> Mabbie on Mabbie with hush in the heart.
> Mabbie on Mabbie to be.
>
> (WGB, p. 14)

An interesting contrast to Mabbie's ballad is "Stand Off, Daughter of the Dusk":

> Stand off, daughter of the dusk,
> And do not wince when the bronzy lads
> Hurry to cream-yellow shining.
> It is plausible. The sun is a lode.
>
> True, there is silver under
> The veils of the darkness.
> But few care to dig in the night
> For the possible treasure of stars.
>
> (WGB, p. 121)

If metaphor is a way to utter the unutterable, then "cream-yellow shining" and "veils of darkness" hint at it, but both are needlessly quaint, drawing attention away from the subject. Not one of her best or most interesting poems, it does articulate the notion of rejection without preaching a sermon about it. In "The Anniad," by contrast, the mood is sardonic and words are ablaze with a passion to kill, both the situation and one's tendency to be undone by it.

The male lover's ultimate choice to betray "sweet and chocolate" leads Annie's "tan man" to what he would consider the better stuff:

> Gets a maple banshee. Gets
> A sleek slit-eyed gypsy moan.
> Oh those violent vinaigrettes!
> Oh bad honey that can hone
> Oilily the bluntest stone!
> Oh mad bacchanalian lass
> That his random passion has!
>
> (*WGB*, p. 88)

Clever synecdoche works here for the poet rather than against her, as it does in "Stand Off," and its comic distortions are reinforced by slant rhyme in the last two lines of the stanza. "Bad" honey is the best kind in colloquial parlance, "bad" having appropriated its antonym, and in the midst of "vinaigrettes" and "bacchanalian lasses," it is a sharp surprise. "Tan man" himself gets similar treatment:

> And a man of tan engages
> For the springtime of her pride,
> Eats the green by easy stages,
> Nibbles at the root beneath
> With intimidating teeth.
> But no ravishment enrages.
> No dominion is defied.
>
> Narrow master master-calls;
> And the godhead glitters now
> Cavalierly on his brow.
> What a hot theopathy
> Roisters through her, gnaws the walls,
> And consumes her where she falls
> In her gilt humility.
>
> How he postures at his height;
> Unfamiliar, to be sure,
> With celestial furniture.
> Contemplating by cloud-light
> His bejeweled diadem;
> As for jewels, counting them,
> Trying if the pomp be pure.
>
> (*WGB*, pp. 84–85)

Rodent, knight, god, by turn, "Tan man" is seen from a triple exposure: his own exaggerated sense of self-worth, the woman's complicity with it, and the poet's assessment, elaborated in the imaginative terms implied by the woman's behavior. Given the poem's logic, the woman and the man are deluded on opposing ends of the axis of self-delusion. As it turns out, he is not the hot lover "theopathy" would make him out to be, but Annie denies it, fearing that to say so would be to evoke an already imminent betrayal:

> Doomer, though, crescendo-comes
> Prophesying hecatombs.
> Surrealist and cynical.
> Garrulous and guttural.
> Spits upon the silver leaves.
> Denigrates the dainty eves
> Dear dexterity achieves.
>   . . .
> Vaunting hands are now devoid
> Hieroglyphics of her eyes
> Blink upon a paradise
> Paralyzed and paranoid.
> But idea and body too
> Clamor "Skirmishes can do.
> Then he will come back to you."
>   (WGB, pp. 85–86)

This scene of "ruin," brought on by sexual impotence, gains a dimension of pathos because it anticipates the woman's ultimate loneliness, but this judgment is undercut by the caricature of the male.

In order to fully appreciate the very pronounced contrast between other Brooks poems and this one, we should note the quality of images in "The Anniad." The dominant function of imagery here is auditory rather than visual, because Brooks, as well as the reader, is so thoroughly fascinated with the sound of words: for example, "Doomer, though, crescendo-comes / Prophesying hecatombs." This heavy word-motion is sustained by the most unlikely combinations—"surrealist and cynical," "garrulous and guttural," etc. The combinations are designed to strike with such forceful contrariness that trying to visualize them would propel us toward astigmatism. We confront a situation where the simple image has been replaced by its terministic equivalent, or by words that describe other words in the poem.[5]

Brooks's intensely cultivated language in "The Anniad" appears to rely heavily on the cross-reference of dictionaries and thesauruses. Lexis here is dazzling to the point of distraction, but it is probably a feature of the poem's moral ferocity. It is clear that the poet, like others, has her eye on the peculiar neurosis that often prevails in sexual relationships. Rather than dignify it, she mocks its vaunted importance, exaggerating its claims nearly beyond endurance. In effect, exaggeration destroys its force, desanctifying hyperbolean phallic status. At the same time, it appears that a secondary motivation shadows the primary one—the poet's desire to suggest a strategy for destroying motives of inferiority in the self. This psychological motif in Brooks's early poetry is disturbing. At times it appears to verge on self-hatred, but style conceals it. "Men of Careful Turns" offers an example, I think, by depicting an interracial love affair corrupted by racism and certain intervening class loyalties. To conceal her disappointment, the black female narrator claims moral superiority over the white male, but in this case, as in "The Anniad," the literal situation is carefully disguised.

In the hands of a lesser poet, Brooks's pyrotechnics would likely be disastrous, but Brooks achieves her aims by calibrating the narrative situation of the poem to its counterpoint in the "real" world. Grounded in solidly social and human content, the poem is saved from sliding off into mere strangeness. The mischievous, brilliantly ridiculous juxtapositions achieve a perspective, and we gain thereby a taste for, rather than a surfeit of, exaggeration toward a specific end: to expose the sadness and comedy of self-delusion in an equally deluded world.

By contrast, a poem whose principle of composition is based on continuity of diction is another of the sonnets, "still do I keep my look, my identity . . ." A model of precision, the poem reworks a single sentence to elaborate its message:

> Each body has its art, its precious prescribed
> Pose, that even in passion's droll contortions, waltzes,
> Or push of pain—or when a grief has stabbed,
> Or hatred hacked—is its, and nothing else's.
> Each body has its pose. No other stock
> That is irrevocable, perpetual
> And its to keep. In castle or in shack
> With rags or robes. Through good, nothing, or ill.
> And even in death a body, like no other
> On any hill or plain or crawling cot
> Or gentle for the lilyless hasty pall
> (Having twisted, gagged, and then sweet-ceased to bother),
> Shows the old personal art, the look. Shows what
> It showed at baseball. What it showed in school.

> (*WGB*, p. 49)

This concentration on a single notion is essential to the working out of the poem, and the qualifying phrases, which establish momentum, create the effect of the poem's being made in front of us. The careful structuring of the body's lines, imitated in time and space, is inherently strategic.

In its directness of presentation, "still do I keep my look" (like "Gay Chaps at the Bar") may be relegated to the category of what might be called Brooks's "pretty" poems: the sword has been blunted by a closer association to the expected. An excerpt from "the old marrieds" provides another example:

> But in the crowding darkness not a word did they say.
> Though the pretty-coated birds had piped so lightly all
>   the day.
> And he had seen the lovers in the little side-streets.
> And she had heard the morning stories
>   clogged with sweets. . . .
>
> (WGB, p. 3)

The opening poem of *A Street in Bronzeville*, "the old marrieds," belongs to Brooks's early career. Its tender insistence is matched elsewhere: for instance, "In Honor of David Anderson Brooks, My Father" and "The Bean Eaters," both from the volume *The Bean Eaters.* An aspect of the poet's reality, this compassionate response to the lives of old people has its complement in her version of the heroic. Two poems from *After the Mecca*, "Medgar Evers" and "Malcolm X" are celebratory:

> The man whose height his fear improved he
> arranged to fear no further. The raw
> intoxicated time was time for better birth or
> a final death.
>
> Old styles, old tempos, all the engagement of
> the day—the sedate, the regulated fray—
> the antique light, the Moral rose, old gusts,
> tight whistlings from the past, the mothballs
> in the Love at last our man forswore.
>
> Medgar Evers annoyed confetti and assorted
> brands of businessmen's eyes.
>
> The shows came down: to maxims and surprise.
> And palsy.

Roaring no rapt arise-ye to the dead, he
leaned across tomorrow. People said that
he was holding clean globes in his hands.
                                    (*WGB*, p. 410)

A poem for the slain civil-rights leader of Mississippi, "Medgar
Evers" reconciles celebration and surprise. Brooks has not exaggerated a feature of reality—Evers's heroism—but has invested that
reality with unique significance. A similar notion works for "Malcolm X," with a touch of the whimsical added:

Original
Ragged-round.
Rich-robust.

He had the hawk-man's eyes.
We gasped. We saw the maleness.
The maleness raking out and making guttural the air
and pushing us to walls.

And in a soft and fundamental hour
a sorcery devout and vertical
beguiled the world.

He opened us—
who was a key,

who was a man.
                                    (*WGB*, p. 411)

In these two poems, as well as others from the later volumes,
Brooks explores various kinds of heroism by means of a shrewd
opposition of understatement and exaggeration. From *The Bean
Eaters*, "Strong Men, Riding Horses" provides a final example:

Strong Men, riding horses. In the West
On a range five hundred miles. A Thousand. Reaching
From dawn to sunset. Rested blue to orange.
From hope to crying. Except that Strong Men are
Desert-eyed. Except that Strong Men are
Pasted to stars already. Have their cars
Beneath them. Rentless, too. Too broad of chest
To shrink when the Rough Man hails. Too flailing
To redirect the Challenger, when the challenge
Nicks; slams; buttonholes. Too saddled.

I am not like that. I pay rent, am addled
By illegible landlords, run, if robbers call.

What mannerisms I present, employ,
Are camouflage, and what my mouths remark
To word-wall off the broadness of the dark
Is pitiful.
I am not brave at all.

(*WGB*, p. 313)

This brilliant use of familiar symbols recalls the staccato message of movie advertisements. It conjures up heroes of the Western courtly love tradition from Charlemagne to Gawain to John Wayne to Superman. Counterpoised against this implied pantheon of superstars is a simple shrunken confessional, the only complete declaratives in the poem. That the speaker pits herself against the contrived heroes of a public imagination suggests that the comparison is not to be taken seriously. It is sham exactly because of the disparity between public idealism and the private condition, but the comic play-off between the poet's open, self-mocking language (a pose of humility) and the glittering, delirious "dig-me-brag" of the "strong men" is the demonstration, more precisely, of the opposing poles of reality—exaggeration and understatement. In the world of Gwendolyn Brooks, the sword is double-edged, constantly turning.

Only a fraction of the canon, the poems discussed in this essay represent the poet's range of strategies to demonstrate her linguistic vitality and her ability to allow language to penetrate to the core of neutral events. The titles of Brooks's volumes, from *A Street in Bronzeville* to *In the Mecca*, suggest her commitment to life in its unextraordinary aspects. Reworking items of common life, Brooks reminds us that creative experience can be mined from this vast store of unshaped material. To see reality through the eyes of the clichéd or the expected, however, is not to revisit it but to hasten the advance of snobbery and exclusion. In her insistence that common life is not as common as we sometimes suspect, Brooks is probably the democratic poet of our time. That she neither condescends nor insists on preciousness is rewarding, but, above all, her detachment from poetry as cult and cant gives her access to lived experience, which always invigorates her lines. By displacing the familiar with the unfamiliar word, Brooks employs a vocabulary that redefines what we know already in a way we have not known it before. The heightened awareness that results brings to our consciousness an interpenetration of events which lends them a new significance.

Some of Brooks's poems speak directly to situations for which black women need names, but this specificity may be broadened to define situations that speak for other women as well. The magic of irony and humor can be brought to bear by any female in her most dangerous life-encounter—the sexual/emotional entanglement. Against that entanglement, her rage and disappointment are poised, but often impotently, unless channeled by positive force. For women writers, decorum, irony, and style itself are often mobilized against chaos. Thus, women don't cry in Brooks's poetry nor does she cry over them, but the poet is remarkably alive and questioning in the dialectical relationship she poses between feeling and thinking. Hers is a tough choice of weapons because it has little use for the traditional status of women—connubial, man-obsessed. The style of Brooks's poetry, then, gives us by implication and example a model of power, control, and subtlety. No ideologue, Brooks does not have to be. Enough woman and poet, she merges both realities into a single achievement. Comedy and pathos, compassion and criticism are not estranged integers in this poetry, but a tangled skein of feeling, both vital and abstract, imposed on a particular historical order. With a taste for the city and an ear for change, Gwendolyn Brooks restores the tradition of citizen-poet.

Notes

1. Gwendolyn Brooks, *Report from Part One: An Autobiography* (Detroit: Broadside Press, 1972), p. 183. Hereinafter cited in the text as *Report.*
2. Gwendolyn Brooks, *The World of Gwendolyn Brooks* (New York: Harper and Row, 1971), p. 315. Hereinafter cited in the text as *WGB.*
3. Brooks's reading of "We Real Cool" is somewhat different from my own (*Report*, p. 185).
4. Northrop Frye, "Emily Dickinson," in *Fables of Identity: Studies in Poetic Mythology* (New York: Harcourt Brace Jovanovich, 1963), p. 202.
5. Kenneth Burke, "On Words and the Word," in *The Rhetoric of Religion: Studies in Logology* (Berkeley: University of California Press, 1970), pp. 14ff.

III

"Daughter of the Dusk":

Maud Martha

—— 17 ——

Nuance and the Novella: A Study
of Gwendolyn Brooks's Maud Martha

*M*aud Martha, Gwendolyn Brooks's only novel, appeared in 1953, the same year that *Go Tell It On the Mountain*, James Baldwin's first novel, was published. By that time, Brooks had already published two books of poetry, *A Street in Bronzeville* (1945) and *Annie Allen* (1949), for which she won the Pulitzer Prize. But although she was an established poet, Brooks's novel quietly went out of print while Baldwin's first publication was to become known as a major Afro-American novel. Brooks's novel, like Baldwin's, presents the development of a young urban black into an adult, although Brooks's major character is female and Baldwin's is male. Brooks's understated rendition of a black American girl's development into womanhood did not arouse in the reading public the intense reaction that Baldwin's dramatic portrayal of the black male did. Yet Paule Marshall (whose 1959 novel, *Brown Girl, Brownstones*, is considered by many critics to be the forerunner of the Afro-American woman's literary explosion of the 1970s), would in 1968 point to *Maud Martha* as the finest portrayal of an Afro-American woman in the novel to date, and as a decided influence on her work.[1] To Marshall, Brooks's contribution was a turning point in Afro-American fiction, for it presented for the first time a black woman not as a mammy, wench, mulatto or downtrodden heroine, but as an ordinary human being in all the wonder of her complexity.

Why is it that *Maud Martha* never received some portion of the exposure that Baldwin's novel did, or why is it still, to this date, out of print, virtually unknown except to writers like Marshall and a small but growing number of black literary critics? Even within the context of black studies or women's studies, Brooks's novel is unknown or dismissed as "exquisite," but somehow not particularly worthy of comment. One could say, of course, that *Maud Martha* was not significant enough to receive such attention. However, comments such as Marshall's tend to nullify that argument. Or one could say that Brooks's accomplishment as a poet overshadowed, perhaps eclipsed, her only novel, although the novel shares so many of her poetic characteristics that one would think that it would attract a similar audience. I am inclined to believe that, ironically, the fate of the novel has precisely to do with its poetic qualities, with the compressed ritualized style that is its hallmark, and as importantly, with the period when it was published.

George Kent tells us in his essay, "The Aesthetic Values of Gwendolyn Brooks," that her pre-sixties poetry was published at a time when the small number of blacks reading black poetry—or any poetry—expected that it be "the expression of interest in the universal, but without the qualifications or unstated premises or doubts regarding Blacks' humanity."[2] And the larger white audience "reflected happiness when they could assure the reading public that the artistic construct transcended racial categories and racial protest . . . and yet paradoxically insisted upon the art construct's informative role, by asserting that the Black artist was telling us what it meant to be a Negro."[3] These observations would, I believe, also apply to the anticipated reading audience of *Maud Martha*, a poetic novel, of the 1950s without any of the sensationalism that characterized popular novels about blacks—a novel that would be considered art. But although *Maud Martha* certainly does have these perspectives, it provides another dimension in that it focuses on a young black girl growing into womanhood without the employment of Afro-American female stereotypes found previously in the novel. While poetry was expected to transcend racial boundaries and aspire toward universality, the novel, by definition, dealt with a specific individual's interaction with her society. The type of interaction that even the small literate audience was used to in the "Negro Novel" was not at all present in *Maud Martha*.

In the novels written by black women in the first half of the century, most featured tragic or not-so-tragic mulattas, as in the Harlem Renaissance novels of Nella Larsen and Jessie Fauset, or the oppressed and finally tragic heroine, as in a protest novel like Ann Petry's *The Street* (1945). Dorothy West's *The Living Is Easy* (1949), the closest in time to Brooks's *Maud Martha*, focuses on a central protagonist who resembles the heroine of the Renaissance period in that an almost histrionic investment in social mobility and decorum is her principal value. And even in that innovative novel of the 1930s

Their Eyes Were Watching God (1937), Zora Neale Hurston imbues her major character with an extraordinary life. However, Brooks's major character is neither an aspiring lady, the major's wife, nor a necessarily beautiful and doomed heroic figure. She lives, like so many of us, an ordinary life, at least on the surface. An excerpt from the novel distinguishes its stance from its predecessors. "On the whole, she felt, life was more comedy than tragedy. . . . The truth was, if you got a good Tragedy out of a lifetime, one good, ripping tragedy, thorough, unridiculous, bottom-scraping, *not* the issue of human stupidity, you were doing, she thought, very well, you were doing well."[4]

In its insistence on examining the supposed "trivia" that makes up the lives of most black women, their small tragedies and fears notwithstanding, *Maud Martha* ran counter to the tone of "the Negro Novel" that both blacks and whites would have expected in 1953. Brooks replaced intense drama or pedestrian portrayal of character with a careful rendering of the rituals, the patterns, of the ordinary life, where racism is experienced in sharp nibbles rather than screams and where making do is continually juxtaposed with small but significant dreams.

Brooks's portrayal of a black woman whose life is not characterized as "tragic" was perhaps partly because of two overlapping trends in Afro-American life and thought of the 1950s. One was the integrationist thrust that culminated in the Supreme Court decision of 1954. In *From the Dark Tower* Arthur P. Davis points out the complexity of this thrust. On the one hand, black writers, like Wright, Hughes, Himes, and Brooks had participated, through their literature, in the protest movement of the 1940s against racism and poverty, especially its manifestations in the urban ghetto. To some extent, the effect of that literature was the development of an *apparent* climate in the country out of which full integration could develop. Emphasis on the overall black protest movement of that period had been on securing equality through the law, thus the significance of the 1954 Supreme Court decision. On the other hand, "there was surface and token integration in many areas, but the everyday pattern of life for the overwhelming majority remained unchanged. . . . In the meantime he [the Negro literary artist] had to live between two worlds, and that for any artist is a disturbing experience."[5]

In the 1940s, black writers like Richard Wright had presented the everyday pattern of life for the overwhelming majority of blacks in as dramatically tragic a form as possible in an attempt to affect the philosophical underpinnings of America towards its black native sons. One unwanted result of this dramatization was white America's tendency to stereotype blacks as creatures entirely determined by their oppression, a tendency that undermined blacks' humanity as much as the previous attitude that they were genetically inferior. Many black intellectuals' reaction to this "protest" stereotype was to emphasize those qualities blacks shared with all other human beings. Thus the "expression of interest in the universal" could be seen in the major books of the 1950s published by already established writers: for example, Wright's *The Outsider* (1953), in which he attempted to weave together the impact of racism on the black man with philosophical issues about the existential nature of all men, or Ann Petry's *The Narrows* (1953), which is set not in the urban ghetto of *The Street* (1945), but in a small New England city, and which focuses on the relationship between a black man and his white mistress. And *Invisible Man* (1952), perhaps the most influential Afro-American novel of the period, emphasizes this double-pronged approach among blacks, for Ralph Ellison consciously weaves together motifs of both Afro and Euro-American culture as the foundation of the novel's structure. Afro-American writers, in other words, were trying out new settings, approaching new subjects. In general, these new approaches attempted to break the image of the black person as an essentially controlled and tragic individual as well as to dramatize the variety of his or her experiences. The political tone of integration and the literary striving to portray black people's many-sided experiences went hand in hand.

One aspect of these strivings was a return to the chronicle of the black family that was apparent in some of the Renaissance novels of Jessie Fauset. But while her novels were entirely about the upper middle class, whose conventions supposedly mirrored those of their white counterparts, the novels of the 1950s featured lower-middle-class folk set against the background of coherent specifically black communities. Unlike the conventional novel of the 1920s or the protest novels of the 1930s and 1940s, the novel of the fifties put more and more stress on the black community as community. Still, novels like Chester Himes's *The Third Generation* (1954) traced the maturation of a black boy within a family that attempts to restrict his growth.

In fact, many of the novels of the late 1940s and 1950s put some portion of the blame for the conflicts of the main characters on the black wife and/or mother, who is depicted as a powerful embodiment of white-middle-class values. Variations on this theme appear not only in Himes's *Third Generation*, but also in West's *The Living Is*

Easy and in *The Outsider*, novels that precede the infamous Moynihan Report (1966). In the popular arena, the image of the aggressive castrating black female who is bent on making the male toe the line was made popular through Sapphire, a major character in the "Amos n' Andy" radio programs of the late 1940s and 1950s.

Interestingly, the Sapphire image, a variant of the old plantation mammy, became current at a time when sociology, one of the major image-makers of blacks, paid little attention to the black family. As Andrew Billingsley points out in *Black Families in White America* (1966), sociology did not discover the black family until the 1930s, and by the 1950s had virtually abandoned it. The academic view on the black family, the context within which most studies of the black woman were initially conducted, was, during the 1940s and 1950s, represented by E. Franklyn Frazier's *The Negro Family in the U.S.* (1948) and Horace Cayton and St. Clair Drake's *Black Metropolis* (1948).[6] Both studies emphasized the strength of the black mother, her coping with adversities such as poverty, poor housing, and desertion, which ironically was interpreted by many to mean that she was more powerful than the black man and therefore too powerful. And although this attitude would not be fully developed or officially authorized until the Moynihan Report, one can in hindsight see the process by which this view gained currency during the 1950s.

But just as Brooks's Maud Martha is not a tragic figure, neither is she a domineering personality. As daughter and then as a mother, she exhibits little of the willfulness associated with Sapphire or even Cleo, the major character of *The Living Is Easy*. Her strength is a quiet one, rooted in a keen sensitivity that both appreciates and critiques her family and culture. Brooks's portrayal of an ordinary black girl, then, who cherishes the rituals of her community even as she suffers from some of its mores, both conformed to and deviated from the family chronicles of the late 1940s and 1950s. Her emphasis on the black girl within the community is a prefiguring of black women's novels of the sixties and seventies, which looked at the relationship between the role of woman in society and the racism that embattled the black community.

Yet a description of *Maud Martha* as a work of such grand intentions would undercut its peculiar quality. In keeping with its smallness, more precisely its virtual dismissal of the grand or the heroic, *Maud Martha* is a short novel. Properly speaking, it should be called a novella, not only because of its length, but also and more important, because of its intention. Brooks is not interested in re-creating the broad sweep of a society, a totality of social interaction, but rather in painting a portrait in fine but indelible strokes of a Maud Martha. In an interview in 1969 with George Stavros, editor of *Contemporary Literature*, Brooks says of her process: "Well, I had first written a few tiny stories, and I felt that they would mesh, and I centered them and the others around one character. If there is a form I would say it was imposed, at least in the beginning, when I started with those segments, or vignettes."[7] And Brooks goes on to agree with her interviewer when he says that "the unity of the novel is simply the central point of view of Maud Martha herself as she grows up."

Brooks's comments emphasize two points: The centrality of Maud Martha's inner life, for the novella is a revelation of her thoughts, and her reflections on her limited world. Unlike her predecessors, with the exception of Hurston's Janie Stark, Maud Martha is not just a creation of her external world; she helps to create her own world by transforming externals through her thoughts and imaginings. This is a quality seldom attributed to ordinary folk in previous black women's novels. And yet, in illuminating Maud Martha's specific individuality, Brooks must necessarily show her in relation to other people and her physical environment, the basis for the world she knows, imagines, even extends. The other point of emphasis in Brooks's description is her use of the word *tiny* and how diminution affects the form of this novella, the use of segments or vignettes. In all, the 170-page novella is divided into thirty-four chapters, many of which are three or four pages long, few longer than ten pages, "the small prose sections fitting together into something like a mosaic." This double emphasis of the novella is introduced in the first vignette, "description of Maud Martha." Immediately, we are in the midst of Maud Martha's images of fancy and her sense of her own ordinariness and diminutiveness.

> What she liked was candy buttons, and books, and painted music (deep blue, or delicate silver) and the west sky, so altering, viewed from the steps of the back porch; and dandelions. . . . But dandelions were what she chiefly saw. Yellow jewels for everyday, studding the patched green dress of her back yard. She liked their demure prettiness second to their everydayness; for in that latter quality she thought she saw a picture of herself, and it was comforting to find that what was common could also be a flower.
>
> (*MM*, p. 127)

As a prose piece, *Maud Martha* is a fusion of these two qualities, the sensitive and the ordinary, not only in its characterization of its protagonist, but also in the moments the writer chooses to include in her compressed rendition of an urban black woman's life. Yet these moments, as they form a whole, both look back to the novels of the 1940s and towards black women's novels of the 1960s and 1970s. Because the time period of *Maud Martha* is the thirties and forties, it is not surprising that the impact of the depression on black family life (e.g., "home" and " 'at the Burns Coopers' ") are some of the moments Brooks chooses to telescope. But there are also vignettes about a dark girl's feeling of being rejected by her own community ("low yellow," "if you're light and have long hair"), a theme that Toni Morrison would use as the basis for her complex analyses of cultural mutilation in *The Bluest Eye* (1970). There are segments about the relationship between the rituals of a black culture and the development of character ("kitchenette folks," "tradition and Maud Martha"), a structural technique that Paule Marshall would expand and refine in her novels. There are moments that are particularly female ("a birth," "Helen," "Mother comes to call"), themes that would become increasingly important to black women novelists of the seventies. And there are "universal" moments in that human beings, whatever their race, sex, or class, muse about the meaning of existence and the degree of responsibility they must take to shape their own lives ("posts," "on Thirty-Fourth Street"), an underlying theme in Walker's *The Third Life of Grange Copeland* (1970).

Maud Martha then is a work that both expresses the mores of a time passing and prefigures the preoccupations to come. Georg Lukács in his analysis of another novella, Solzhenitsyn's *One Day in the Life of Ivan Denisovich* (1953), points out that novellas often appear at the end of a historical period or at the beginning of a new period, that often they are "either in the phase of a not yet (*noch nicht*) in the artistically universal mastery of the given social world, or in the phase of the no longer (*nichtmehr*).[8] His analysis of the genre is one way of locating the elusive significance of Solzhenitsyn's "exquisite" novella. For in its focus on a single character or situation rather than the totality of a society, and in its economy of presentation, the novella may summarize the essentials of a period that has just ended and be an initial exploration into attitudes that are just forming. The writer, then, although not consciously intending to write a novella, may find that in trying to express the moment of transition from one mode of interpreting reality to another, the present cannot be expressed in the novel of the past, nor is the totality of the new reality understood enough to transform it.

I think that it is important to note that the period of the 1930s and 1940s had been written about in many black novels. Wright's *Native*

Son (1940) is set in that period as is Petry's *The Street* (1945). What Brooks does is to present another version of black life at that time, as she may have experienced it, but also as she could interpret it through the integrationist thrust of the 1950s. Yet she also pointed to future emphases: the sense of the black community as community and the black reaction to imposed white notions of beauty and cultural nationalist concepts of the 1960s, as well as the sensitivity and specificity of the black woman's experience as woman, a pervasive theme of the seventies. In effect, the seeds of these themes were sowed in the thwarted expectations of the integrationist thrust. And although Brooks could hardly foresee the civil rights movement, the black power movement, or the women's movement and their impact on American literature, her experience as she described it in *Maud Martha* was the outline of some of the reasons for the desires and goals of these movements. When Maud Martha's little daughter, Paulette, is rejected by a white Santa Claus and asks "Why didn't Santa Claus like me?" and Maud Martha must try to explain why without saying why, we are witnessing one of the "trivial" but significant reasons for the 1960s black search for nationhood. When Helen, Maud Martha's sister, proclaims to her, "you'll never get a boy friend, . . . if you don't stop reading those books," we hear in Maud Martha's sighs the rumblings of the redefinition of woman that would be attempted in the 1970s. Perhaps, as Arthur P. Davis pointed out, because there was an apparent climate of change but little actual change and the Negro artist of the 1950s was living between two worlds, Brooks's rendition of Maud Martha's life would have to look backward and forward.

Yet Brooks's overt intention in writing *Maud Martha* was not to reinterpret the past or prefigure the future. She tells us that she "wanted to give a picture of a girl growing up—a black girl growing up in Chicago, and of course much of it is wrenched from my own life and twisted . . ." (*Report,* p. 162). In *Report from Part One,* she provides us with a partial list of some of those "twists," how she used her knowledge of her specific community and her perception of her own life and culled from it the essence of "a black girl growing up in Chicago." She also tells us that the first passage she wrote for the novella became the opening of the last chapter (*Report,* pp. 190–93). That passage emphasizes Maud Martha's awareness of the bursting life within her and without her, the result of which is her whisper, "What, *what* am I to do with all of this life?" That question that permeates the entire novella is both its theme and nuance, both the question of all persons in all times, and the question of that specific individual in that specific time. Life was drastically limited for an ordinary black girl in the Chicago of the 1940s, as it was for most ordinary people. And yet, like most ordinary people, there is so much life in Maud Martha. *Whispering* the question emphasizes its ironic truth, for to most institutions, most authorized social processes, even most literature, neither Maud Martha nor her question is at all important.

In a sense, then, the conflict of the novella is contained in its subject, that such a person as Maud Martha is seldom seen as imbued with importance. Thus the question that permeates the entire novella is based not so much on the usual "character in a conflict" motif, but on the gradual unraveling of the life that is in Maud Martha, this ordinary, unheroic girl. The novella does not have intense dramatic rises and falls so much as it is the presentation of a typical life as not at all typical in the flat meaning of the word. And concurrently, it is the embodiment of the idea that a slice of anybody's life has elements of wonder and farce, wry irony and joy. No fire and brimstone need fly. But because the hero or heroine, the exceptional person, has been extolled in most societies, Brooks's orientation is in itself a challenge to a venerated "universal" idea. In framing her intention as she did and in carrying it through in her "tiny" novel, Brooks articulated the value of the invisible Many. The social and literary black movements of the 1960s and 1970s would emerge precisely because these many would insist on the value of their "little" life and would ask the questions, "What, *what* am I to do with all of this life?"

That *Maud Martha* is partially based on Brooks's own experience as a young black girl growing up in the Chicago of the 1930s and 1940s contributes to the authenticity one feels while reading the novel. In other words, Maud Martha is not merely a response to the social images of blacks that were current in the 1950s. It is also a manifestation of Brooks's own philosophy about the relationship between life and aesthetics. She distinguishes a memoir from an autobiographical novel by calling the former "a 'factual' account" while the latter is "nuanceful, allowing." *Maud Martha*, as is true of many novellas, is economical in its presentation. But there are many styles of economic writing. What characterizes this novella is not only its precision but also its nuance, and how these stylistic elements are organic to its underlying theme: the wonderfulness of a Maud Martha.

As a poet, Brooks is known for her precision of language, for the care with which she chooses every word and that "concentration, that crush" in her work. It is not surprising then that *Maud Martha* also shares this characteristic. Brooks says of the poet's unique relationship to language that: "The poet deals in words with which everyone is familiar. We all handle words. And I think the poet, if he wants to speak to anyone, is constrained to do something with these words so that they will 'mean something,' will *be* something that a reader may touch" (*Report*, p. 148).

Her emphasis on the word as being, not as abstraction but as sensory, concrete, underlines her choice of words in her novella as well as her poetry. *Maud Martha* is a compression of images from which the prose radiates. So that in the chapter, "spring landscape: detail" Brooks's description of Maud Martha's school is concrete, sensory: "The school looked solid. Brownish-red brick, dirty cream stone trim. Massive chimney, candid, serious" (*MM*, p. 130).

Most of Brooks's adjectives are certainly concrete. But look at how they move to the words, "candid," "serious," words that are usually abstract but have now become concrete, something you can touch in this spring landscape. And when her description of the solid school is contrasted with the school children whom she describes as "Bits of pink, of blue, white, yellow, green, purple, brown, black, carried by jerky little stems of brown or yellow or brown-black," that blow into the schoolyard, Brooks shows us more than the color or line of this landscape. She evokes the touch, the feel of a configuration of attitudes represented by the solid dullness of the school as opposed to the vibrant playfulness of the children. Hence, the reader is moved from words that may be touched towards nuances that cannot be touched. The precise and the nuance-full work hand in hand.

Not only can one touch Brooks's words, but one can also hear them. Rhythm and sound are not as important to the quality of prose as they are to poetry. However, although *Maud Martha* is written in the form of a prose narrative, Brooks employs many of the techniques she uses in her poetry. The pacing of words through her adroit use of juxtaposition, the alternation of short and longer units, the creation of emphasis through alliteration and imagery, the selection of specific sounds to evoke a certain quality—all these elements are characteristic of the prose of *Maud Martha* and contribute to its quality of nuance. Maud Martha's assessment of her first beau is typical of Brooks's use of rhythm and sound to advance the prose narrative: "For Russell lacked—what? He was—nice. He was fun to go about with. He was decorated inside and out. He did things, said things, with a flourish. That was what he was. He was a flourish. He was a dazzling, long, and sleepily swishing flourish" (*MM*, p. 167).

The emphasis in this two-page chapter is on Maud Martha's recognition of her first beau's grand superficiality, a quality that is not enough to absorb her, although it had vanquished so many others. That the passage quoted above is not just a description of Russell; it is both a process of insight for Maud Martha as well as for the reader. We learn much about her character by feeling her reaction to Russell. Brooks gives us the nuance of Maud Martha's insight as well as the factual through her choice of words, imagery, and sounds. The dashes indicate reflection, the slowing of the pace, as Maud Martha begins her assessment. "He was fun to go about with" is followed by equally short sentences which use repetition to create a gradual quickening of pace, *He* was, *he* did *things*, said *things*, *he was*, until the pace slows down to the moment of recognition "That was what he was." Finally various elements of language, repetition, imagery, alliteration, assonance, combine in the long sentence that summarizes his essence: "He was a dazzling long and sleepily swishing flourish," in which the z's s's and l's, i's evoke Russell as much as the meaning of the words themselves.

Because of her careful use of these poetic devices, Brooks is able to compress the prose narrative, drawing fine outlines of mood, emotions, thought, and events without having to fill in many details. By eliminating the nonessential fact, by creating nuance, we touch, see, hear the whole much in the same way a few deft lines by an accomplished artist can suggest the entire human body. Abstraction of form is only possible because we recognize, know, *what* is being suggested. But even more than recognizing the mood, emotion, event, we can concentrate on its essence without the distraction of the superfluous that can sometimes obscure rather than reveal. And because of Brooks's distillation, our experience is more focused, more intense.

But poetic devices are not enough to make a novella. The form, by definition, involves some kind of narrative, some reflection of external as well as internal reality, some development of character as well as a structure that shows the organic relationship between these elements. So while Brooks employed poetic devices to advantage in *Maud Martha*, she also had to utilize the technique of fiction. Yet the line between her poetic and prose techniques is not a hard one, because her creation of nuance is especially critical to the overall design of the novella. Not only does each vignette evoke the essence of a specific mood, emotion, thought, or event, but it also contributes to a composition that suggests the essence of Maud Martha's character and the pattern that is her life. Brooks's poetic sensitivity is especially apparent in the novella's structure, because she usually selects only those moments that accomplish two things. They reinforce the outline of a pattern that is repeated in many other lines and is being reenacted here, while paradoxically they focus on Maud Martha's individuality. The effect is that of a ritual performed from time immemorial by different actors who can vary the pattern but slightly, the actor this time being this ordinary black girl from Chicago. The tension between these two elements, a pattern that seems prescribed and Maud Martha's transformation of it, moves the narrative.

The pattern of Maud Martha's life is presented in extremely short condensed chapters, thirty-four in all, which are loosely divided into six phases. While Brooks's creation of nuance suggests Maud Martha's inner life, the chapter divisions are the external structure of the novel. These divisions are stages in the universal process of becoming an adult and, therefore, an outline of societal configurations of custom, culture, and historical forces that help to shape that individual. Thus, the phases of early childhood, and school, adolescence, and courtship, work, marriage, the beginning of a family, the impact of the depression of the 1930s and the war of the 1940s are a general outline of life for a young American girl growing up in the 1930s and 1940s. The moments Brooks selects to focus on in these divisions, however, are a reflection to a large extent of her view of that external reality. In concretizing the universal outline, she stresses both the rituals of a black family and community. She outlines the individuality of the girl-woman Maud Martha while emphasizing the impact of the particular concept of beauty, as well as the societal limits of being a woman, upheld by her community on her personality. She focuses on the ordinary tone of Maud Martha's life while stressing the complexity of her inner character. Because we know, in general, the universal concept of growing up; because we know, in general, about family life and community; because we know, in general, the way that girls and women should be, she can evoke these configurations through nuance while emphasizing the uniqueness of Maud Martha's character and context. Thus the "racial element is organic not imposed." And so is her portrayal of womanhood and of the ordinary person.

At the crux of Brooks's composition is the development of her central actor. Of course, the chronology of the novella is its outer movement, but it is Maud Martha's sensibility, her perception of the world that enlivens the narration. Yet Brooks does not use the "I," the first-person point of view. As is her custom in many of her poems (e.g., "the rites for Cousin Vit," "Mrs. Small"), the author creates a character for whom she cares intensely, but from whom she is clearly detached. And although the substance of the novel is told through Maud Martha's eyes, Brooks suggests, by her use of the objective third person, that other eyes see what hers see. While the reader feels intimately connected to Maud Martha, there is constant awareness of the world around her as separate from, and yet connected to, her. Brooks's use of an omniscient narrator who sees through Maud Martha's eyes emphasizes the sensibility of her central actor solidly located in a world of many others. The beginning of the vignette "Tim" illustrates how effective this technique is as a means of establishing Maud Martha's relationship to the outer world:

> Oh, how he used to wiggle!—do little mean things! do great big wonderful things! and laugh laugh laugh.
>
> He had shaved and he had scratched himself through the pants. He had lain down and ached for want of a woman. He had married. He has wiped out his nostrils with bits of tissue paper in the presence of his wife and his wife had turned her head, quickly, but politely, to avoid seeing them as they dropped softly into the toilet, and floated. He had had a big stomach and an alarmingly loud laugh. He had been easy with the ain'ts and sho-nuffs. He had been drunk one time, only one time, and on that occasion had done the Charleston in the middle of what was then Grand Boulevard and is now South Park, at four in the morning. Here was a man who had absorbed the headlines in the *Tribune,* studied the cartoons in *Collier's* and the *Saturday Evening Post.*
>
> These facts she had known about her Uncle Tim. And she had known that he liked sweet potato pie. But what were the facts that she had not known, that his wife, her father's sister Nannie, had not known? The things that nobody had known.
>
> (*MM,* pp. 149–50)

Clearly, Tim and his life exist outside of Maud Martha's head, but it is her language that articulates his individuality. And it is also her language that indicates that she is a woman, is black, and lives in a certain section of Chicago. The way she chooses details that appear trivial on the surface but cumulatively communicate a feeling for and a knowledge of this man—the way she focuses on intimate details that emphasize his relationship with others—are styles of speaking that often indicate a woman's voice. The content of these details tells us that he is a working-class black man who lives in Chicago and is somewhat interested in the world beyond him. And it is typical of Maud Martha's personality that she would ask what was beneath the surface: What were the "things" that nobody had known?

The qualities of Maud Martha's language are, in fact, of considerable importance to the major theme of the novella. Brooks carefully

constructs Maud Martha's voice as that of a woman. The images she
uses throughout the book are often derived from the world of the
home, the world of cooking, flowers, ferns, and furniture, the world of
emotional relationships—worlds that have traditionally been seen as
woman's domain. And much of what Maud Martha says is not said
aloud; it is usually her internal conversations with herself, because
her observations, critiques, and musings are not considered important. There is also a way in which her persistent attention to size
(which sometimes stems from her own feeling of littleness) connotes
"the smaller sex," as well as the ordinary person, a scale that is
reflected in the tininess of the novel itself. And it is often because she
understands that there is sometimes so much in what appears to be so
little that she gleans many insights about herself and her world.

In fact, the critical aspects of Maud Martha's sensibility are her
ability to see beneath the mundane surface of things and to transform
the little that is allowed her into so much more than it originally was.
As Mary Helen Washington puts it, "in her daily life, Maud Martha
functions as an artist. In that way, this novel carries on the African
tradition that the ordinary rituals of daily life are what must be made
into art."[9] In her adolescence, Maud Martha is able to put this insight
into words in the vignette, "at the Regal":

> To create—a role, a poem, picture, music, a rapture in stone: great. But
> not for her.
> What she wanted was to donate to the world a good Maud Martha.
> That was the offering, the bit of art, that could not come from any other.
> She would polish and hone that.
>
> (MM, p. 148)

That awareness of her own being, as valuable, unique, as created by
herself yet connected to those around her, marks her personal development, so that she can refuse to be devalued by her potential
employer, Mrs. Burns-Cooper, although there is only "a pear in [her]
ice box, and one end of rye bread." She can be hurt by her husband's
desire to be a social somebody, understand how that is linked to his
hidden dislike of her dark skin and heavy hair, and yet maintain her
own sense of worth precisely because she has developed her own
standards, her own concept of the valuable.

It is the articulation of this value in Brooks's unheroic ordinary
black girl from Chicago, a value that is celebrated almost only in the
heroic, the extraordinary, the male, that marks the distinctive language, movement, substance of Maud Martha. Through her use of
nuance, Brooks is able to present this celebration in its essential

form, suggesting that Maud Martha is one of any number of ordinary people who, against the limits of the mundane life, continue to create themselves.

Notes

1. Paule Marshall, "The Negro Woman Writer," tape-recorded conference lecture, Howard University, 1968.

2. George E. Kent, "Aesthetic Values in the Poetry of Gwendolyn Brooks," in *Black American Literature and Humanism*, ed. R. Baxter Miller (Lexington: University Press of Kentucky, 1981), p. 84.

3. Kent, "Aesthetic Values," p. 85.

4. Gwendolyn Brooks, *Maud Martha*, in *The World of Gwendolyn Brooks* (New York: Harper and Row, 1971), p. 291. Hereinafter cited in the text as *MM*.

5. Arthur P. Davis, *From the Dark Tower: Afro-American Writers, 1900–1960* (Washington, D.C.: Howard University Press, 1974), p. 138.

6. Gloria Wade-Gayles, "She Who Is Black and Mother: In Sociology and Fiction, 1940–1970," in *The Black Woman*, ed. LaFrances Rodgers-Rose (Beverly Hills, Calif.: Sage Publications, 1980), p. 95.

7. Gwendolyn Brooks, *Report from Part One* (Detroit: Broadside Press, 1972), p. 162. Hereinafter cited in the text as *Report*.

8. George Lukaćs, *Solzhenitsyn*, trans. William David Graf (Cambridge: MIT Press, 1969), p. 7.

9. Mary Helen Washington, "Book Review of Barbara Christian's *Black Women Novelists*," *Signs: Journal of Women in Culture and Society* 8 (Aug. 1982): 179.

18

Maud Martha:

The War with Beauty

Arthur P. Davis's article of December 1962, "The Black-and-Tan Motif in the Poetry of Gwendolyn Brooks," even after twenty years provides a fitting springboard for a discussion of the same motif in Brooks's novel, *Maud Martha*.[1] Davis explores the social theory that among black people the inside color line had tended "to create a problem *within* the group similar to that between colored and white in America."[2] He points out that this color difference within the group caused special problems for the dark girl, who during the early decades of the century was often the object of ridicule among black men.

Davis's social theory is that "as cruel as it was, the whole attitude of ridicule is a natural reaction to the premium which America by law and custom and by its uncivilized institution of segregation had placed on color."[3] To paraphrase and extend Davis's remarks and expand on the literary significance of the social theory, I contend that *Maud Martha* as well as Brooks's poetry makes a sharply ironic commentary on human nature by revealing that in American society rejection is caused less by deep-rooted cultural, religious, or ideological differences than by aesthetic difference, or what we think about body proportions, facial features, skin color, and hair texture. The psychological effect of this familiar and pervasive kind of ridicule and of the standard of beauty in America is explained by psychiatrists William Grier and Price M. Cobbs in "Achieving Womanhood" in *Black Rage*:

> In this country, the standard is the blond, blue-eyed, white-skinned girl with regular features. . . . The girl who is black has no option in the matter of how much she will change herself. Her blackness is the antithesis of a creamy white skin, her lips are thick, her hair is kinky and

short. She is, in fact, the antithesis of American beauty. However beautiful she might be in a different setting with different standards, in this country she is ugly.[4]

Brooks's conscious subscription to this social premise is epitomized by Maud's tendency, like the tendency of the mother in "the children of the poor," to shield, to protect her children from the harshness of the environment. For instance, in Brooks's poem "What shall I give my children? who are poor," when the children

> . . . have begged me for a brisk contour,
> Crying that they are quasi, contraband
> Because unfinished, graven by a hand
> Less than angelic, admirable or sure

the mother laments her powerlessness:

> My hand is stuffed with mode, design, device,
> But I lack access to my proper stone,
> And plenitude of plan shall not suffice
> Nor grief nor love shall be enough alone
> To ratify my little halves who bear
> Across an autumn freezing everywhere.[5]

The same frustration and "baffled hate" are expressed by Maud after her daughter, Paulette, has been virtually ignored by Santa Claus in a department store:

> Maud Martha wanted to cry.
> Keep her that land of blue!
> Keep her those fairies, with witches always killed at the end, and Santa every winter's lord, kind, sheer being who never perspires, who never does or says a foolish or ineffective thing, who never looks grotesque, who never has occasion to pull the chain and flush the toilet.
>
> (*WGB*, p. 203)

Although Maud Martha herself is accepting and supporting as a parent, she never forgets the mild reinforcement of the American standard of beauty by her family. Closely paralleling Brooks's own depiction, Grier and Cobbs further point out the devastating effect when parents wittingly or unwittingly reinforce the standard: "When the feeling of ugliness is reinforced by the rejection of family and society, the growing girl develops a feeling not only of being undesirable and unwanted but also of being mutilated—of having been fashioned by Nature in an ill-favored manner."[6]

Color and color prejudice are also treated from strikingly similar perspectives in the literature of other black writers, particularly black female writers. In her autobiographical novel, *I Know Why the Caged Bird Sings*, for example, Maya Angelou reveals the debasing effect that the pervasive white standard of beauty has on the self-image of black girls. Aware from an early age of the exclusive nature of the standard, Maya thinks that her "new" Easter dress would make her "look like one of the sweet little white girls who were everybody's dream of what was right with the world."[7] As she continues to fantasize, the extent of the demoralization is evident:

> Wouldn't they be surprised when one day I woke out of my black ugly dream, and my real hair, which was long and blonde, would take place of the kinky mass that Momma wouldn't let me straighten? My light-blue eyes were going to hypnotize them. . . . Because I was really white and because a cruel fairy stepmother . . . had turned me into a too-big Negro girl, with nappy black hair, broad feet and a space between her teeth that would hold a number-two pencil.[8]

Maud's own attention to color, features, and hair are paralleled in Brooks's autobiography, *Report from Part One*, and in her poetry.[9] The novel portrays a woman with doubts about herself and where and how she fits into the world. Maud is clearly less concerned with being thought inferior than she is with being perceived as ugly. This concern is filtered through the point of view of an insecure, self-disparaging black woman who feels that she is homely and, therefore, uncherished because she is black and has nappy hair and "Negro features." This perspective leads her to give a disparaging although undue deference to white people and to society's invidious standard of beauty. As I point out in the chapter "Maud Martha" in my introductory study, *Gwendolyn Brooks*:

> She measures herself and her work against the standards of the world and feels that she comes out short inevitably—that white or light beauty often triumphs, though somehow unfairly—and that the deprivation of the beholder is to blame. The book is also about the triumph of the lowly. She shows what they go through and exposes the shallowness of the popular, beautiful, white people with "good" hair. One way of looking at the book, then, is as a war with beauty and people's concepts of beauty.[10]

One of the first casualties of the war is Maud's self-assurance about her own image. Self-doubt is an important part of the novel, providing a rather constant backdrop to almost every vignette. However, the situations where doubt is presented are not simple. Rather, in most cases Brooks holds out something positive such as hope, promise, or comfort, which is then assaulted by the American standard of beauty, leaving a condition of doubt and insecurity that itself often gives way to a grudging deference to whites. Occasionally the positive aspects prevail, leaving a sense of small but sweet victories in individual isolated battles in a larger lost war. This dialectic provides the main tension of the novel.

In "Description of Maud Martha" the stage is set for the war with beauty that is waged throughout the novel by Maud's ready identification with the dandelion, her favorite flower. She refers to them as "yellow jewels for everyday," and "she liked their demure prettiness second to their everydayness. . . ." In so describing the dandelion, she is comparing it to herself, "for in that latter quality she thought she saw a picture of herself, and it was comforting to find that what was common could also be a flower." In this description the word "demure" is important, because it fits the shy, weak nature of Maud's image of her own "prettiness." The everyday or common prettiness of the dandelion contrasts with the more exotic or exquisite beauty of rarer flowers even as Maud's own shy prettiness contrasts with white beauty. Although she thinks the dandelion is pretty, she is aware that others consider it plain or ugly—a weed.

The dialectic potential of this vignette extends to Maud's desires, for "to be cherished was the dearest wish of the heart of Maud Martha Brown. . . ." Because the plain, common dandelion could be cherished, Maud had hope that she, too, could be cherished, although plain. The reader, however, is immediately aware of the tenuous nature of this hope, because it lasts only while Maud is looking at the dandelions. Otherwise, she has doubts that the ordinary dandelion is "as easy to love as a thing of heart-catching beauty." Ironically, it is in Maud's own everyday life when she cannot look at the dandelions to boost her morale that she has the greatest doubts about herself:

> And could be cherished! To be cherished was the dearest wish of the heart of Maud Martha Brown, and sometimes when she was not looking at dandelions (for one would not be looking at them all the time, often there were chairs and tables to dust or tomatoes to slice or beds to make or grocery stores to be gone to, and in the colder months there were no dandelions at all), it was hard to believe that a thing of only ordinary allurements—if the allurements of any flower could be said to be ordinary—was as easy to love as a thing of heart-catching beauty.
>
> (*WGB*, p. 128)

Doubt about the ability to be loved is a permeating theme in the novel, affecting Maud's relationship with her friends and family.

The prime example of a familiar relationship affected by Maud's doubt is that with her sister, Helen. From the earliest descriptions of

Helen she is presented as the exquisite, "heart-catching" beauty—a foil and frequently an adversary to Maud. "Helen" suggests Helen of Troy, the ideal beauty, to contrast the common plainness of a girl whose very name suggests drabness. Helen was not one of those "graven by a hand / Less than angelic, admirable or sure." The rub, however, is that Helen is "easy to love" simply because she is "a thing of heart-catching beauty." The relationship between beauty as it is perceived in the Western world and being loved or cherished is very positive. To further emphasize the importance of beauty in the formula for being loved, Maud points out that in all other considerations, she and Helen were about equal:

> a thing of heart-catching beauty.
> Such as her sister Helen! who was only two years past her own age of seven, and was almost her own height and weight and thickness. But oh, the long lashes, the grace, the little ways with the hands and feet.
>
> (*WGB*, pp. 128–29)

These are not terms of endearment.

Helen's natural proximity as a sister facilitates discussion of the efficacy of beauty. One of the numerous instances that helps to convince Maud that being beautiful brings favors as categorically as being ugly brings rejection is Maud's experience of being rejected by Emmanuel for a ride in his wagon while Helen is accepted. Emmanuel, riding his wagon, approaches the two young girls and asks, "How about a ride?" When the shy Maud uncharacteristically responds with, "Hi, handsome!" Emmanuel scowls and says, "I don't mean you, you old black gal. . . . I mean Helen." Helen gets the ride because she is beautiful—not because she otherwise deserves it any more than Maud. This experience visits and revisits Maud many times during her life. Years later the memory hurts as Maud observes that Helen makes $15 a week as a typist while she, Maud, makes $10 a week as a file clerk. She realizes that the basic situation has never changed. "Helen was still the one they wanted in the wagon, still 'the pretty one,' 'the dainty one.' The lovely one."

Helen remains the favored one because of her beauty. Maud makes the efficacy of Helen's beauty clear by removing all of the other variables:

> She did not know what it was. She had tried to find the something that might be there to imitate, that she might imitate it. But she did not know what it was. I wash as much as Helen does, she thought. My hair is longer and thicker, she thought. I'm much smarter. I read books and newspapers and old folks like to talk with me, she thought.

But the kernel of the matter was that, in spite of these things, she was poor, and Helen was still the ranking queen, not only with the Emmanuels of the world, but even with their father—their mother—their brother. She did not blame the family. It was not their fault. She understood. They could not help it. They were enslaved, were fascinated, and they were not at all to blame.

(*WGB*, pp. 160–61)

Maud is more than merely equal to Helen in all other variables. She deserves Harry's loyalty, but Helen gets it. Their father prefers Helen, although Maud really works harder at getting love and respect by doting on her father and sympathizing with him. Even against these odds, however, Helen's beauty triumphs, making Maud the pauper and Helen the "ranking queen."

One result of continually having life's situations assailed by measurement against an alien and artificial standard is not merely to doubt the possibility of positive evaluations, but to develop the inclination to project the likelihood of negative evaluations. Maud Martha begins as a young girl to project toward the portentous rather than the propitious. In observing those around her, she begins to attribute thoughts and motives to them that are not always self-evident from their behavior. For example, as her thoughts dwell on Helen and her advantages, she assumes that she knows her father's thoughts: "It did not please her, either, at the breakfast table, to watch her father drink his coffee and contentedly think (oh, she knew it!), as Helen started on her grapefruit, how daintily she ate, how gracefully she sat in her chair, how pure was her robe and unwrinkled, how neatly she had arranged her hair. Their father preferred Helen's hair to Maud Martha's (Maud Martha knew) . . . (*WGB*, pp. 162–63). Maud's doubts progressively give rise to more elaborate and more depreciative thinking about her physical appearance. Chapter 13, "low yellow," consists almost entirely of her thoughts like the following about Paul Phillips's thoughts about her color, hair, and features:

I know what he is thinking, thought Maud Martha, as she sat on the porch in the porch swing with Paul Phillips. He is thinking that I am all right. That I am really all right. That I will do. . . .

But I am certainly not what he would call pretty. . . . Pretty would be a little cream-colored thing with curly hair. Or at the very lowest pretty would be a little curly-haired thing the color of cocoa with a lot of milk in it. Whereas, I am the color of cocoa straight, if you can be even that "kind" to me.

He wonders, as we walk in the street, about the thoughts of the people

who look at us. Are they thinking that he could do no better than—me?
Then he thinks, Well, hmp! Well, huh!—all the little good-lookin' dolls
that have wanted *him*—all the little sweet high-yellows that have
ambled slowly past *his* front door—What he would like to tell those
secretly snickering ones!—That any day out of the week he can do better
than this black gal.

(*WGB*, pp. 178–79)

The title of this chapter, "low yellow," accurately and rather bluntly
reflects the subject that weighs heavily on Maud's mind for a significant portion of the novel. There are some moderately auspicious
projections of Paul's assessment of Maud, such as his thinking that
"she will do," or that Maud is "sweet," or that she has "nice ears."
She is also optimistic that she will "hook him" in spite of his predilection for "the gay life, spiffy clothes, beautiful yellow girls, natural hair, smooth cars, jewels, night clubs, cocktail lounges, class."
Still, Maud's realization that she embodies the antithesis of Paul's
"idea of pretty" does not bode well for her sense of security.

In chapter 19, "if you're light and have long hair," Maud is even less
subtle and more pessimistic in her projections. Whereas in "low
yellow" she is able to perceive some benefit of the doubt that she
feels, in "if you're light" she imputes only the most negative interpretation to Paul's behavior. When Paul is invited to attend what to
him is the most important social event imaginable, the Foxy Cats
Dawn Ball, Maud is filled with trepidation and doubt about whether
he will want to take her. Although they are married at the time, she
believes that Paul will take her only grudgingly. She does not feel that
she will fit in with the "beautiful girls, or real stylish ones" at the
ball. She speculates that he will take her only out of a sense of
obligation, and that if he could assemble the right words, he would
tell her that he could tolerate the marriage only as long as he was free.
She further believes he wants to humor her only because she is
pregnant.

In Maud's mind, Paul's behavior at the ball can only mean that he
would rather not be with her. When after their second dance he leaves
her sitting, "she sat, trying not to show the inferiority she did not
feel." Maud is even more concerned when Paul dances closely with
Maella, who is "red-haired and curved, and white as a white." A dark
man dances with Maud, but she hardly notices him for watching Paul
and Maella. The dark dance partner tries to make small talk, and even
tells her, "You're a babe. . . . You're a real babe." Again Maud hardly
notices, but she does notice Paul and Maella and begins to project:
"But it's my color that makes him mad. I try to shut my eyes to that,

but it's no good. What I am inside, what is really me, he likes okay. But he keeps looking at my color, which is like a wall. He has to jump over it in order to meet and touch what I've got for him. He has to jump away up high in order to see it. He gets awful tired of all that jumping" (*WGB*, pp. 213–14).

Whether the threat to their marriage is real or generated out of Maud's insecurity, it is clear from the symbolism of the gradual demise of a snowball bush that Maud believes the threat is real. She is escorted to a chair near a rubber plant, where she sits and briefly considers violently attacking Maella. However, her final thought on the matter suggests that she perceives the problem with Paul's standard of beauty—and consequently with their marriage—to extend far beyond Maella. As she puts it, "But if the root was sour what business did she have up there hacking at a leaf?"

Maud's doubts and her self-deprecating projections attend most of the major events of her life. When her daughter, Paulette, is born, for instance, Maud notices that her mother, Belva Brown, "looked at the newcomer in amazement. 'Well, she's a little beauty, isn't she!' she cried. She had not expected a handsome child." Maud is so sensitive about color and other aspects of appearance that she interprets possibly well-meaning statements as pejorative. Another time Maud imagines that she sees Paul's eye-light take leave of her, and she projects his rejection of her and the life they live together. "She knew that he was tired of his wife, tired of his living quarters, tired of working at Sam's, tired of his two suits." She thinks that Paul's boredom occurs partially because "the baby was getting darker all the time." But that fear could be just as easily attributed to Maud herself, for Maud as mother is very concerned with the war and the battles that Paulette will have to fight as a black girl.

One such battle occurs early in Paulette's life. Maud and Paulette go to a store where there is a Santa Claus. Santa's high enthusiasm for the children suddenly dies when Paulette's turn comes. When Santa is coldly indifferent to Paulette, Maud takes her away. As they leave the store, Paulette wonders why Santa does not like her. Maud finds herself in the same position as the parent in "children of the poor," "holding the bandage ready for your eyes." She lies to Paulette, telling her, "Baby, of course he liked you." Maud views this kind of battle as something peculiar to her. She realizes that neither Helen nor Paul, two people who are very close to her, would have reacted with the same venom with which she reacted. For different reasons neither of them would have had to fight nor to appreciate the same kind of battles that Maud Martha had fought. But the problem for Maud is too real to ignore and too complex to unravel: "She could neither resolve nor dismiss. There were these scraps of baffled hate in her, hate with no eyes, no smile and—this she especially regretted, called her hungriest lack—not much voice" (*WGB*, p. 302).

In spite of the "baffled hate" resulting from fighting and losing many skirmishes in the war with beauty, Maud Martha, being part of the society she fights, ironically subscribes in part to the same standard of beauty that she fights. In spite of herself, she gives a kind of deference to whites and to the society's standard of beauty.

While throughout the novel Maud is overly concerned about other's perceptions of her, she is especially concerned with the perceptions that whites have not only of her, but also of black people in general. That she is aware of and concerned about their perceptions is evident in chapter 5, "you're being so good, so kind," by her hesitancy and fear concerning the visit of Charles, her white schoolmate. She feels that "she was the whole 'colored' race, and Charles was the personalization of the entire Caucasian plan." She defers to him by dashing about straightening up the house and raising all the windows because she is aware that whites often say that "colored people's houses necessarily had a certain heavy, unpleasant smell." Her inordinate concern about the general appearance of her home and the odor in the house is a product of her projecting Charles's thoughts on the situation. When he rings hesitantly, she further ascribes thoughts to Charles that further reveal her doubt that she can be considered favorably, especially by this representative white: "No doubt regretting his impulse already. No doubt regarding, with a rueful contempt, the outside of the house, so badly in need of paint. Those rickety steps" (*WGB*, p. 144). Her deference proceeds to the extent that she is "sickened" to realize that she is grateful for his coming to visit her "as though Charles, in coming, gave her a gift."

Although Maud is sickened at her own fawning behavior during Charles's visit, she makes no comment during David McKemster's soliloquy on the virtues of the good life—"a picture of the English country gentleman"—versus the depravity in the ghetto. This chapter, "second beau," reveals the extent to which one can become unreasonably enamored with a given standard. Beyond his wanting to master the American literary critic, Vernon Paddington, David wishes to adopt white ideals, to emulate the white-middle-class lifestyle.

McKemster's desire in "second beau" to change his style to escape his own heritage (like Satin-Legs Smith) is somewhat comparable to Maud's own desire to change whatever she can to be accepted—to be cherished. The contrast is that although McKemster can effectively affect white styles, Maud will always be plain Maud.

There are times when Maud also engages in the desire to escape her situation. The glitter and shine in Maud's perception of New York in "Maud Martha and New York" is not unlike McKemster's idealized description of the white section east of Cottage Grove. "People were clean," he says, "going somewhere that mattered, not talking unless they had something to say." Maud, meanwhile, sees the material and stylistic splendor of New York as a symbol of what life should be like—jeweled. She, like McKemster, even makes an allusion to the lustrous style of the English as perhaps the accepted pinnacle of style and class. Both McKemster and Maud are products of the ghetto, who dream, realistically or unrealistically, of escaping their situations. It is ironic that in both cases the places and things that they would escape to or through are associated with the very aesthetic that condemns them for being what they are—black Americans. McKemster would shed his black background where his mother had said, "I ain't stud'n you," and his father "hadn't said anything at all," where "he himself had had a paper route. Had washed windows, cleaned basements, sanded furniture, shoveled snow, hauled out trash and garbage for the neighbors." McKemster's dream of changing his life is more materialistic and attainable: "He wanted a dog. A good dog. No mongrel. An apartment—well-furnished, containing a good book-case, filled with good books in good bindings. He wanted a phono-graph, and records. The symphonies. And Yehudi Menuhin. He wanted some good art. These things were not extras. They went to make up a good background. The kind of background those guys had" (*WGB*, p. 172). The fallacy is that one comes with a background. A background is not simply superimposed with the acquisition of cer-tain material things.

Maud's fantasy is more to escape a stultifying mental and aesthetic environment: "What she wanted to dream, and dreamed, was her affair. It pleased her to dwell upon color and soft bready textures and light, on a complex beauty, on gemlike surfaces. What was the matter with that? Besides, who could safely swear that she would never be able to make her dream come true for herself? Not altogether, then!—but slightly?—in some part?" (*WGB*, p. 177). Maud would keep her background, but would have others to evaluate her by a different standard of beauty.

Maud Martha never gets to New York, but David McKemster does take steps toward the fulfillment of his dream. Several years after their first conversation about McKemster's need to acquire a new background, he is ensconced at the University of Chicago. In "an encounter," Maud meets him by chance on the campus. She is hesitant to strike up a conversation because "this was the University world, this was his element. Perhaps he would feel she did not belong here, perhaps he would be cold to her." He is cold to her because she too is part of the black past that he has illusions of shedding. He merely tolerates her company glumly for a few minutes "till they met a young white couple. . . . David's face lit up," and McKemster comes alive with cultured conversation as viewed by Maud Martha: "Had they known about the panel discussion? . . . Tell him, when had they seen Mary, Mary Ehrenburg? Say, he had seen Metzger Freestone tonight. . . . (He lit a cigarette.) Say, he had had dinner with the Beefy Godwins and Jane Wather this evening. Say, what were they doing tomorrow night? . . . (He took excited but carefully sophisticated puffs.). . . . Say, how about going to Power's for a beer?" (*WGB*, p. 255). Maud senses that he wishes to be rid of her. Having completely subscribed to the white values he had idealized earlier, McKemster views Maud as old, excess baggage.

When McKemster offers to have a cup of coffee with Maud and the young white couple, Maud assumes that he is trying to pacify her before "disposing" of her. Maud interprets the young white man's stare as saying, "Well! and what have we here!" Maud Martha's "baffled hates" make her suspect of disparaging, benign, or even friendly gesture alike. It is not easy to be kind to Maud Martha. Maud sees the young white lady as "attractive," suggesting once again that she subscribes to the prevailing standard of beauty even while she fights the effects of it. Maud sees her as bold and confident: "She leaned healthily across the table; her long, lovely dark hair swung at you; her bangs came right out to meet you, and her face and forefinger did too (she emphasized, robustly, some point)" (*WGB*, p. 257).

The references to health and robustness in describing the girl's behavior suggest that Maud would like to be this way. But Maud has not the white face, the "summer-blue eyes. . . . lovely dark hair" nor the confidence (which is itself a testimony to the efficacy of beauty) to do so. She instead describes her own behavior in terms as sharply contrasting as her own physical description would contrast that of the girl. "But herself stayed stuck to the back of her seat, and was shrewd, and 'took in,' and contemplated, not quite warmly, everything" (*WGB*, p. 257). Maud's discomfort is exacerbated by McKemster's attempt to "look down" on her physically as he had been socially, although "when they sat their heights were equal."

Maud's war with beauty, then, is partially internal, for not only does she rail against the standard, but she also grapples with her own ambivalent aesthetic sense in order not to see whites as beautiful and, more critically, in order not to see herself and her daughter, Paulette, as ugly. The crudest application of the standard of beauty is to see whites as beautiful and to see blacks, the antithesis, as ugly. Application of this standard, however, is complicated by the varying degrees to which blacks can approximate the physical attributes that are associated with the standard. Hence, Maud often sees her white or light-skinned rivals as "attractive," "lovely," or "beautiful." In "low yellow," little doubt is left about the deference that Maud and Paul both give to the white standard of beauty. They are contemplating marriage and the kinds of children they would have:

> "I am not a pretty woman," said Maud Martha. "If you married a pretty woman, you could be the father of pretty children. Envied by people. The father of beautiful children."
> "But I don't know," said Paul. "Because my features aren't fine. They aren't regular. They're heavy. They're real Negro features. I'm light, or at least I can claim to be a sort of low-toned yellow, and my hair has a teeny crimp. But even so I'm not handsome."
> No, there would be little "beauty" getting born out of such a union.
> (*WGB*, p. 180)

They both idealize light skin, wavy or straight hair, and fine or regular features. Likewise, it is clear from their conversation that black skin, nappy hair, and "real Negro features" make them less than beautiful in their own eyes.

Well after they are married Maud and Paul continue to show their perhaps unwitting but nonetheless real deference to whites. Being black in a white environment is central in "we're the only colored people here." Maud's only hesitation in asking Paul to go downtown to a movie is that he will object that there are "too many white folks." Once there, they feel conspicuous and alone. They stand in the lobby looking sheepishly about and whispering. Immediately Maud notices the refined "cooked, well cared-for" appearance of the whites and contrasts it favorably to that of the ghetto blacks. At one point Paul is hesitant to approach a white girl at the candy counter to ask about tickets. He is afraid of intruding or even of her coldness. From Maud's point of view she is described as "lovely and blonde and cold-eyed, and her arms were akimbo, and the set of her head was eloquent." Maud and Paul both defer to her whiteness, her beauty. Maud contrasts the white and black environments almost enviously but certainly qualitatively or valuatively. They attribute an uplifting effect just to being in the theater frequented by whites:

> But you felt good sitting there, yes, good, and as if, when you left it, you would be going home to a sweet-smelling apartment with flowers on little gleaming tables; and wonderful silver on night-blue velvet, in chests; and crackly sheets; and lace spreads on such beds as you saw at Marshall Field's. Instead of back to your kit'n't apt., with the garbage of your floor's families in a big can just outside your door, and the gray sound of little gray feet scratching away from it as you drag up those flights of narrow complaining stairs.
>
> (*WGB*, p. 203)

As they leave the theater, they are very concerned with not making the whites feel intruded upon:

> the Negroes stood up . . . looked about them eagerly. They hoped they would meet no cruel eyes. They hoped no one would look intruded upon. They had enjoyed the picture so, they were so happy, they wanted to laugh, to say warmly to the other outgoers, "Good, huh? Wasn't it swell?"
>
> This, of course, they could not do. But if only no one would look intruded upon . . . .
>
> (*WGB*, p. 204)

This kind of deference is associated closely with their sense of aesthetic worth. Both before and after the movie they are self-conscious and apologetic about the appearance of their color, hair, features, clothes, and even, through extension, their very habitats.

Maud continues to defer to whites in various ways such as continued projection of disparaging thoughts into the minds of white people whom she encounters. One such incident occurs in "Millinery," when Maud visits a shop and attributes the following negative thoughts to the white manager: "Oh, not today would she cater to these nigger women who tried on every hat in her shop, who used no telling what concoctions of smelly grease on the heads that integrity, straightforwardness, courage, would certainly have kept kinky" (*WGB*, p. 281). To Maud, the manager is yet another critic finding only fault.

In encountering the manager in the millinery shop Maud is facing her main adversary—the white woman. Therefore, she determines that she can and will win some small victory in the ongoing war with beauty. In Maud's mind the manager cannot bring herself to say that the hat Maud tries on makes Maud beautiful. "Looks lovely on you," she says. "Makes you—" She stops, perhaps searching for the right

word. In her effort to sell the hat to Maud the manager assures her of
what a bargain the hat would be at "seven ninety-nine," and that she
is doing Maud a favor because "you looked like a lady of taste who
could appreciate a good value." At another point when she "looked at
Maud Martha, it was as if God looked." Maud starts twice for the
door. On both occasions the manager stops her with another pitch.
The last ploy is to say that she will "speak to the—to the owner,"
who "might be willing to make some slight reduction, since you're an
old customer." Even when Maud assures the manager that she has
never been in the store before, the manager "rushed off as if she had
heard nothing." Maud's cynical mind completes the act: "She rushed
off to consult with the owner. She rushed off to appeal to the boxes in
the back room" (*WGB*, p. 282).

After having the manager go through the difficulty of finally agree-
ing on the price that Maud has indicated, Maud is delighted to calmly
tell her, "I've decided against the hat." She has made a decision—a
firm, unflinching decision after the white woman has tried in every
way she could to make Maud feel obligated to buy the hat. The
terrible frustration of the manager is captured in the final scene:

> "What? Why, you told—But, you said—"
> Maud Martha went out, tenderly closed the door.
> "Black—oh, black—" said the hat woman to her hats—which, on the
> slender stands, shone pink and blue and white and lavender, showed off
> their tassels, their sleek satin ribbons, their veils, their flower coquettes.
> (*WGB*, pp. 282–83)

All the while the terrible frustration is contrasted with the peaceful
physical background that is unbiased and indifferent, an ironic reflection of that gentle and genteel side of the white woman that her
terrible anger and frustration belie.

It is obvious that Maud's reaction is quite different from Sonia
Johnson's in "the self-solace." When a young white woman comes
into Sonia Johnson's beauty shop to sell lipstick, Sonia listens to her
pitch and finally orders some lipstick. Maud, who is in the shop at the
time, is furious for several reasons. One is that Sonia did not use the
opportunity for a small victory over this young white woman with
what Maud thinks of as "beautiful legs." Maud knows that some
beauticians, glad to have the white saleswomen at their mercy if only
for a few minutes, would make them crawl. They are sometimes
insulting, brusque, and then they "applied the whiplash." "Then
they sent the poor creatures off—with no orders. Then they laughed
and laughed and laughed, a terrible laughter." A second reason Maud

is furious is that the saleswoman sells the order to Sonia, saying that "this new shade . . . is just the thing for your customers. For their dark complexions." Maud wonders if the saleswoman realizes that the "Negro group" included all complexions from those lighter than her own, to "brown, tan, yellow, cream which could not take a dark lipstick and keep their poise." But Maud is primarily furious because the saleswoman has used the word "nigger" and has not been taken to task by Sonia. She has said, "I work like a nigger to make a few pennies." Sonia has an opportunity for a small victory in the continuing war, but she does not take it.

"At the Burns-Coopers" presents Maud with a chance for a small although Pyrrhic victory. Driven by desperation caused by Paul's unemployment and her not being able to find more suitable work, Maud seeks a job as a domestic. Mrs. Burns-Cooper is very superior and authoritative and particularly condescending and unwittingly insulting. Bearing her insults in silence is barely manageable for Maud. Both Mrs. Burns-Cooper and her mother-in-law complain that the potato parings are too thick and proceed to treat Maud like a child: "As though she were a child, a ridiculous one, and one that ought to be given a little shaking, except that shaking was—not quite the thing, would not quite do. One held up one's finger (if one did anything), cocked one's head, was arch. As in the old song, one hinted, 'Tut tut! now now! come come!' " (*WGB*, pp. 288–89).

Maud does not return to the Burns-Coopers'. She says that she cannot explain why to Mrs. Burns-Cooper. Like the millinery shop manager and the lipstick saleswoman, Mrs. Burns-Cooper does not understand that there is a war. As long as they can perceive black women as inferiors who ought to be grateful for the opportunity to work or to buy, they will not even be conscious of the war nor of any casualties on the black side. When there is "retaliation" that amounts only to failure to comply with the wishes of the white women, they are shocked and see Maud and her kind as belligerent and uncooperative. It is hard to fight a war with an enemy who does not know a war is being fought, but who nevertheless has all of the weapons and continues to inflict casualties. Maud's explanation, which would certainly have escaped Mrs. Burns-Cooper, is simply that she is a human being:

> One walked out from that almost perfect wall, spitting at the firing squad. What difference did it make whether the firing squad understood or did not understand the manner of one's retaliation or why one had to retaliate?

Why, one was a human being. One wore clean nightgowns. One loved one's baby. One drank cocoa by the fire—or the gas range—come the evening, in the wintertime.

(*WGB*, p. 289)

The last vignette of *Maud Martha*, "back from the wars!" provides a fitting final comment on the various kinds of war that rage among people. Because World War II is over and her brother, Harry, has returned, she, like others, exults. She does notice, however, that some wars are continuing. "And the Negro press (on whose front pages beamed the usual representations of womanly Beauty, pale and pompadoured) carried the stories of the latest of the Georgia and Mississippi lynchings . . ." (*WGB*, p. 305). This passage, in addition to suggesting that all the wars are not over, refers to the war of black people for freedom and dignity and to the specific war that black women wage with the standards of beauty (which Brooks capitalizes for emphasis).

In the midst, however, of Maud Martha's concern with lynching and color prejudice, she is optimistic. On a sun-filled spring day her hope lies in the fact that man's foolishness cannot destroy even "the basic equanimity of the least and commonest flower: for would its kind not come up again in the spring? come up, if necessary, among, between, or out of—beastly inconvenient!—the smashed corpses lying in strict composure, in that hush infallible and sincere" (*WGB*, p. 305).

The "commonest flower" is the dandelion with which she identifies in the book's first vignette, "description of Maud Martha." Her war continues against "the usual representation of womanly Beauty, pale and pompadoured."

The image is like that of the Phoenix, rising from its ashes, or like the sun and the children in "spring landscape: detail," who on a gray spring day are "little silver promises somewhere up there, hinting," able to shut out all the world's inhibitions and ridiculousness. These images cause Maud to end on a note of hope and promise:

And was not this something to be thankful for?
And, in the meantime, while people did live they would be grand, would be glorious and brave, would have nimble hearts that would beat and beat. They would even get up nonsense, through wars, through divorce, through evictions and jiltings and taxes.
And, in the meantime, she was going to have another baby.
The weather was bidding her bon voyage.

(*WGB*, pp. 305–6)

Notes

1. Arthur P. Davis, "The Black-and-Tan Motif in the Poetry of Gwendolyn Brooks," *College Language Association Journal* 6 (Dec. 1962): 90–97.

2. Davis, "The Black-and-Tan Motif," p. 90.

3. Ibid.

4. William Grier and Price Cobbs, *Black Rage* (New York: Basic Books, 1968), pp. 40–41.

5. Gwendolyn Brooks, *The World of Gwendolyn Brooks* (New York: Harper and Row, 1971), p. 100. Hereinafter cited in the text as *WGB.*

6. Grier and Cobbs, *Black Rage*, p. 52.

7. Maya Angelou, *I Know Why the Caged Bird Sings* (New York: Random House, 1969), pp. 1–3.

8. Angelou, *I Know Why*, p. 2.

9. Gwendolyn Brooks, *Report from Part One* (Detroit: Broadside Press, 1972).

10. Harry B. Shaw, *Maud Martha* in *Gwendolyn Brooks* (Boston: Twayne Publishing, 1980), p. 165.

SELECTED BIBLIOGRAPHY

I. Works by Gwendolyn Brooks

POETRY

A Street in Bronzeville. New York: Harper and Brothers, 1945.
Annie Allen. New York: Harper and Brothers, 1949.
Bronzeville Boys and Girls. New York: Harper and Brothers, 1956.
The Bean Eaters. New York: Harper and Row, 1960.
Selected Poems. New York: Harper and Row, 1963.
In the Mecca. New York: Harper and Row, 1968.
Riot. Detroit: Broadside Press, 1969.
Aloneness. Detroit: Broadside Press, 1971.
A Broadside Treasury: 1965–1970. Detroit: Broadside Press, 1971.
Family Pictures. Detroit: Broadside Press, 1970.
Jump Bad: A New Chicago Anthology. Detroit: Broadside Press, 1971.
The World of Gwendolyn Brooks. New York: Harper and Row, 1971.
The Tiger Who Wore White Gloves. Chicago: Third World Press, 1974.
Beckonings. Chicago: Third World Press, 1975.
Primer for Blacks. Chicago: Brooks Press, 1980.
To Disembark. Chicago: Third World Press, 1981.

PROSE

Maud Martha. New York: Harper and Brothers, 1953.
The Black Position: An Annual. Detroit: Broadside Press, 1971.
Report from Part One. Detroit: Broadside Press, 1972.
A Capsule Course in Black Poetry Writing. Detroit: Broadside Press, 1975.
Young Poet's Primer. Chicago: Brooks Press, 1980.

II. Critical Sources

BOOKS

Abel, Elizabeth, Marianne Hirsch, and Elizabeth Langland, eds. *The Voyage In: Fictions of Female Development.* Hanover, N.H.: University Press of New England, 1983.

Baker, Houston A., Jr. *Singer of Daybreak: Studies in Black American Literature.* Westport, Conn.: Greenwood Press, 1980.

Bell, Roseann P., Bettye J. Parker, and Beverly Guy-Sheftall, eds. *Sturdy Black Bridges: Visions of Black Women in Literature.* New York: Doubleday, 1979.

Bigsby, C. W. E. *The Second Black Renaissance: Essays in Black Literature.* Westport, Conn.: Greenwood Press, 1980.

———. *The Black American Writer,* vol. 2: *Poetry and Drama.* Baltimore: Penguin Press, 1971.

Bowles, Juliette, ed. *In the Memory and Spirit of Frances, Zora, and Lorraine: Essays and Interviews on Black Women and Writing.* Washington, D.C.: Howard University Press, 1979.

Brown, Patricia L., Don L. Lee, and Francis Ward, eds. *To Gwen with Love: An Anthology Dedicated to Gwendolyn Brooks.* Chicago: Johnson Publishing, 1971.

Christian, Barbara. *Black Feminist Criticism: Perspectives on Black Women Writers.* Elmsford, N.Y.: Pergamon Press, 1985.

———. *Black Women Novelists: The Development of a Tradition, 1892–1976.* Westport, Conn.: Greenwood Press, 1980.

Davis, Arthur P. *From the Dark Tower: Afro-American Writers, 1900–1960.* Washington, D.C.: Howard University Press, 1974.

Drotning, Phillip T., and Wesley W. South. *Up from the Ghetto.* New York: Cowles Book Company, 1970.

Evans, Mari, ed. *Black Women Writers: A Critical Evaluation 1950–1980.* New York: Anchor Press/Doubleday, 1984.

Gayle, Addison, Jr., ed. *Black Expression.* New York: Weybright and Talley, 1969.

Gilbert, Sandra M., and Susan Gubar, eds. *Shakespeare's Sisters: Feminist Essays on Women Poets.* Bloomington: Indiana University Press, 1979.

Gould, Jean. *Modern American Women Poets.* New York: Dodd, Mead, 1984.

Gross, Theodore L., and James A. Emmanuel, eds. *Dark Symphony.* New York: Free Press, 1968.

Henderson, Stephen E., ed. *Understanding the New Black Poetry.* New York: William Morrow, 1973.

Jackson, Blyden, and Louis D. Rubin, Jr. *Black Poetry in America: Two Essays in Historical Interpretation.* Baton Rouge: Louisiana State University Press, 1974.

Juhasz, Suzanne. *Naked and Fiery Forms: Modern American Poetry by Women: A New Tradition.* New York: Harper and Row, 1975.

Kent, George E. *Blackness and the Adventure of Western Culture.* Chicago: Third World Press, 1972.

Kufrin, Joan. *Uncommon Women.* Piscataway, N.J.: New Century Publishers, 1981.

Lee, Robert A. *Black Fiction: New Studies in the Afro-American Novel Since 1945.* London: Vision Press, 1980.

Littlejohn, David. *Black on White: A Critical Survey of Writings by American Negroes.* New York: Grossman Publishers, 1966.

Miller, R. Baxter, ed. *Black American Literature and Humanism.* Lexington: University Press of Kentucky, 1981.

———. *Langston Hughes and Gwendolyn Brooks: A Reference Guide.* Boston: G. K. Hall, 1978.

Murphy, Rosalie, and James Vinson, eds. *Contemporary Poets of the English Language*. New York: St. Martin's Press, 1970.

Ostendorf, Berndt. *Black Literature in White America*. Totowa, N.J.: Barnes and Noble Books, 1982.

Pryse, Marjorie, and Hortense J. Spillers, eds. *Conjuring: Black Women, Fiction, and Literary Tradition*. Bloomington: Indiana University Press, 1985.

Redmond, Eugene B. *Drum Voices: The Mission of Afro-American Poetry*. New York: Doubleday, 1976.

Rollins, Charlemae. *Famous American Negro Poets*. New York: Dodd, Mead, 1965.

Shaw, Harry B. *Gwendolyn Brooks*. Boston: Twayne Publishers, 1980.

Tate, Claudia. *Black Women Writers at Work*. New York: Continuum Publishing, 1983.

Vinson, James, ed. *Contemporary Novelists*. New York: St. Martin's Press, 1972.

Wade-Gayles, Gloria. *No Crystal Stair: Visions of Race and Sex in Black Women's Fiction*. New York: Pilgrim Press, 1984.

ARTICLES

Andrews, Larry R. "Ambivalent Clothes Imagery in Gwendolyn Brooks' 'Sundays of Satin-Legs Smith.'" *College Language Association Journal* 24 (Dec. 1980):150–63.

"Artists, Friends, Admirers Gather in Tribute to Poetess Gwendolyn Brooks." Illus. *Jet*, 25 Feb. 1971, pp. 16–17.

Baker, Houston, A., Jr. "The Achievement of Gwendolyn Brooks." *College Language Association Journal* 16 (Sept. 1972):23–31.

Barrow, W. "Five Fabulous Females." *Negro Digest* 12 (July 1963):78–83.

Bird, Leonard G. "Gwendolyn Brooks: Educator Extraordinaire." *Discourse* 12 (Spring 1969):158–66.

Brown, Frank L. "Chicago's Great Lady of Poetry." *Negro Digest* 10 (Dec. 1961):53–57.

Budd, Louis J. "The Not So Tender Traps: Some Dilemmas of Black American Poets." *Indian Journal of American Studies* 3 (June 1973):47–57.

Clark, Edward. "Studying and Teaching Afro-American Literature." *College Language Association Journal* 16 (Sept. 1972):96–105.

Crockett, Jacqueline. "An Essay on Gwendolyn Brooks." *Negro History Bulletin* 19 (Nov. 1955):37–39.

Davis, Arthur P. "The Black-and-Tan Motif in the Poetry of Gwendolyn Brooks." *College Language Association Journal* 6 (Dec. 1962):90–97.

———. "Gwendolyn Brooks: Poet of the Unheroic." *College Language Association Journal* 7 (Dec. 1963):114–25.

Duffy, John. "Style and Exasperation." *Spirit* 30–31 (1963–65):47–48.

Ford, Nick Aaron. "Battle of the Books: A Critical Survey of Books by and about Negroes Published in 1960." *Phylon* 22 (Summer 1961):128–29.

Fuller, Hoyt W. "Primer for Blacks." *First World* 2, no. 4 (1980):43.

———. "The Negro Writer in the United States." *Ebony*, Nov. 1964, pp. 126–28, 134.

Furman, Marva R. "Gwendolyn Brooks: The 'Unconditioned' Poet." *College Language Association Journal* 17 (Sept. 1973):1–10.

Gregory, Carole. "An Appreciation of Gwendolyn Brooks." *Black Collegian*, Dec. 1981, pp. 22–23.

Hansell, William H. "Aestheticism versus Militancy in Gwendolyn Brooks' 'The Chicago Picasso' and 'The Wall.'" *College Language Association Journal* 17 (Sept. 1973):11–15.

———. "Gwendolyn Brooks' 'In the Mecca': A Rebirth into Blackness." *Negro American Literature Forum* 8 (Summer 1974):199–207.

———. "The Role of Violence in Recent Poems of Gwendolyn Brooks." *Studies in Black Literature* 5 (Summer 1974):21–27.

———. "Essences, Unifyings, and Black Militancy: Major Themes in Gwendolyn Brooks' *Family Pictures* and *Beckonings*." *Black American Literature Forum* 11 (Summer 1977):63–66.

———. "The Poet-Militant and Foreshadowings of a Black Mystique: Poems in the Second Period of Gwendolyn Brooks." *Concerning Poetry* 10 (Fall 1977):37–45.

Harriott, Frank. "The Life of a Pulitzer Poet." *Negro Digest* 8 (Aug. 1950):14–16.

Harris, Victoria F. "The Voice of Gwendolyn Brooks." *Interpretations* 11 (Fall 1979):55–66.

Hudson, Clenora F. "Racial Themes in the Poetry of Gwendolyn Brooks." *College Language Association Journal* 17 (Sept. 1973):16–20.

Hull, Gloria T. "A Note on the Poetic Technique of Gwendolyn Brooks," *College Language Association Journal* 19 (Dec. 1975).

Kent, George E. "Gwendolyn Brooks—Portrait, in Part, of the Artist as a Young Girl and Apprentice Writer." *Callaloo* 2 (Oct. 1979):74–83.

———. "The Poetry of Gwendolyn Brooks: Part I." *Black World* 20 (Sept. 1971):30–43.

———. "The Poetry of Gwendolyn Brooks: Part II." *Black World* 20 (Oct. 1971):36–48.

Lattin, P. H., and V. E. Lattin. "Dual Vision in Gwendolyn Brooks' *Maud Martha*." *Critique* 25 (Summer 1984):180–88.

Lee, Don L. "The Achievement of Gwendolyn Brooks." *Black Scholar* 3 (Summer 1972):32–41.

Loff, Jon N. "Gwendolyn Brooks: A Bibliography." *College Language Association Journal* 17 (Sept. 1973):32–41.

Lupack, Alan C. "Brooks' 'Piano After War.'" *The Explicator* 36 (Summer 1978):2–3.

Madhubuti, Safisha N. "Focus on Form in Gwendolyn Brooks." *Black Books Bulletin* 2, no. 1 (Spring 1974):24–27.

Mahoney, Heidi L. "Selected Checklist of Materials by and about Gwendolyn Brooks." *Negro American Literature Forum* 8 (Summer 1974):210–11.

Melhem, D. H. "Gwendolyn Brooks: The Heroic Voice of Prophecy." *Studies in Black Literature* 8 (Spring 1977):1–3.

Miller, Jean Marie A. "Gwendolyn Brooks—Poet Laureate of Bronzeville U.S.A." *Freedomways* 10 (First Quarter 1970):63–75.

Miller, R. Baxter. "Define . . . The Whirlwind: *In the Mecca*—Urban Setting, Shifting Narrator and Redemptive Vision." *Obsidian* 4 (Spring 1978): 19–31.

Mootry, Maria K. "Brooks' 'A Bronzeville Mother Loiters in Mississippi. Meanwhile, a Mississippi Mother Burns Bacon.'" *The Explicator* 42 (Summer 1984):51–52.

O'Neale, Sondra A. "Race, Sex and Self: Aspects of *Bildung* in Select Novels by Black American Women Novelists." *Melus* 9 (Winter 1982):25–37.

Park, Sue S. "A Study in Tension: Gwendolyn Brooks' 'The *Chicago Defender* Sends a Man to Little Rock.'" *Black American Literature Forum* 11 (Spring 1977):32–34.

Rivers, Conrad K. "Poetry of Gwendolyn Brooks." *Negro Digest* 13 (June 1964):67–69.

Shands, Annette Oliver. "Gwendolyn Brooks as Novelist." *Black World* 22 (June 1973):22–30.

Shaw, Harry B. "Gwendolyn Brooks." *Black American Literature Forum* 13 (Spring 1981):116–18.

Sims, Barbara B. "Brooks' 'We Real Cool.'" *The Explicator* 34 (April 1976):58.

Smith, Gary. "Gwendolyn Brooks's *A Street in Bronzeville*, The Harlem Renaissance, and the Mythologies of Black Women." *Melus* 9 (Fall 1983):33–46.

———. "Brooks' 'We Real Cool.'" *The Explicator* 43 (Winter 1985):49–50.

Star, Jack. "The Proud Poet of Bronzeville." *Chicago Magazine* 6 March 1981, pp. 132–37.

Stetson, Erlene. "Songs After Sunset" (1935–1936): The Unpublished Poetry of Gwendolyn Elizabeth Brooks." *College Language Association Journal* 24 (Sept. 1980):87–96.

Towns, Saundra. "Black Autobiography and the Dilemma of Western Artistic Tradition." *Black Books Bulletin* 2, no. 1 (Spring 1974):17–23.

Washington, Mary H. " 'Taming All That Anger Down': Rage and Silence in Gwendolyn Brooks' *Maud Martha*." *Massachusetts Review* 24 (Summer 1983):453–66.

Werner, Craig. "Gwendolyn Brooks: Tradition in Black and White." *Minority Voices* 1 (Fall 1977):27–38.

Williams, Gladys M. "Gwendolyn Brooks' Way with the Sonnet." *College Language Association Journal* 26 (Dec. 1982):215–40.

INTERVIEWS

Angle, Paul M. *We Asked Gwendolyn Brooks.* Chicago: Illinois Bell Telephone, n.d.

Brooks, Gwendolyn. "Interview (autobiography)." *Triquarterly* 60 (Spring/Summer 1984):405–10.

Brown, Martha H. "Interview with Gwendolyn Brooks." *Great Lakes Review* 6 (Summer 1979):48–55.

Garland, Phyl. "Gwendolyn Brooks: Poet Laureate." *Ebony*, July 1968, pp. 48–56.

Hull, Gloria T., and Posey Gallagher. "Update on Part One: An Interview with Gwendolyn Brooks." *College Language Association Journal* 21 (Sept. 1977):19–40.

"Interview with Gwendolyn Brooks." *Black Books Bulletin* 2, no. 1 (Spring 1974): 28–35.

Kufrin, Joan. "Our Miss Brooks," *Chicago Tribune Magazine* 28 March 1982.

Stavros, George. "An Interview with Gwendolyn Brooks." *Contemporary Literature* 11 (Winter 1970).

BOOK REVIEWS

A Street in Bronzeville
Derleth, August. "A Varied Quartette." *Voices* (Sept.–Dec. 1957):44–66.

Hazard, Eloise P. "A Habit of 'Firsts.'" *Saturday Review*, 20 May 1950, p. 20.

Humphries, Rolphe. "Bronzeville." *New York Times Book Review*, 4 Nov. 1945, p. 14.

Nelson, Starr. "Social Comment in Poetry." *Saturday Review*, 19 Jan. 1946, p. 15.

Shapiro, Harvey. "A Quartet of Younger Singers." *New York Times Book Review*, 23 Oct. 1960, p. 32.

"Blues Songs and Funeral Chants." *Chicago Daily News*, 22 Aug. 1945.

Wilder, Amos N. "Sketches from Life." *Poetry* 67 (Dec. 1945):164–66.

Annie Allen
Deutsch, Babette. "Six Poets." *Yale Review* 39 (Dec. 1949):361–65.

Hughes, Langston. "Name, Race, and Gift in Common." *Voices* 140 (Winter 1950):54–56.

Humphries, Rolphe. "Verse Chronicle." *The Nation*, 23 Sept. 1949, p. 306.

Kunitz, S. "Bronze by Gold." *Poetry* 76 (April 1950):52–56.

Lechlinter, Ruth. "Love Songs." *New York Herald Tribune*, 25 Sept. 1949, p. 44.

McGinley, Phyllis. "Poetry for Prose Readers." *New York Times Book Review*, 22 Jan. 1950, p. 7.

Redding, J. Saunders. "Cellini-Like Lyrics." *Saturday Review*, 17 Sept. 1949, pp. 23, 27.

Maud Martha
Bradley, Van Allen. "Negro's Life Here Effectively Portrayed in First Novel." *Chicago Daily News*, 30 Sept. 1953, p. 26.

Butcher, Fanny. "Swift, Sharp Prose by a Poet." *Chicago Sunday Tribune Magazine*, 4 Oct. 1953, p. 41.

Monjo, Nicholas. "Young Girl Growing Up." *Saturday Review*, 30 Oct. 1953, p. 41.

Rosenberger, Coleman. "A Work of Art and Jeweled Precision." *New York Herald Tribune Book Review*, 18 Oct. 1953, p. 4.

Bronzeville Boys and Girls

Libby, Margaret S. "Bright Is the Ring of Words When the Right Person Rings Them." *New York Herald Tribune Book Review*, 18 Nov. 1956, p. 2.

Rollins, Charlemae. *Chicago Sunday Tribune Magazine*, 11 Nov. 1956, p. 20.

The Bean Eaters

Bock, Frederick. "Prize Winning Poet Fails to Measure Up." *Chicago Sun Times Sunday Magazine*, 5 June 1960, sec. 4, p. 12.

Burke, Herbert. *Library Journal* 85 (April 1960):1599.

Dana, Robert P. "Double Martini and Broken Crank Shaft." *Prairie Schooner* 35 (Winter 1961–62):357–62.

Hartman, Geoffrey. "Les Belles Dames Sans Merci." *Kenyon Review* 22 (Autumn 1960):691–94.

Nathan, Leonard E. "Four Books." *Voices* (Sept.–Dec. 1960):44–47.

Parker, John W. "Saga of the Bronzeville Community." *College Language Association Journal* 4 (Sept. 1960):59–61.

Webster, Harvey Curtis. "Pity the Gods." *The Nation*, 1 Sept. 1962, p. 967.

Selected Poems

Alderson, Sue Ann. "Selected Poems." *West Coast Review* 10 (Oct. 1975): 45–47.

Cutler, Bruce. "A Long Reach, Strong Speech." *Poetry* 103 (March 1964):387–93.

Morse, Carl. "All Have Something to Say." *New York Times Book Review*, 6 Oct. 1963, p. 28.

Nyren, Dorothy. "Review of *Selected Poems*." *Library Journal* 88 (July 1963): 2708.

Simpson, Louis. "Don't Take a Poem by the Horns." *Bookweek*, 27 Oct. 1963, pp. 6, 26.

In the Mecca

Benson, Brian J. "In the Mecca." *College Language Association Journal* 13 (Dec. 1969):203.

Laing, Alexander. "The Politics of Poetry." *The Nation*, 7 July 1969, p. 2628.

Rosenthal, M. L. "In the Mecca." *New York Times Book Review*, 2 March 1969, p. 14.

A Broadside Treasury

Golden, Bernette. "Broadside Treasury." *Black World* 23 (April 1974):51.

Family Pictures

Skeeter, Sharyn J. "Family Pictures: Book Review." *Essence*, June 1971, p. 72.

The World of Gwendolyn Brooks

Gayle, Addison, Jr. "Making Beauty from Racial Anxiety." *New York Times Book Review*, 2 Jan. 1972, pp. 51–52.

Kent, George E. "Notation Concerning *The World of Gwendolyn Brooks.*" *Booklist*, 15 Nov. 1971, p. 277.

Miller, Jean Marie A. "The World of Gwendolyn Brooks." *Black World* 21 (Jan. 1972):51–52.

Report from Part One

Bambara, Toni Cade. "*Report from Part One.*" *New York Times Book Review*, 7 Jan. 1973, pp. 1, 10.

Farrison, W. Edward. "*Report from Part One.*" *College Language Association Journal* 16 (June 1973):527–29.

Hortense, D. Lloyd. "Report from Part One." *Negro Educational Review* 24 (July–Oct. 1973):166.

Shands, Annette O. "*Report from Part One*: The Autobiography of Gwendolyn Brooks." *Black World* 22 (March 1973):70–71.

Washington, Mary H. "*Report from Part One*: The Autobiography of Gwendolyn Brooks." *Black World* 22 (March 1973):51–52, 70.

Beckonings

Henderson, Stephen E. "Beckonings." *Black Books Bulletin* 3 (Winter 1975): 34–35.

Towns, Saundra. "Beckonings." *Black World* 25 (Nov. 1975):51–52, 87–88.

To Disembark

Kent, George E. "To Disembark." Illus. *Black Books Bulletin* 7, no. 3 (1981): 44–46.

Martin, Herbert W. "To Disembark." *Great Lakes Review* 9 (Fall 1983):109–12.

DISSERTATIONS

Alexander, Estella C. "Tell Them So You'll Know." Ph.D. diss., University of Iowa, 1984.

Clark, Norris B. III. "The Black Aesthetic Reviewed: A Critical Examination of the Writings of Imamu Amiri Baraka, Gwendolyn Brooks and Toni Morrison." Ph.D. diss., Cornell University, 1980.

Clyde, Glenda E. "An Oral Interpreter's Approach to the Poetry of Gwendolyn Brooks." Ph.D. diss., Southern Illinois University-Carbondale, 1966.

Hansell, William H. "Positive Themes in the Poetry of Four Negroes: Claude McKay, Countee Cullen, Langston Hughes, and Gwendolyn Brooks." Ph.D. diss., University of Wisconsin, 1972.

Hemingway, Beulah Smith. "The Universal Wears Contemporary Clothing: The Works of Gwendolyn Brooks." Ph.D. diss., Florida State University, 1981.

Keizs, Marcia V. "The Development of a Dialect: Private and Public Patterns in the Work of Margaret Walker and Gwendolyn Brooks." Ed.D. diss., Columbia University Teachers College, 1984.

Lynch, Charles H. "Robert Hayden and Gwendolyn Brooks: A Critical Study." Ph.D. diss., New York University, 1977.

Melhem, D. H. "Gwendolyn Brooks: Prophecy and Poetic Process." Ph.D. diss., City University of New York, 1976.

Moore, Maxine F. "Characters in the Works of Gwendolyn Brooks." Ph.D. diss., Emory University, 1983.

Schuchat, Marjorie Jane Smock. "Gwendolyn Elizabeth Brooks: A Janus Poet." Ph.D. diss., Texas Woman's University, 1982.

Shaw, Harry B. "Social Themes in the Poetry of Gwendolyn Brooks." Ph.D. diss., University of Illinois at Urbana-Champaign, 1972.

Stratton, Kathryn Alice Abels. "Woman as A: Woman as B." Ph.D. diss., Indiana University of Pennsylvania, 1982.

ACKNOWLEDGMENTS

"Madimba: Gwendolyn Brooks," by Michael S. Harper, is reprinted by permission of Johnson Publishing Company, Inc., © 1971.

We wish to thank the following publishers for permission to reprint essays that they originally published, sometimes in slightly different versions:

"Aesthetic Values in the Poetry of Gwendolyn Brooks," by George E. Kent, in *Black American Literature and Humanism*, ed. R. Baxter Miller (Lexington: University Press of Kentucky, 1981).

" 'Does Man Love Art?': The Humanistic Aesthetic of Gwendolyn Brooks," by R. Baxter Miller, in *Black American Literature and Humanism*, ed. R. Baxter Miller (Lexington: University Press of Kentucky, 1981).

"The Women of Bronzeville," by Beverly Guy-Sheftall, in *Sturdy Black Bridges*, ed. Roseann P. Bell, Bettye J. Parker, and Beverly Guy-Sheftall (New York: Anchor Press/Doubleday, 1979).

"Gwendolyn the Terrible: Propositions on Eleven Poems," by Hortense J. Spillers, in *Shakespeare's Sisters*, ed. Sandra M. Gilbert and Susan Gubar (Bloomington Indiana University Press, 1979).

"Nuance and the Novella: A Study of Gwendolyn Brooks' *Maud Martha*," by Barbara Christian, in *Black Feminist Criticism* (New York: Pergamon Press, 1985).

We also wish to thank the editors of the following journals for permission to reprint essays that they originally published, sometimes in slightly different versions:

"The Achievement of Gwendolyn Brooks," by Houston A. Baker, *College Language Association Journal* 16 (Sept. 1972).

"The Poet Militant and Foreshadowings of a Black Mystique: Poems in the Second Period of Gwendolyn Brooks," by William H. Hansell, *Concerning Poetry* (Fall 1977).

"*Songs After Sunset* (1935–1936): The Unpublished Poetry of Gwendolyn Elizabeth Brooks," by Erlene Stetson, *College Language Association Journal* 24 (Sept. 1980).

This book was made possible by many people. In particular, we would like to thank the late Professor George E. Kent, whose early essay, "The Poetry of Gwendolyn Brooks," was a pioneering effort in Brooks scholarship, and who encouraged us to undertake the project. Professors J. Saunders Redding, Samuel W. Allen, and Richard F. Peterson offered generous commentary on the form of the text. Magnolia Broadnax and Pauline J. Duke of Southern Illinois University-Carbondale, and Ann Larson of Evanston, Illinois typed drafts of the manuscript; the SIU-C Office of Research and

Development provided financial assistance in the form of a Project Completion Grant; and the College of Human Resources provided valuable material resources.

Finally, we want to express our profound gratitude to Gwendolyn Brooks, to whom this volume is appropriately dedicated.

BIOGRAPHICAL CHRONOLOGY

1917   Gwendolyn Brooks, the first child of David and Keziah Brooks, was born June 7 in Topeka, Kansas. One month later, family moved to Hyde Park in Chicago.

1918   Brother Raymond born.

1921   Family moved to a house on Chicago's South Side, where Gwendolyn lived until she married.

1930   First poem, "Eventide," published in *American Childhood* magazine.

1932   Enrolled in predominantly white Hyde Park High School, later transferred to all black Wendell Phillips High School, then to integrated Englewood High School.

1933   Met James Weldon Johnson, black writer and activist of the Harlem Renaissance, who advised her to read the modernist poets T. S. Eliot, Ezra Pound, and E. E. Cummings. Later met Langston Hughes, who encouraged her writing and became her literary mentor.

1934   Began weekly contributions to black newspaper, the *Chicago Defender*, in which she published nearly eighty of her poems in a weekly poetry column; graduated from Englewood High School.

1936   Graduated from Wilson Junior College.

1937   Two poems appear in anthologies of American poetry.

1938   Married Henry Blakely, a fellow aspiring poet, and moved to kitchenette apartment on Chicago's South Side.

1940   First child, Henry Jr., born on October 10.

1941   Attended Inez Stark's writer's workshop on Chicago's South Side and was introduced to *Poetry* magazine and the practice of modernist poetry.

1943   Won Midwestern Writer's Conference Poetry Award in Chicago.

1945   First collection of poetry, *A Street in Bronzeville*, published by Harper and Row. Won four awards at Midwestern Writer's Conference at Northwestern University, selected one of *Mademoiselle* magazine's "Ten Young Women of the Year," and received Society of Midland Authors' "Patron Saints" Award.

1946   Won Guggenheim Fellowship and made a Fellow of the American Academy of Arts and Letters.

1947   Won second Guggenheim Fellowship.

1948   Began to write literary reviews for several Chicago newspapers.

1949   *Annie Allen*, her second volume of poetry, published by Harper and Row. Won *Poetry* magazine's Eunice Tietjens Prize.

1950   Won Pulitzer Prize for *Annie Allen*; the first and, to date, only black American poetry volume to be so honored.

1951   Second child, Nora, born on September 8.

1953   Published *Maud Martha* (novel); family moved into house at 7428

South Evans Avenue on Chicago's South Side, where she continues to live.

1956 Published book of poetry for children, *Bronzeville Boys and Girls.*

1959 Father, David Brooks, died.

1960 *The Bean Eaters,* her third volume of poetry, published by Harper and Row.

1962 Invited by President John F. Kennedy to read at a Library of Congress Poetry Festival; met Robert Frost, who praised her work.

1963 *Selected Poems* published by Harper and Row. Accepted first teaching job, a poetry workshop at Chicago's Columbia College; later taught creative writing at Elmhurst College and Northeastern Illinois State College; at Columbia University and City College of New York; and at the University of Wisconsin as Rennebohm Professor of English.

1964 Received first honorary degree, Doctor of Humane Letters, from Columbia College. Won Friends of Literature Award for Poetry and Thormond Monsen Award for Literature.

1967 Attended Fisk University Second Black Writers' Conference and experienced "awakening" into Black Arts Movement, after she heard poets and writers Imamu Baraka, John Oliver Killens, and David Llorens, who articulated the "black aesthetic."

1968 *In the Mecca* published by Harper and Row. Appointed Poet Laureate of Illinois.

1969 *Riot* published by Broadside Press.

1971 *Family Pictures* published by Broadside Press; collected works, *The World of Gwendolyn Brooks,* her last Harper and Row volume, published. Edited *The Black Position* (a periodical), *Jump Bad* (poetry), and *A Broadside Treasury* (poetry for Broadside Press). Made a "pilgrimage" to East Africa. *To Gwen with Love* published by admirers, many of whom were members of Chicago's Organization of Black American Culture workshop. Recognized as mentor of the Chicago Black Arts Movement, which included activist poets Don L. Lee (Haki Madhubuti) and Carolyn Rodgers. Gwendolyn Brooks Black Cultural Center named for her at Western Illinois University. Second children's book, *Aloneness,* published by Broadside Press.

1972 *Report from Part One,* her autobiography, published by Broadside Press.

1974 *The Tiger Who Wore White Gloves* (children's book) published by Third World Press.

1975 *Beckonings* and *A Capsule Course in Black Poetry Writing* published by Broadside Press.

1976 Brother, Raymond Brooks, died.

1978 Mother, Keziah Brooks, died.

1980 *Primer for Blacks* and *Young Poet's Primer* published by Brooks Press.

1981 *To Disembark* published by Third World Press.

1985 Appointed Poetry Consultant to the Library of Congress.

CONTRIBUTORS

Houston A. Baker, Jr., is the Albert M. Greenfield Professor of Human Relations at the University of Pennsylvania. His recent critical work, *Blues, Ideology, and Afro-American Literature,* explores the prospects of a "vernacular" theory of Afro-American cultural expression. His third volume of poetry is *Blues Journey Home.*

Barbara Christian is associate professor in the Afro-American Studies Department at the University of California, Berkeley. She has published two books, *Black Women Novelists, The Development of a Tradition,* and *Black Feminist Criticism: Perspectives on Black Women Writers,* as well as numerous essays on black women writers.

Norris B. Clark is director of black studies and associate professor of English at Bradley University. He has published essays on Amiri Baraka, Gwendolyn Brooks, Michael S. Harper, and Toni Morrison.

Beverly Guy-Sheftall is director of the Women's Research and Resource Center and assistant professor of English at Spelman College. She is co-editor of *Sturdy Black Bridges: Visions of Black Women in Literature* and founding co-editor of *Sage: A Scholarly Journal on Black Women.*

William H. Hansell is associate professor in the English Department of the University of Wisconsin Center—Sheboygan County. He has published articles and book reviews in *Black American Literature Forum, College Language Association Journal, Concerning Poetry, Obsidian, Phylon,* and *Studies in Black Literature.*

Michael S. Harper is I. J. Kapstein Professor of English at Brown University. He has published eight poetry collections, including *Dear John, Dear Coltrane, Images of Kin,* and most recently, *Healing Song for the Inner Ear,* and has co-edited *Chant of Saints.*

Gayl Jones is the author of two novels, *Corregidora* and *Eva's Man,* a collection of short stories, *White Rat,* and three volumes of poetry, *Song for Anninho, The Hermit Woman,* and *Xarque and Other Poems.*

George Kent was a professor of English at the University of Chicago. He published *Blackness and the Adventure of Western Culture* and numerous essays on Afro-American writers.

R. Baxter Miller is professor of English and director of the Black Literature

Program for the University of Tennessee at Knoxville. He is the author of the *Reference Guide to Langston Hughes and Gwendolyn Brooks* and editor of *Black American Literature and Humanism*.

Maria K. Mootry is assistant professor of black American studies at Southern Illinois University-Carbondale. She has published in *Obsidian, College Language Association Journal, Phylon, Massachusetts Review,* and *Open Places*.

Harry B. Shaw is associate dean of the College of Liberal Arts and Sciences and associate professor of English at the University of Florida. He has published articles as well as a book on Gwendolyn Brooks's poetry.

Gary Smith is assistant professor of English at Southern Illinois University-Carbondale. He has published articles on Gwendolyn Brooks, Sterling Brown, Robert Hayden, and Melvin Tolson. He has also published a volume of poetry, *Songs for My Fathers*.

Hortense Spillers teaches at Haverford College, Haverford, Pennsylvania. She has published essays, reviews, and short stories in a number of anthologies, journals, and magazines. She has also co-edited a collection of critical essays on black American women writers, *Conjuring: Black Women, Fiction, and Literary Tradition*.

Erlene Stetson is professor of English at Indiana University. She has edited *Black Sister*, a collection of poetry.

Claudia Tate is associate professor of English at Howard University. She is the author of *Black Women Writers at Work*. She has published essays in *Black American Literature Forum, College Language Association Journal, Essence, Ebony,* and *The Washington Post*.

Gladys M. Williams has taught at Talladega College and Spelman College, Indiana University in Indianapolis, Brooklyn College, and LaGuardia Community College in New York City. Her articles and reviews have appeared in *English Journal, Reading Teacher, Obsidian,* and *College Language Association Journal*.

Kenny J. Williams is professor of English at Duke University. She is the author of *They Also Spoke: An Essay on Negro Literature, From the City of Men: Another Story of Chicago, Prairie Voices: A Literary History of Chicago from the Frontier to 1893,* and *Chicago's Public Wits: A Chapter in the American Comic Spirit*.